Exploiting Chaos

**Cashing in on the Realities
of Software Development**

D1305002

Exploiting Chaos

*Cashing in on the Realities
of Software Development*

Dave Olson

VNR VAN NOSTRAND REINHOLD
New York

Copyright © 1993 by Van Nostrand Reinhold

Library of Congress Catalog Card Number 92-14997
ISBN 0-442-01112-1

I⟨T⟩P   Van Nostrand Reinhold is an International Thomson Publishing company.
        ITP logo is a trademark under license.

Printed in the United States of America

Van Nostrand Reinhold   ITP Germany
115 Fifth Avenue   Königswinterer Str. 418
New York, NY 10003   53227 Bonn
                                         Germany

International Thomson Publishing   International Thomson Publishing Asia
Berkshire House,168-173   38 Kim Tian Rd., #0105
High Holborn, London WC1V 7AA   Kim Tian Plaza
England   Singapore 0316

Thomas Nelson Australia   International Thomson Publishing Japan
102 Dodds Street   Kyowa Building, 3F
South Melbourne 3205   2-2-1 Hirakawacho
Victoria, Australia   Chiyada-Ku, Tokyo 102
                                          Japan

Nelson Canada
1120 Birchmount Road
Scarborough, Ontario
M1K 5G4, Canada

16 15 14 13 12 11 10 9 8 7 6 5 4 3 2

Library of Congress Cataloging-in-Publication Data

Olson, Dave.
   Exploiting chaos : cashing in on the realities of software
development / by Dave Olson.
       p.   cm.
   Includes bibliographical references and index.
   ISBN 0-442-01112-1
   1. Computer software—Development. I. Title.
QA76.76.D47048   1992
005.1—dc20   92-14997
                                         CIP

Contents

Preface

In 1991 you wouldn't find "fractal" in most dictionaries—it's too new a word. "Fractal" is a word that has been coined to describe the ordered chaos (or chaotic order) in things that appear disorderly but are actually views of an underlying mathematical order that has not been well understood. "Fractal" refers to the entire set of patterns of order and disorder in a unified, chaotic whole.

Usage of other words in this book may differ slightly from what is recommended in dictionaries. Much of software development is goal-directed activity. When I describe particular activities as "retrograde," I mean that these activities are apparently directed contrary to the overall goal being pursued at the time. Often, apparently retrograde efforts can be highly productive in reaching the project's goals. Also, the term "order" has two meanings that are appropriate to the book. One of these meanings encompasses the mathematics of chaos, while the other relates to the observable behavior of things and the question of whether there are obvious patterns in those behaviors. Usually, when I talk about things being "orderly" or "disorderly" I'll be talking about the appearances. I fully intend the overtones in these usages, making the distinction between things as we like them (orderly) and things as we don't like them (disorderly). When I want to talk about the mathematical order in chaos, the unity of order and disorder, I'll try to be explicit and say so. I'll frequently use the word "fractal" in this case. We have to play word games like these simply because we don't really have the right words to express the concepts of "chaos in a form and environment where we like the results" and "chaos in a form and environment where we consider the results to be unacceptable."

The initial audience for this book is the software development community, including technical and nontechnical staff. While I recognize that software development is only an example of what goes on in the world at large, my immediate purpose is to suggest and document ways that the software development community can improve its software development efforts.

The observations in this book are in accord with the comments made by Frederick P. Brooks, author of *The Mythical Man-Month* and IBM manager for the development of OS/360 in his article "No Silver Bullets." However, the book continues from that point, taking a more positive and prescriptive approach. It provides a new model for the software development process, which leads to improved productivity and response to customer needs in today's dynamic environment.

The single most important message in this book is in the importance of achieving balance and conformance in long- and short-term efforts. Factors and things to be balanced include the following and more.

Problems	Management	Customers
Processes	Planning	Users
Technologies	Development	Ideas
Businesses	Maintenance	Solutions

Constant efforts to achieve a working balance will minimize the disruption caused by chaotic situations and maximize the benefits to be found in riding fractal waves to the future. Everything in this book is specifically intended to carry this point and to show how some unconventional approaches (pre-1991) can be used to discover more productive balances in software development. Even though the examples and thrust of the book are mainly on the technical side of software development, the reader will easily see that the examples and results relate to people in all kinds of human endeavor.

Closure Questions

At the end of each section or chapter, you will find closure questions. Closure questions are intended to help you to relate the covered material to your business or personal situation, consolidating what you've read with your own experience. Will your responses to these questions tell you anything about the level of reading you're using? About your interest in the ideas being presented? Will they allow you to explore your own experiences related to fractal things?

Acknowledgments

The contributions to this book are many and varied. James Gleick described the fractal framework that I used to hang my experiences on, Tom Peters showed some of the ways that apparent chaos in organizations can be a sign of vitality, Dick Berg asked questions that spurred me to tie things together that I hadn't recognized as belonging together, Martin Chetlen and Jim Soldini gave outstanding review feedback and criticism (Martin also contributed "attacks of irreverence" that helped to keep the fun in the work), Jack Skinner independently derived a development process so similar to my first fractal one that I knew I was on a good track, Mike Barnhouse provided excellent views on getting customers involved in the process, W. Edwards Deming provided key thoughts I used to solidify (but I hope not ossify) my understanding of chaotic behavior within bounded processes, Dr. Perry Buffington clearly showed the human need for order in everyday life, and my wife not only encouraged me to pursue these thoughts but helped me to make available the time that was necessary to do so. To all of these people, and everyone else that I learn from every day, I extend my thanks.

Figures

Side Comments

1

Chaotic Foundations

Chaos is a mess. In common language, chaos is confusion and disorder; "chaos" describes things that have no apparent rhyme or reason. For lay mathematicians, even the definitions of chaos are in confusion and disorder. All agree that chaos is the result of feedback in systems. Beyond that, some say that chaos is only found in the disorderly parts of the systems. Others say that the systems are entirely chaotic. We get further confusion from the claim that chaos is only to be found in deterministic systems.

Benoit Mandelbrot (*The Fractal Geometry of Nature*) gave us one escape from the chaos of defining chaos. He coined the word "fractal" to describe the entire field of systems that display chaotic behavior, without excluding any parts because they might or might not appear to be orderly. We invent another escape by using the terms "orderly" and disorderly" to describe things we like and things we don't like. Ignoring determinism, we provide ourselves with another escape and assume that chaos still exists, in accord with our everyday experience.

You'll read about the Mandelbrot set several times as you work your way through *Exploiting Chaos: Cashing in on the Realities of Software Development*. The Mandelbrot set has a visual representation that is recognized as the visual representation of chaos in publications today. You'll see a representation of the Mandelbrot set on page 20.

Boxes throughout the book will show ideas and examples to help you. James Gleick's work is noted in the first box. Other boxes in this chapter show how aspects of software development involve feedback and so are chaotic.

James Gleick traces the development of the science of chaos (Chaos, Making a New Science. New York: Viking Penguin Inc., 1987.) using stories of its practitioners and pioneers. While the vehicle is the stories of the people, the information carried along leads to an intuitive understanding of chaos, what it is, how it acts, and how it applies to our everyday lives. The book is clear and understandable for the lay scientist (a person who has a basic understanding of mathematics and science but who may not be an expert practitioner in any of the specifically mentioned fields).

As noted in the acknowledgments, Gleick's book was a triggering influence in the development of this book. The concepts of chaos and feedback showed shapes and behaviors that I found familiar in my experience in computer-related work. The natural chaos in software development is something to be understood and exploited, not suppressed or ignored.

Closure Questions:

How often do you read literature outside of computer science to find ideas that can provide a new perspective on your work?

Can you exploit such transference of ideas from physics, psychology, history, language studies, journalism, and political science?

Which will you explore next?

Box 1. *James Gleick:* Chaos, Making a New Science

INTRODUCTION TO CHAOS

We know what feedback is. The output of a system is fed back into the system and has some effect on the future of the system. Examples of feedback systems include the thermostat in your home, the grip you use when you hold your coffee cup, a microphone and loudspeaker in an auditorium, and the behavior of employees when counselled by management.

When the feedback is applied in a self-correcting way, the system displays some stability and order; your home stays at a comfortable temperature, you drink your coffee, the loudspeakers clearly amplify what you say into the microphone, and employees and managers pursue mutually agreeable goals. When the feedback is applied in other ways, the system displays little stability or order; your home gets too hot or too cold, you crush or drop your coffee cup, the loudspeakers squeal, and employees mutiny or quit.

Engineers characterize feedback according to what it does for them. They often want a system to be stable in a particular way. When feedback pushes the system toward that particular kind of stability, they call it negative feedback; it opposes the drift away from stability. When feedback pushes the system away from that particular kind of stability, they call it positive feedback: it adds to the drift away from stability. The interesting thing about the engineering definition is that the difference between positive feedback and nega-

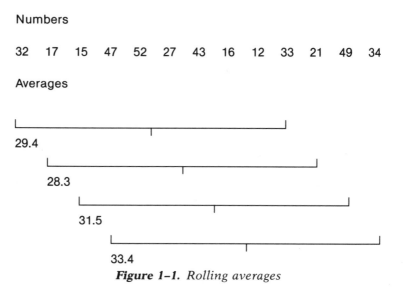

Figure 1–1. *Rolling averages*

tive feedback usually is the result of very minor changes in simple controls. It's not a difference in kind, it's a difference in degree.

When I was a Data Base Administrator for an IMS (IBM's Information Management System, a data base and application support system) installation, part of my job was to measure the IMS part of the overall system with great vigor. Measurements included counting transactions, counting data base calls for transactions, and keeping track of the processing time required for transactions. Then, with the understanding gleaned from all those measurements, I was to help improve the performance of the system.

When I started, I had no idea that I would run into chaos.

One of the key measurements was the number of transactions that were processed every day. An initial hope was that the numbers would display some nice kind of pattern and be useful for tuning the system, but it didn't work out that way. The problem was that transaction counts varied all over the map. There were no patterns of numbers of transactions by day of the week, no steady trends that could be seen in the daily data; the whole set of statistics looked chaotic.

So it was time to try something else. Maybe, even if the daily numbers didn't show trends, averaging transactions over a week would point them out in the weekly counts. But I had no such luck. Every chosen set displayed the same chaotic behavior.

Since averaging didn't work, more imagination was called for. Instead of using a set of data for an average, I tried an average in a moving window. I took data from several consecutive days and averaged it together. Then, I took out the data for the oldest day and put in the data for the next day in sequence, giving a new average. I experimented to see how many days should be in the rolling average to damp out the chaos. The average would eventually flatten out because the numbers that are close together in the sequence of averages have much the same basis for their values.

Clearly you need to have quite a bit of accumulated data to use this technique, but I had lots of data. Also, if the data is fairly well behaved, you would expect that the rolling averages would quickly become meaningless, or at least not useful. But the search was for trends, so trying it was worthwhile.

After several trials and computations, the chaotic behavior in the numbers settled down, showing trends with a 30-day rolling average. Anything less than 30 days and the chaotic behavior was still overwhelming; anything more and the curves got too flat to be useful.

Stop and think about this number 30. If you try this averaging scheme, you'll probably think that four or five common numbers would keep the averages close together. Try to visualize how drastic the change in numbers has to be if it takes 30 of them to get the averages close together. I was absolutely amazed that it took 30 common numbers to find the trends.

It's easy to think that people do about the same amount of work each day. It's easy to think that systems respond consistently day after day. It's easy to think that combining the workload of many groups in a single system will tend to have a stabilizing effect on the whole system. But none of these things are necessarily true. Systems respond quickly one day and slowly the next. People adjust their work for what they think will happen, so after a good day a system will tend to become bogged down. Note carefully that people, responding to the smooth running of the system, proceeded to add an extra burden to that system.

This is chaos. There are three things to notice about chaos. First, it is not predictable. Second, it depends on or arises from feedback. Third, whether it looks orderly or disorderly, you can still work with it and make things happen.

Closure Questions:

> How do you decide when you will use a computer system to do your work?
> Can you exploit fast times when they occur, or do you even think about the performance of a computer system when you devise your plans?
> Do you expect your computer support to run like clockwork?

CHAOS IN CLOCKS—CHAOS IS ALWAYS THERE

Let's look at an orderly process: the ticking of a grandfather clock. This time-honored time piece was considered to be the most accurate of clocks until quite recent times. Surely, there's no chaos to be found in a grandfather clock.

The heart of the regularity of the grandfather clock is the pendulum. Mathematicians have devised nice formulas for describing the regularity of the pendulum's motion, but the equations are based on some assumptions. They assume that the masses involved—Earth and the pendulum's knob—are point masses, which is not quite true. They assume that the pendulum's shaft is massless—also not true. They assume that there is no friction to impede the motion of the pendulum, which again is not true. Finally, they assume that the pendulum just swings along with no external forces being applied. But the pendulum is kept in motion by giving it a little kick (or pull or push, depending on the mechanism) at just the right moment in each swing. We can't have perpetual motion, after all, and the kick keeps the pendulum swinging; something has to overcome the friction that the equations ignore. The "right moment" is determined by the swing of the pendulum itself, using a latch and hook arrangement that is coupled with the top of the pendulum. The latch and hook also moves the gears that move the hands of the clock to tell us what time it is.

From the very beginning, software development is a feedback, chaotic process.

Some people think you just take a class in programming and you're a software developer. But it doesn't work that way. You take the class and try to apply what you learned, but your programs fail. As you try various techniques, some work and some fail.

You get feedback from the programs you write, and you adjust your view of programming accordingly.

Your learning curve is an example of chaos. You can't predict the shape of your final understanding of the programming language. Each step of the way, you are surprised and you adjust.

Closure question:

How would you recognize a part of your job that wasn't chaotic?

Box 2. *Learning how to program*

Given the regularity in the pendulum of a grandfather clock, can we look for and find chaos there? The answer is yes. You find the chaos by carefully measuring the differences in the swings of the pendulum. You can use the distance the pendulum moves, or the time it takes for a full swing; either measurement will work. Looking at the differences between successive measurements, you see apparent chaos.

The equations try to show how the movement of the pendulum is governed by the laws of gravitation. They give us numbers for the time and distance of the swing of the pendulum, regular numbers. But the equations do not account for the additional forces of friction and the timing and magnitude of the force used to keep the pendulum in motion.

Friction and the clock mechanism change the movement of the pendulum during every swing. Highly significantly, the changes in the motion of the pendulum are dependent on the motion of the pendulum itself. Even with every part of the mechanism firmly under control, this feedback will lead to unpredictability.

If you start two grandfather clocks that were made carefully, using the same design, and adjust them as carefully as you can so that their pendulums each duplicate the motion of the other, do you expect that they will continue to tick together for one minute? Ten minutes? One hour? Half a day? A whole day? A week? As you go through those time intervals, your confidence in a "yes" answer becomes lower and lower.

The lowered confidence reflects our knowledge that we can't make things correspond exactly. But while this lack of precision is real, an even more significant impact comes from the fact that small changes in initial conditions in feedback systems lead to significant differences in ultimate outcomes. Even if two clocks could truly be made to be identical, differences in initial conditions would still lead to unsynchronized ticking. This unpredictability is an inherent part of a feedback system.

One description of this unpredictability in chaotic behavior comes from the weather-oriented description of "the butterfly effect": the movement of a butterfly's wings that causes a thunderstorm half a world away. This illustrates the sensitivity to initial conditions and the unpredictability of chaotic behavior. Small initial differences lead to immense later differences. Behaviors are somewhat predictable in the near future, but are highly unpredictable in the far future, on whatever scale you want to use.

Now, it is true that the level of chaos in a grandfather clock is low. This is the first demonstration of one of the features of chaos: changes in chaotic behavior with differing circumstances.

With the grandfather clock, you would expect to see more disorderly behavior if you were to increase the kick given to the pendulum on each swing, or if you were to kick it more often. This is why we tend to get more accuracy from a grandfather clock with a longer pendulum. The swing of the pendulum is closer within the bounds of the order-predicting equations, each swing takes a longer time, and the longer time allows feedback effects to die down between kicks. In effect, you can reduce the apparent chaos, sometimes, if you carefully impose boundaries on the system.

The temptation is to say that the chaos is strictly noise, the result of errors in measurement or practice, and should be ignored. Indeed, in many practical applications, as with grandfather clocks and hospital drip chambers, the chaos *is* ignored because the results are "close enough." W. Edwards Deming differentiates between a system that is in statistical control (the chaos is bounded and close enough) and one that is chaotic (the chaos extends beyond desirable bounds). See page 40.

However, the chaos is not noise, it is not the result of errors in measurement or practice, and it cannot be ignored as a matter of course. Further, apparent chaos and apparent order are very close together when measured by changes in particular controlling circumstances. Thus, one of the big lessons of chaos is that a slight change in circumstances can lead to a massive change in the orderliness and predictability of the results.

Another lesson is that chaotic behavior is fully compatible with useful behavior. That is, chaos is not bad or necessarily the same as being out of con-

Set up an experiment to create water drops. This, we would think, would be as precise, orderly, and regular as anything could possibly be. After all, we know about the irritation of the legendary faucet that drips so constantly and regularly, and the hospital use of drip chambers in measuring the intravenous rate of delivery of medications, fluids, and nutrients.

In spite of all of this, the chaos in dripping water is closer to the surface than it is in the ticking of the grandfather clock. Measure the time between drops, and you will again find that there's a level of unpredictability to be found in the data.

The size of the drops and the time taken to form one are both dependent on what happened to the previous drop. Surface tension and weight work together to determine the size of a drop. Then, when that drop falls, surface tension causes a rebounding of the water, a third factor in the formation of a drop. These all are part of feedback between drops.

If you increase the flow rate, you will see increasing chaos in the timing between drops. The measurements show more and more disorderly behavior. Graphs of the measurements begin to show patterns that are characteristic of chaos. These patterns are the best mathematical indications of chaotic behavior.

Closure questions:

Can you adjust the water flow so that it produces all and only drops of water, yet any increase in the flow becomes a stream with no drops?

Is the boundary between the two flow rates orderly or disorderly?

Box 3. *Dripping water and mathematical chaos*

trol. Rather, it is a phenomenon to be recognized, understood, and possibly exploited.

Closure Questions:

How many places can you observe feedback that is supposed to keep things neat and orderly?

If you observe feedback systems closely, can you see chaotic behavior within the bounds set by the feedback?

Can you identify some natural examples of feedback and chaos?

CHAOS IN WATER AND WAX— CONTROL OFTEN EXAGGERATES CHAOS

As a final example, let's talk about water. The example is one that many of us have actually seen—a stream of water running across the waxed hood of a car. We don't need careful apparatus for this one; no fancy lab equipment and measuring tools are required. All we need is a car, a garden hose, and our eyes. Actually, you can do the same thing with a shower, a bathtub, a plastic drinking tumbler, an umbrella, and any number of other devices, but your car is dirty and you can do this experiment when you get around to washing it.

You have to watch out for requirements—gathering them is chaotic. When you start to pursue them, you never quite know where you'll end up.

If you start with lists of functions, gathering requirements seems easy. However, someone will interpret every item on your list differently than you do. Together, you can explore the item in more detail, and draw your interpretations closer together, but the limit of that exploration is the actual implementation.

As you gather requirements, with any luck you interact with customers or surrogates for the customers. We've already seen that simple learning is a feedback, chaotic activity. Gathering requirements, learning someone's application need and the possible solutions to that need, is even more so. Instead of getting feedback from something consistent like a computer, you're getting feedback from someone who keeps changing, your customer. Your understanding and your customer's understanding both adjust to your efforts. You know you'll end up at some understanding, but you can't possibly predict where.

Closure question:

    If you can think of ways to avoid the feedback of gathering requirements, why do you have any confidence that the resulting requirements will be useful?

Box 4. *Requirements feedback*

First, wash and wax your car (since you obviously put business before pleasure). If your car is already clean and you don't want to run the hose on it, go to your kitchen sink. Run water over the outside of a plastic bowl, or across a plastic cutting board or some other squeaky-clean surface. Adjust the flow of water anywhere from a trickle to a torrent, and direct it across the surface. If you have a trickle, look at the whole flow. If you have a torrent, look at the edges of the flow. You will see the flow (or edge) take its own path, a path that sometimes looks as if it is forced by the curvature of the surface and sometimes looks as if it has a mind of its own and chooses to go against the curvature. Often, the flow will change its course or position, independent of how you change it. Make a slight change in its direction and watch what happens to it. Some parts of the flow will move in a direction that corresponds to the change you made, but some parts will change in the opposite direction. For a real challenge, try to predict how you can change the flow to cause a specific desired change in the actual flow path some distance downstream.

The sources of chaos in this example are the same surface tension we discussed in the drops, the momentum of the water as it flows, surface irregulari-

Picture a software development group of moderate size. Assume that everyone in the group wants the project to be successful, and that everyone has agreed to "plan the work, then work the plan."

The plan is put in place, in significant detail. Initially, everything goes according to plan, but then the first unexpected occurrence occurs. People start to scramble to adjust to the occurrence so they can get back on track with the plan. Then the second surprise arrives, before everyone has quite recovered from the first one. Now people really dig in to get back on course, but the third surprise proves that a piece of the design is wrong.

With little effort, we can visualize people holding the project on schedule by violating the plan. We can imagine all kinds of strange things being done to achieve project success. But notice that some of the surprises might have been opportunities. Maybe taking some of the opportunities could have made the project better and more successful. But adherence to the plan made it impossible to take the opportunities, increasing the chaos within the project group.

Closure question:

How would you know if your project control kept you from seizing opportunities?

Box 5. *Chaos and software development control*

ties encountered by the flow, interrelations among all of these, and feedback between them and the flow of the water. Playing with this example also shows the sensitivity to "controlling" conditions, as did the example of the drops of water. A message in this observation is that many situations, particularly the ones we think are tightly controlled and nicely bounded, can easily switch between orderly and disorderly behaviors. We need to remember this when we come to discussions of software development.

These examples are nice, and there are many more, but my purpose is not to steal James Gleick's thunder. His book is an excellent one and explains much more than I need to here. (See box 1, on page 2.) The book includes descriptions of researchers who have looked at "disorderly" behavior and found an underlying order. Notice that this is not predictability, but order. Notice also that the order is an underlying order, not necessarily an apparent order.

What do these examples show that might be of interest to us?

First, they show that natural processes are not always as regular and neat as we might think. We should notice that people at work are not "unnatural" and many might well be expected to be somewhat irregular and less than tidy.

Second, the examples clearly illustrate the observation that bounded phenomena tend to look much more regular than unbounded phenomena. We have some justification in believing that a controlled environment can have a stabilizing influence on what happens within it.

Third, they demonstrate that feedback can be both an instrument of order and an instrument of disorder, but will always lead to unpredictability over the long run.

Finally, each example displays chaotic, unstable behavior that is ignored and assumed to be unimportant for normal purposes. Yet that chaotic, unstable behavior can easily be seen all around us if we care to look.

Closure Questions:

> Are there disorderly parts of your job that you routinely ignore or adjust for because they don't fit in with the official things you are supposed to do?
>
> Is your performance rated better when you ignore these things or when you adjust for them and make the process look better?

CHAOS IN A RAINSTORM—ADJUST TO CHAOS OR YOU'LL BE ALL WET

A few years ago, as I was learning about chaos, I watched a rainstorm through my office window. The patterns of rain hitting the top of a nearby parking ramp were fascinating. It looked as if there were rings of water running across the concrete. Each ring would run for a while and then collapse. This happened over the entire expanse of concrete, so there were rings forming and collapsing all the time.

The feedback of rain forming in a rain cloud is well documented. Rising air blows water drops up through the cloud until they're too heavy to be carried any higher, and then they fall. After some cycles, the rain leaves the cloud and heads for some newly washed car.

But I was seeing different evidence of feedback, with clearly identifiable areas I would call orderly and disorderly. As the rain fell, air movement and other drops of rain apparently worked together so that it didn't fall uniformly. Instead, it fell in the rings I observed. I saw no splashing raindrops in the center of any ring. The edge of each ring had lots of splashing raindrops. The center of each ring looked like a desirable area, one in which I could stay dry, an area of order. The edge of each ring looked like an undesirable area, an area in which I could get really wet, an area of disorder.

The thought occurred to me that it might be possible to pick one of those rings and run with it. If that were possible, we really could "run between the raindrops" and stay dry in the midst of a storm. That thought sounds ludicrous in the midst of a rainstorm, doesn't it? No one I know has ever successfully run through a rainstorm and stayed dry. But, watching those rings run around, it was an intriguing thought.

The parallel thought in software development is even more seductive. It is more common than not to see software development organizations working in the midst of their private area of order, assuming that area of order will continue forever.

With the thought of running between the raindrops, I looked more closely to see if I could see a ring of rain that I could occupy from one edge of the concrete to the other. There were none. It was as if bubbles of air provided shelter for a while, but were soon overcome by the weight of the rain. It would be impossible to run from one edge of the concrete to the other and remain completely dry. The best that could be done, if it were possible to see the rain on its way down, would be to run in one ring, jump through the edge to another ring, and work across the concrete that way. The runner would still get wet, but not as wet as if she had walked across and let the rings sweep over her.

Now let's think about software development some more, with examples.

When programming was first invented, people made a giant leap from hard-wired computers to internally stored programs. The programs were stored as bits, and programmers had to figure out all the bits and feed them into the computer. This area of order opened up when programming was invented, and effectively closed when symbolic programming was invented.

Symbolic programming released programmers from the need to figure out all the bits to feed to the machine. The programmer used symbols for instructions and symbols for addresses, and an assembler program figured out which bits to feed to the machine. This area of order opened up when symbolic programming was invented, and effectively closed (for the majority of programming jobs) when higher-level languages came into common use.

I won't belabor the idea of generations of languages here. (I do that in box 13 on page 47.) We could make the same point with computer memory and the techniques used to exploit that memory. We could make the point with design and development disciplines and the impact they've had on application software.

The history of software development is full of examples of areas of order that opened up, were carried forward for a time, and then closed up. In each case, changing from one area of order to another required new knowledge, new skills, and a trip across an area of disorder to get to the new area of order. It seems particularly unlikely to me that we will never again have to move from our comfortable existing areas of order to areas we've never experienced before.

Closure Questions:

What does your organization do to see if its areas of order are about to close up or to find new areas of order that might be productive?

What tools and concepts do you have to help you exploit existing areas of order?

How will you find or create new areas of order when you need them?

2

Flow and Change

CATASTROPHE THEORY

Brace yourself—we're going to lean toward the mathematical for a minute or two. But relax, we're not going to make you do equations and stuff, just use some words a little differently from what you're accustomed to. The word for this section is "catastrophe."

The snap of your fingers, the sharp boundary between a meadow and the adjacent woods, the tree line up on a mountain, the software effort that suddenly falls into place, and the slippage of a fault line leading to an earthquake are all examples of one common phenomenon: catastrophic transition. These are what catastrophe theory is about—sudden, inescapable transitions.

Think about balancing a coin on its edge on a flat table. You can do it because the coin's edge is wide enough to keep its center of gravity over its edge in a stable way. Now think of balancing the same coin on its edge when the table is tipped just a little. You can't do it—there's no area to sit under the coin's center of gravity in a stable way. This is the simplest and lowest order of catastrophe. You can get as close as you want to balancing the coin, but the balanced state is unstable. Reaching the balance point, you find that you pushed the coin through the unstable state to the stable state on the other side (falling on its head or tail).

Now look at something a little more complex. When you washed your car earlier you played with running streams of water over a waxed surface. (See page 7.) Now look at the hood or top of the car where the metal forms kind of a dome (a very shallow dome, but still a dome). If you lean on the dome, what happens? (If you don't want to lean on your car, you can experience the same things by squeezing the sides of a steel or aluminum soft drink can. When the exercise says to push on the dome, squeeze the sides of the can.) You will find that you can avoid the catastrophic transitions, but you can also make them happen at will. When you put a little weight on the dome, it gives a little, but it's still a dome. Add a little more weight and it gives a little more. If you keep adding weight, very slowly, very gradually, what happens?

As you add weight, the dome deforms downward. At some point, the dome can't support the weight any more and the metal snaps from the dome shape to a saucer shape. This is a catastrophic transition. Now we can illustrate the difference between a catastrophe and a disaster. Snapping from the dome to the saucer was a catastrophe. If you remove the weight and the metal snaps back to the dome shape, that's another catastrophe. If you remove the weight and the metal remains caved in to the saucer shape, that's a little disaster.

Now if you've ever done any auto body work or seen any auto body work done, you know that you can sometimes pull dents out of a car body. With shallow dents (maybe like the little disaster above) a plumber's friend can do the job; apply a little suction and pull the dent out. When you do that, assuming that it works, the little disaster wasn't really a disaster, it was just a little scare that was fixed by another catastrophe. But if you can't pull, push, punch, or flatten out the dent, that's a disaster, for which I apologize. (If you want to see a good book on catastrophe theory, albeit one with more mathematics than some would appreciate, look at P. T. Saunders' *An Introduction to Catastrophe Theory*.)

The point is that a catastrophe has something to do with software development (that's catastrophe, not disaster). To understand this, look at a couple of key characteristics of a catastrophe.

A catastrophe is possible when there is a situation that includes a force for change and a force resisting the change. For your car or soft drink can, the shape of the metal carried in it a force resisting your push. That's the first key characteristic. As the force for change becomes stronger, there comes a point where the resisting force can't resist the change any more. That's the second key characteristic. For your car, that's when you added enough weight to snap the dome into a saucer shape. The final key characteristic is that there must be stable states on either side of the transition but no stable state at the transition point. That's the snap of your fingers, the whomp sound when the metal in your car adopts the saucer shape, the clicks as you drive people crazy with your soft drink can, and the slippage in an earth fault that makes an earthquake happen.

It's worthwhile to focus a little more on the critical point of a catastrophic transition. At the critical point, a very small change in force (or resistance) leads to a drastic change in state. Software development may not know where critical points are, so even small changes in process or systems should have follow-up. Where this isn't practical (there are always places where that is

When Harlan Mills first introduced structured programming, the group to which he introduced it was reluctant to accept it. Structured programming appeared to be esoteric beyond reason, or at least beyond the experience of the group.

But Harlan Mills' push and the development group's cooperation (even if it was to give the boss enough rope to hang himself) were the forces for change. The resistance to change was in the habits of the developers and their skepticism about the new technology. Even though they practiced the new techniques, their attitudes remained firmly attached to their older techniques.

The catastrophic transition came when the product was delivered with higher-than-traditional quality and on schedule (not necessarily a common occurence in software development). The group snapped from their old view to the structured programming view, never to return, and could not sit on the fence between the two.

In the words of one of the participants, "No one straddled the fence. You either bought in completely to structured programming or you didn't buy it at all."

Closure questions:

How could you marshall forces like Mills' and make change happen in your organization?

What would you do if the transition happened to you rather than to the organization?

Box 6. *A structured programming catastrophe*

true), periodic sanity checks on processes and systems will help to discover any catastrophic transitions that may have occurred.

In software development, a development process is a force to fend off disorder. If the development process is not well suited to the problem, the developers, the environment, or the customers, then that mismatch with reality is the force for change that is opposed to the force of the development process. Using this example, the catastrophe comes when the development process breaks and either fails to deliver a suitable product or has to be discarded in favor of another process.

Now we've used the terms, let's tie catastrophe theory back to chaos, software development, and people. Chaos has areas of order and areas of disorder with the disorder separating the areas of order. Catastrophe theory talks about transitions between areas of order. The disorder between areas of order is not a stable place for people to work. (There is more on this on page 16.) With no stability between them, the transition from one area of order to another will often be a catastrophic transition.

This tells us that the next-to-worst thing we can do in software development

Areas of order are conceptual things. If we were forced out of an area of order, we will adopt or define concepts for a new area of order. We could dodge the responsibility of the transition, abandon all of our organizing concepts and decide to simply react to anything that happens.

We would thus trivialize our work and effectively stall in an area of disorder. As programmers, we would then code increasingly complex special cases for the rest of our so-called careers. Our customer-perceived productivity would be low and our products tricky to use, but we'd comfort ourselves that we had jobs—while they lasted.

Closure questions:

What might you do if you were a programming leader and your team members demonstrated that they just wanted to code for explicit requests?

What similarity do you see between this view and an organization that is firmly in crisis management mode?

Box 7. *Catastrophic sidetrack*

is to cling unthinkingly to a specific area of order when we encounter forces for change. If the forces for change overwhelm us, we won't know what area of order we will snap into and we won't have any idea of what kind of disorder we'll have to go through to reach our new areas of order. Our responses to the forces for change will be the least orderly and the least productive this way.

The next best thing to the involuntary change would be to seek some awareness of areas of order other than the ones we're using. That way, we will be somewhat prepared to respond if the forces for change do overwhelm us. We actually may be comfortable with the world after the change, even if we don't help to make the change happen.

If we actively seek areas of order that are suitable to our project, our people, our circumstances, and our customers, we will be far more likely to work in an area of order that is stable for the duration of our project than in the prior cases. This is one of the key points of exploiting chaos in software development: selecting our areas of order for best results. And whatever area of order we occupy, it's important to keep looking for two things: sources of changes (incompatibilities between what we need to do and the way we're working), and new areas of order (new havens if a catastrophic transition should become necessary).

These areas of order usually correspond to world views or paradigms. What we've just discussed is a reason why paradigm changes are so difficult for people, why the transition through the areas of disorder generally are painful. Despite that, it is essential to cultivate a tolerance for paradigm changes in order to allow for productive software development in a changing world.

World changes are coming so quickly that it's no longer acceptable for "the old guard" to die out and so make way for the new. (See page 21.) We have to expand our views one level (that's probably a big enough step for beginners like us) to see multiple areas of order in software development and choose between them for our projects.

Closure Questions:

What was the cause of the last failure in software development you experienced?

In retrospect, can you see the key characteristics of a catastrophic transition in that situation?

How can you help to prepare your group to survive and thrive if a catastrophic transition is forced on it?

BUBBLES AND FUNCTION CHARTS

Draw a chart of the functions supported in a commercially viable application package. Use bubbles for each function, and use the size of each bubble to indicate the depth and breadth of coverage for that function within that package. Try, as possible, to have each bubble touch other bubbles where they have an interface or dependency.

You'll find that the chart probably has one large bubble in the center, representing the primary function of the package, with many smaller bubbles around the edges, as necessary to tie the main function to the user world. For example, if the main function is text manipulation, peripheral functions will include printing, file manipulations, maybe some graphics, some operating system command facilities, and so on. Another package, with a different primary purpose, might have the graphics capabilities as the main bubble and the text manipulation as a minor bubble.

A conclusion I used to draw from bubble charts like this was that the ultimate application package would have every bubble be the best possible implementation for its function. If we're trying to build a package that has heavy-duty support for several functions, we could be tempted to select heavy-duty functions from several packages and put them into the new package with minimal change.

This is the best of best of breed (BoBoB) approach. No, that's not a typographical error. The BoBoB approach assumes that we can take the best functions from the best of breed products and combine them to end up with "Super-Product." That's a seductive theory, but it is simplistic. The result will not form a coherent whole. Why? Peripheral functions are always tailored for the world view of their respective main functions. That support has to be carried to the resultant product.

Each formerly central function will retain its own printing support, because the kinds of data being handled are different and the printing routines will have been optimized for the differences.

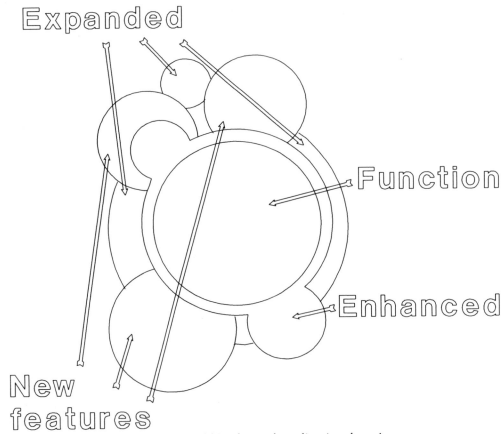

Figure 2–1. *Bubble chart of application function*

Each formerly central function will retain its own text manipulation support, again because the support was optimized for the individual use of text within each original function.

Thus, the combined product will actually have duplicated functions scattered throughout.

The simplistic conclusion ignores boundary conditions between the functions (with the details that always fall into such boundaries), and it evokes the view that all the bubbles are the same size. It is a conclusion that is likely to fail in the face of real products and real customer use. In other words, the result of that approach to creating a comprehensive package would directly show its chaotic nature.

Areas of order—Each major function represents an area of order and consistency; user interfaces are consistent within the function, as is the user conceptual view. Similarly, the peripheral functions represent smaller areas of order.

As suggested by a reviewer (I love feedback) there is a balance to be achieved between optimizing a total system and optimizing its component parts. Interested readers can refer to the field of optimization theory.

One of the results of optimization theory is that the best optimization for individual components is often the worst possible optimization for the total system. Similarly, optimization of the total system can cause some components to have unacceptable performance or to be unusable.

Notice something about getting a working balance of optimization. If the people doing the optimization focus their attention on individual components and the system by turns, they set up a feedback situation that leads to chaos such that their jobs may never be done. Only by handling the cross-effects of optimization carefully will they achieve a satisfactory balance for both the system and all of its components.

Closure questions:

> *Which of the decisions that you make routinely are optimization decisions?*

> *How might you know whether your decisions bring order or disorder to your organization?*

Box 8. *Local optimization*

Areas of disorder—Compared with the major functions, the collection of peripheral functions are less orderly. For example, peripheral print functions will probably not look at all alike, graphics need print control that differs from what is required for text or spreadsheets, and the parameters and controls on peripheral functions will be confusing to the novice user.

Self similarity—Functions that are peripheral to major functions will show some similarities to the corresponding major function; within limits they will even have their own ties to other peripheral functions. Further, with the central functions and supporting peripheral functions, major functional groups will be structurally similar to each other. (Look at their bubble charts).

Self dissimilarity—Even as corresponding major and peripheral functions show similarities of purpose, they will still betray their origins and have differences in details and user interface that may require users to understand those origins in order to be able to use them.

Even if a heavy-duty package isn't compounded from different existing packages, the same kinds of effects will be seen. Consider what is required to support printing relative to multiple major functions. Different needs in each of the major functions will cause differences in the information required to print their information.

The only thing that can prevent this kind of disorder is the adoption of a

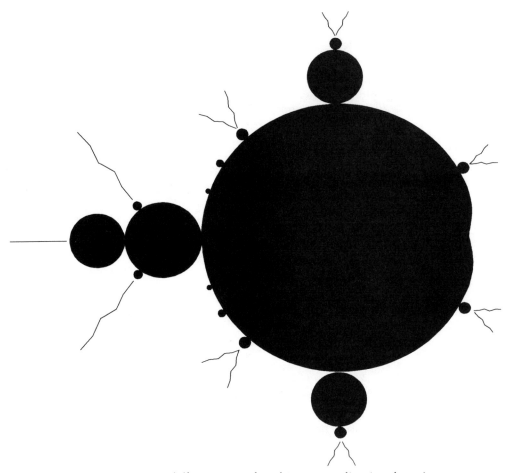

Figure 2–2. *Mandelbrot set as the ultimate application function*

common conceptual view for the entire package. That is, the conceptual views for the individual functions must be abandoned in favor of a single unifying view. This, however, is not a step to be taken without considerable care. The common conceptual view might detract from the efficacy of the individual functions. It might alienate users of existing products because it would differ from the views for all existing products. It might cause problems in selling the product because there would be no single application view that would entice novice users. On the other hand, the common conceptual view might make the product easier to use and more attractive to the expert or the general user.

A better view might be that the full-function ultimate application set is a collection of bubble charts (individual applications). The biggest bubbles correspond to the clear areas in plots of the Mandelbrot set as introduced on page 1, while boundaries in the plot correspond to the smaller bubbles and the areas where the bubbles come together.

Note that the different concentrations of application function may not require that the user interface be different. While there are application functions that are more productive with different user interface techniques than other functions might require, the current state of the art in user interface calls for more similarity of design, not for excuses to be different.

Closure Questions:

> Do you know of any useful application that consists of a single function with no peripheral supporting functions?
> What is required of a utility support function that is useful with multiple major applications?
> Would you expect the same data structures to work in different applications that are based on different paradigms?

PARADIGMS AND WORLD VIEWS

Thomas S. Kuhn studied changes in scientific thought through history and came to the startling conclusion that those changes didn't happen very smoothly. We're startled by this because we've spent our entire lives learning how one set of ideas leads naturally to another set of ideas. But Kuhn's book, *The Structure of Scientific Revolutions* blows holes in all that. We do stand on the shoulders of giants, but getting up there is no smooth elevator ride.

Kuhn's basic idea is that the endeavors of scientists are coordinated and focused by a commonly accepted world view, called a paradigm, and that a change in paradigms is always accompanied by distress and disorientation among the scientists until the new paradigm is acceptably entrenched.

A paradigm is highly useful because it orients the normal work that must be done in a field. Normal exploration within the field is directed toward discoveries that will reconfirm the validity of the paradigm and expand the way the paradigm covers the field for ever more productive results. Paradigms adjust and their details accumulate as part of the practice of the normal work done within them.

Near the time when a paradigm changes, anomalies raise their ugly heads, standing out in stark contrast to the order of the old paradigm. Adherents of the old paradigm try to dismiss the anomalies as noise or the failure to apply sufficient discipline. But those on the fringes of the old paradigm start looking for a new one that will explain the anomalies and provide a more satisfactory understanding of the world. For this very reason, an older paradigm is a straitjacket for those who feel that a different world view would be more productive. Paradigms are replaced when more attractive (seductive, elegant, comprehensive . . .) paradigms are set forth, usually in response to unexplained and anomalous (according to the old paradigm) observations. The anomalies were ugly ducklings in the old view, but they become swans in the new.

Looking at current information and things not stated by Kuhn, there are three significant comments to be made.

First, Kuhn reported only on researchers in pure science. Being very careful about this, he didn't report the fact that he described the normal human condition. That is, we can use his observations in everything that we do.

Second, Kuhn didn't explore what happens with concurrent paradigms. There really are lots of groups working in parallel, each with its own paradigm. The collection of paradigms forms a mosaic structure.

The complete set of paradigms in existence at a particular time can be likened to the Mandelbrot set—there are areas of consistency (order) and areas of chaos (apparent disorder). The mosaic has a coherent structure, as does each piece. Looking more closely at areas of disorder or boundary areas between order and disorder, you can see sub-areas that display all of the characteristics noted in the original view.

Starting with the mosaic view of all of the paradigms in force at any particu-

---

The story goes that baby ducks are imprinted with the first moving object that they see. That object is forevermore accepted (and all others are rejected) as the duckling's mother.

There's a parallel tendency for software developers to be imprinted with the first technology, the first language, and the first organization in which they had any success at all. A developer will measure the value of other development organizations, technologies, and languages in terms of the original imprinting.

However, there are exceptions to this tendency. Some developers are perpetual mavericks, people who never quite got imprinted on any of their projects. These people will have their biases (don't we all?) but their egos will not be involved with any particular imprinting.

Some developers go through the traumatic experience of finding their original imprinting to be untenable. Whether the original imprinting was hopelessly ineffective or the developer found projects where the original imprinting implied career suicide makes little difference. The surviving developer shifts paradigms, either adopting a new imprinting or joining the ranks of the perpetual mavericks.

A person's flexibility and imprinting are key characteristics to be considered when forming a new team or adding people to an existing team. Mismatches can be disastrous.

Closure questions:

How would you identify developers with desirable imprints for your projects?

What might you do with developers who are imprinted in ways that will conflict with your project needs?

Box 9. *The baby duck syndrome*

lar time, paradigm changes are like growth or size reduction in areas of order or disorder in the Mandelbrot set. This reminds me of the rainstorm noted on page 10. A paradigm change in one area might have a negligible effect on the paradigm in a second area while completely overwhelming the paradigm in a third.

Finally, Kuhn has laid some important groundwork. The concepts he provides are robust, and they are easily combined with newer information to aid in understanding how people work and how to cope with human institutions.

Closure Questions:

> How many paradigms (world views) can you identify in the current field of computer science?
> How often do such theoretical dichotomies as Reduced Instruction Set Computers and Complex Instruction Set Computers prevent practical implementations?
> Do you have a blind spot because of your own current specialty?
> How would you step above a possible blind spot to see if it existed?

LAYERS OF REALITY

World views provide an overlay of reality. No person now alive is able to look at all human artifacts and tell exactly what each artifact will do under any specified circumstance. We have only to look at computer systems to realize this, since those who built the systems are often mystified by their behaviors. The chaos of reality will have areas of order and areas of disorder, as will the chaos of any particular world view.

The areas of order and different world views actually become layered. For example, a physical reality is interpreted by the world view of a particular culture. Within that culture, a community of experts in particular matters adopts a world view that is specific to the community. Within that community, each individual will have a unique world view that differs from all the others, whether they are individual, community, or cultural. Even individuals will often have several world views, depending on what they're doing at any particular time. Moreover, they will usually be aware enough of the surrounding world views to be able to communicate (somewhat) with others within the community or the surrounding culture.

Each of these world views will recognize areas of order and try to ignore areas of disorder. Because of the layering, however, it is safe to say that the areas of order at one level will often disagree with the areas of order at other levels. Where a cultural view of a polished marble surface might see smoothness with an interesting pattern, the community of marble workers might see the original roughness of the quarried stone and the potential breakage that might have occurred during cutting and polishing, while a sculptor might see the potential to use the fracture lines in the marble to reshape it into the likeness of a flying bird. At each level, the features of the marble are viewed differently, as beauty, peril, and opportunity.

If one layer has an area of order where an underlying layer has an area of disorder, we can sometimes see the superimposed layer dominating the disorder and suppressing it. This is not unreal. In an overview of software development, lines of code can be used to estimate effort, complexity, and the resources that will be required to produce a product. However, at the detailed level of software development, lines of code are of little use and actually may be harmful as a measurement.

Think in terms of the feedback that is the proximate cause for chaos. An imposed world view changes the feedback, and the change in feedback can change the behavior of the system. Of course, there's always the risk that the change can increase rather than decrease the disorder, but that is also in accord with our experience with human institutions.

If the superimposed layer has a broad-brush generality to it, it will often ignore or not account for the funny little things that happen at the lower level. Often this is acceptable because the superimposed layer gives significant assistance in dealing with the world. Where the underlying details are important, people often make the necessary adjustments without even noticing that there is anything missing from the superimposed layer. Those who doubt this need only consider the bureaucracy that works: policies are broad enough for general work, but caring people keep things running smoothly.

Where the superimposed layer matches an underlying layer or even reaches through to a still deeper layer and matches *that*, the results can be immensely productive and pleasing. We can exploit the match. The learning curve will be quite fast for the software system that is in accord with the culture that will use it. We see this occur frequently when the implementation model is natural for users, but seldom when the implementation model is imposed by developers.

This formulation also indicates areas of trouble. When one layer is in conflict with another layer and neither can adjust, the resultant disorder will exceed what should be expected by either. These kinds of situations can usually be characterized as fictions imposed on misunderstood realities.

We can easily see the results in the competition between American and Japanese companies in the 1980s. Where those in control failed to recognize the realities of their situations, they were displaced by others who had more productive views of those realities. Given the choice between adjusting to changes in the world and clinging to prior views, the losers made the second choice. The most frequently cited example of this phenomenon is the automobile industry in the early 1980s. Japanese companies adopted the most productive view, and American companies are still trying to catch up.

A world view that works for a while is not guaranteed to work forever. Reality itself changes in a competitive world because of the advances and dynamic interaction (feedback) between all of the competitors in that world. It is necessary to know that our world views will always differ from reality and that a competitive position is based on a conformance between our world view and reality. Since reality is constantly changing, we must be ready—even eager—to change our world views. As with the rainstorm on page 10, we can't run in the same area of order forever. In very practical terms, this leads to a technique for exploiting chaos. Try on a different world view for size, or adjust your own, and then look to see and understand whether the changes reduced the disorder you have to deal with or moved some of that disorder to a place that might be more convenient for you or your customers.

Closure Questions:

> How might you know if your world view interfered with solutions to your design problems?
>
> When was the last time some novice asked a question out of ignorance and you responded, "Why didn't I think of that?"
>
> What techniques could help you to remember other points of view?

GAUSE WINDOWS

At a quality course chaired by IBM's Marty Fisher, Dr. Don Gause presented a concept that shows great promise for organizing thoughts on designing software. He drew a window with four areas and associated each area with the knowledge that people have of the application being developed.

Along the top edge, he divided the window according to whether the application developer does or doesn't know pertinent information. Along the left edge, he divided the window according to whether the application client or user does or doesn't know the pertinent information. (See Figure 2–3.)

In the upper left area, both the user and the developer know what's going on. This should be good news, as there is clear communication, the requirements are known, and the developer can build exactly what the client/user needs and wants.

The upper right area is labelled "the area of lost opportunity." This is the area where the user knows what is going on but the application developer doesn't. Because the application developer is in the dark, the area is not supported in the product and the user will feel much dissatisfaction. The user isn't supported and the developer has missed some opportunities.

The lower left area is labelled "the area of surprises." In this area, the developer knows what's going on but the client/user doesn't. In past systems, this is where the developer has provided great support for functions and the user has stumbled all over the place trying to locate entirely different functions. Dr. Gause illustrates this with an imaginary phone system. The system has a message for him, but he has no way of finding it because he has to know a password that only he can find—only if he knows the password. You see lots of Catch 22 situations in "the area of surprises." This is also where developers don't understand why a user has problems.

The fourth area, the lower right, is labelled "the area of nature's last laugh."

	Developer's Knowledge	
	Known	Unknown
Known	Area of Good News	Area of Lost Opportunity
Unknown	Area of User Surprises	Area of Nature's Last Laugh

(Left vertical label: Client or User's Knowledge)

Figure 2–3. *The Gause Window*

This is the area where neither the developer nor the client/user knows what's going on. This area leads to such occurrences as Galloping Gerty (the Tacoma Narrows Bridge, which vibrated itself to pieces in a 40-mile-an-hour cross-wind), early jet airplanes blowing up (because of metal fatigue in their skins), and a highway patrolman shooting an innocent motorist (because a license number had been reissued to a vehicle owned by someone who was not "armed and dangerous").

Looking at what we can do with each of the areas within the Gause Window, at least two things become apparent.

First, developers need to try to reduce the "unknown" portion of their windows. That is, a developer should try to understand the application. This is particularly true in a competitive environment. We can't afford a large area either of "lost opportunity" or "nature's last laugh." Neither is profitable and nature's last laugh tends to be a pratfall or worse.

Second, developers need to understand what it is that they know that the client/user doesn't. Consider what happens if a developer builds a system (or tool) that makes everything equally accessible and easy to use. If the client/user doesn't understand very much about the application, most attempts to use the system will result in surprises. Unfortunately, in such situations the surprises are frequently unpleasant.

The less a user knows about what developers provide, the more mysterious the whole product will be. Such products tend to be dominated by things that mean nothing to users. Faced with such a situation, developers often claim that the user needs to learn how to use the product. While there's truth in this claim, it is too often used to deny that developers could make the product easier to use and understand. This doesn't have to be a source of conflict.

We can realize a mutually advantageous resolution when we keep the Gause Window in mind.

We can design a system (tool) so that the basics (what the client/user knows) are covered in the most natural and accessible part of the tool. We can design the additional parts of the system so that getting to them is a logical process that grows out of what the user already knows. That is, the user can understand more and more about the system so that there are no big and unpleasant surprises. Learning can be a series of small and pleasant surprises.

Self-similarity is probably the most productive way to handle the design of applications between the areas that the application developer knows about. If the sub-area that the user doesn't know about follows the pattern of the area the user does know about, the entire application is accessible to the user.

Closure Questions:

> What product has given you the pleasure of using an application tool that fits Don Gause's ideas, where learning more about the tool was simple because it extended what you first learned?
> What products have required you to learn whole new sets of rules and thoughts?
> Which did you like better?
> What is it about people that makes the second kind of product so much more common than the first?

MYOPIA—SOME LIMITS ON WHAT WE SEE

One of my favorite observations is "Everyone is myopic; we are all bounded by what we've seen and what we can imagine." You can see some significant aspects of this in Chapter 9, particularly in the sections on Designer's Sources and Pedantry and Design Skills, but the effect is even more pervasive than those sections would indicate. Myopia is a significant part of our everyday lives. Further, that myopia severely limits our achievements and value in an environment that requires innovation.

On the face of it, this observation is a self-defining truth. Taking the word "myopic" as a visual metaphor for thought and conceptual exploration, it is obvious that we should include everything we've ever experienced in forming our current and future thoughts. This is a minimal definition. For the maximal definition, it's difficult to conceive of the possibility that we could think about something we can't imagine. So, it might appear that my observation isn't of much use since it is trivial.

However, we can follow the observation with some questions that can help to turn it into something much more useful for us. For example, "Are the bounds inviolate and immutable? Are the bounds so fixed and unchangeable that we are forever and always limited to what we have experienced today and to what we imagine today?"

The answer to those questions definitely should be no. If the answer were yes, then there would be a time in our lives when there would be no new situations, no new people, no new challenges, and no new jobs to do. If someone argues with these specific examples to argue the general statement, we can easily pick similar examples to illuminate the unreality of any bounds he or she chooses to set, either by differences that can be found within the bounds, or by the intrusion of reality on unreal assumptions.

So we can safely say that the bounds can and will change over time. This should be a red flag for us. We should realize that we can choose to stay up with the tides of change or we can ignore them and be overwhelmed.

Another question to ask is "How can we get around these bounds?"

There are many answers to this question, probably as many as there are people who ask it. In general, though, the answer is to look intentionally beyond those bounds. Recognizing that they are composed of what we've experienced and what we can imagine, we can extend the bounds by experiencing more and by learning to imagine more.

If this still sounds trivial, look around you. There are people with whom you work who firmly believe that their jobs are completely defined and will be so forever. There are people with whom you work who firmly believe that their current tools are exactly the ones required for their jobs and that nothing else could possibly be better. As an example, a person like this, using a paper spreadsheet, would not believe that the electronic version was possible. Similarly, a person like this, using a hammer and a nail, would not believe that a staple gun or a nail gun would be possible.

There are many ways to broaden your experience: books, personal interactions, courses, hobbies, individual explorations, and so on. For software developers, direct contact with a knowledgeable end user is one of the most surprising and profitable ways to broaden experience. Individual explorations can involve such things as trying a new tool and seeing where a particular application model leads, or they can be like the exploration done by Stephen W. Hawking in theoretical physics. Flights of the mind and mental explorations have opened many famous doors to thought and practice.

Experience provides that basis and the raw materials that imagination manipulates, but you can extend your bounds by working directly with your imagination itself. Rather than waiting for ideas to occur to you, you can practice any of a number of techniques for pursuing them. *Are Your Lights On?* by Donald C. Gause and Gerald M. Weinberg, *Conceptual Blockbusting* by James L. Adams, and *Patterns of Problem Solving* by Moshe F. Rubinstein are excellent texts that can help you discover techniques for expanding your imagination. Look for ideas that transfer from one environment to another (use microcode principles in application software, for example, or use a desired organizational structure as the structure of an application). Or suspend your critical facilities for a while and make long lists of silly ideas about a problem (brainstorming); when you look back over the silly list, you'll find that some of the ideas aren't so silly after all and may in fact be eminently practical.

So we're all myopic. We can let our myopia be a mental straitjacket, holding us in the past, or we can expand the bounds of our myopia to grow into the future.

Closure Questions:

If you have problems to be solved, do you want them to be solved by people whose myopic bounds are smaller than or the same as yours?

How might you find people with different myopic bounds who could contribute to your projects?

Having seen changes in the past, do we have any reason to believe that the future will involve no further change?

SIMULATED ANNEALING

I beg your pardon. I'm about to do it to you again. This section is based on some mathematical ways to deal with problems and it uses an idea taken from metallurgy. But read on anyway, this is where we find that we can make progress by moving backwards.

Some problems require the evaluation of large numbers of alternatives, so many that analytic solutions are not practical. Many of these deal with combinations of possibilities. One of the most familiar of these problems is the attempt to minimize the cost of a salesperson who covers a multicity territory. Solutions to these problems are found by starting with any solution, then looking for ways to change to better solutions. An overall cost function gives a measurement for how much each change might improve or degrade the overall cost.

The straightforward approach to finding a "best" solution is to try changes and incorporate those changes that reduce the cost. This, unfortunately, often ends in a local rather than a global minimum—a solution that looks good compared to all immediate changes but still is not the best overall solution.

An example is that of water in Utah, trying to get to the lowest possible place. The water follows one rule—it obeys the law of gravity. That straightforward rule leads much of the water in the state to the Great Salt Lake, rather than to the lower (and so more desirable) ocean. The Great Salt Lake is a local minimum, the ocean a more global minimum.

Crystals in metals lead to structural weakness and other undesirable properties. Crystals form when hot metal is cooled nonuniformly or too rapidly, allowing the atoms in the metal to form local alignments—crystals—instead of achieving a uniform alignment throughout the part. If the metal cools slowly and uniformly, the atoms align uniformly and the crystals don't form— local optima are bypassed in favor of the desired global solution. Annealing is the controlled cooling process whereby metal parts are formed without internal crystallization.

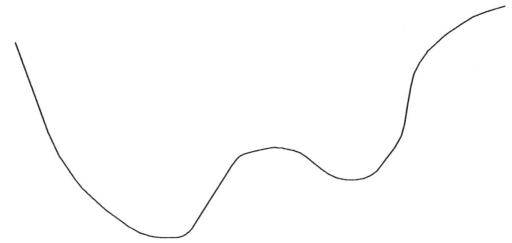

Figure 2–4. *Curve with local minimum*

The parallels between metallurgy and combinatorial problems are in the avoidance of local optimizations and the gradual tightening of controls.

In the combinatorial situation, a local optimum can be viewed as a cup. (This concept is described in *Simulated Annealing: Theory and Applications* by P.J.M. van Laarhoven and E.H.L. Aarts.) The depth of the cup is the cost difference between the solutions at its bottom (locally minimal cost) and the solutions that allow a set of changes, with some ending inside the cup and some ending outside it. The goal is to be able to choose sequences of solutions that can escape from cups.

The Simulated Annealing answer is to accept solution changes that may result in increased cost. This is done by controlling "temperature." Temperature, for simulated annealing, is defined in terms of controls on how much of a cost degradation will be allowed. Typically, there are two aspects to this— the amount of cost degradation allowed, and the probability of accepting a degraded solution.

In a straightforward solution to a combinatorial problem, there is zero probability of accepting a solution that costs more than a known solution.

In simulated annealing, solutions with higher cost than a known solution may be accepted to allow solutions to escape from cups. A probability function is used for this, a function that can be controlled so that it gradually reduces to zero. The result is that sequences of solutions have finite probabilities of escaping from cups, and computing for "long enough" will ensure that the remaining solutions are not in cups.

To ensure that a sequence of solutions doesn't jump around so much that it ends back in a cup, we limit the cost degradations. By gradually tightening the restrictions on the size of the allowed cost degradation and the probability of accepting cost degradations, the sequence of solutions will have a high probability of leading to a global rather than a local optimum. Gradually reducing the "temperature" allows the improvement of the final solution.

Looking back at the example of the water in Utah, the local optimum (cup) is the Great Salt Lake, the global optimum the Pacific Ocean. With the simulated annealing concept, water would be allowed to flow uphill (with some probability, and within limits). It would have some chance of getting out of the Great Salt Lake to someplace else. However, the limits on how far uphill it could go would prevent water from getting from the ocean back into the lake. The result would be that water that left the lake would never get back to it so all the water would eventually end up in the ocean.

Simulated annealing is often used in association with artificial intelligence. However, the idea has considerable value for us in software development. Rather than taking a forced march to a locally optimal solution to a software problem, we need to take a larger view and allow ourselves to get out of our cups.

Closure Questions:

> How might you use the concept of simulated annealing to overcome a cultural aversion to risk taking?
>
> What kinds of results would you expect from any project that is not allowed to back away from bad or less than optimal decisions?

3

Order and Boundaries

So far, we've talked about chaos and catastrophes. However, as strange as it might seem in a book with such beginning headings, the real message of *Exploiting Chaos: Cashing in on the Realities of Software Development* is about order. That's what we'll talk about in this chapter. As you'll soon see, the need for order is a basic human and business need. But, just as order is basic for human endeavor, the various areas in chaos are inherently bounded. This is one of the most fascinating aspects of chaos from a business point of view. Allowing for chaos allows us to remain productive and on track in achieving what we need to achieve, while failing to allow for it often leaves us so badly swamped in our own efforts that we can't produce.

THE PSYCHOLOGY OF ORDER

Dr. Perry Buffington is a PhD in child psychology, lecturer, talk show host ("Doc Rock"), writer for *Sky* magazine, and all-around good guy. In his outstanding talk on the psychological aspects of leadership, Dr. Buf (his preferred moniker) discusses what it takes to be a charismatic leader.

Dr. Buf asserts that people will do almost anything if they are given authoritative reasons for doing it. Examples include such extremes as lining up for electroshock treatments, running death camps, inflicting pain on test subjects, and taking poison in Jonestown.

In software development, we can expect that the same kinds of phenomena will occur. We will see people following development processes whether they "believe" in the processes or not. (See box 6 on page 15.) We will see leaders who compel entire organizations to do smart (or stupid) things.

All of this ties in with a key point in Dr. Buf's description of a charismatic leader: a charismatic leader provides order (or at least the illusion of order) to his or her followers. Let's put that another way. People will do almost anything if their leaders will give them authoritative endorsement in an area of apparent order. In fact, people will do almost anything to remain in an area of order, whether there's a leader to tell them to do that or not. This is a basic characteristic of people; *people function only when they perceive order in their enterprises*.

The natural conclusion we can draw from this portion of Dr. Buf's work is that people will always develop software in an area of order, according to their world views and perceptions. Now, think back to the section on catastrophe theory. We talked about a catastrophic sidetrack—people "stalling" between areas of order—in box 7 on page 16. They really didn't stall in an area they considered to be an area of disorder. Rather, their perception, "I'm doing my job, I handle exceptions," defines their area of order.

If you see people who appear to be disruptive to software development, the direct conclusion is that they are either using a different world view (hence a different area of order) than you are, or that they are not involved in software development at all (perhaps they have another agenda). The latter is the easier guess to make, as it allows us to retain our view that we are personally correct in our world view and those who disagree are troublemakers. Unfortunately for our sense of balance, the former is more often the reality.

Closure Questions:

What will you see in your organization if it is actively pursuing an area of order?

What key factors can you use to resolve apparent disruptions in the organization?

BOUNDS OF CHAOS

Chaos, in useful cases, is bounded. There are boundaries in terms of areas where things are orderly and conventionally predictable. There are also boundaries in terms of the results of processes that are wildly disorderly yet never exceed those boundaries. Further, since chaos is the result of feedback, we can be assured that the full range of chaotic behavior will cover both a process and any attempts to dynamically modify that process. This, in effect, can push the bounds of a chaotic process to wider boundaries than might be desirable.

The other boundaries on chaotic behavior that we should never forget are the natural limits that even the most chaotic processes don't exceed. Trees, for example, are very chaotic in their growth (including size, placement, and shape) but can be counted on to remain within particular ranges of sizes in particular growing conditions. The fact that these boundaries can sometimes be very precise is shown by the existence of the "tree line" on a mountain, that altitude above which no trees grow.

In software development, one of the key boundaries comes from the complexity of communication. If the number of people who need to communicate is small, the potential for disorderly behavior is also small. But if the number of people who need to communicate is large, the probability of disorderly results becomes a near certainty. This is one of the concepts that Frederick P. Brooks explores. (See box 20 on page 77.)

Chaos, in useful cases, has a variety of dimensions. Real world problems (and particularly the kinds of things found in software development) have complex feedback from a variety of factors. We can view each of the factors in complex situation as being a dimension. By the inherent nature of feedback, a change in any individual factor will probably have an effect on the process as a whole. Further, the results of any particular change will vary depending on what the rest of the factors are doing.

Basically, all of this means not only that we have to be careful, but also that we have to take a few risks.

The area where we have to exercise care is in the controls we place on a

---

A friend of mine who has a swimming pool teaches us about how control can lead to chaotic behavior. This friend dutifully measured the chemical balance of the pool water and every day he added the right amounts of chemicals to lead to the right chemical balance. Being an intelligent person, he soon noticed that he and his wife were spending less time than they desired in the pool because it was not in the proper balance for use. Despite his good intentions, the chemical and biological balance of the pool fluctuated wildly.

He tied his observation to his behavior and decided to take a more stabilizing approach. He acted on his measurements less often and used less than the prescribed amount when he did add chemicals. In effect, he allowed the pool's responses to stabilize somewhat before he intervened again. The result was that he no longer found it necessary to frequently put in massive doses of chemicals to kill runaway algae growth, and he no longer had to avoid the pool because it was too much of a chemical soup. By restraining his intervention, he reduced the bounds of the chaotic behavior and increased his use of his pool.

Closure question:

> *If your group is gyrating wildly, how will you know whether to introduce an exciting, unifying idea to your people or to take them away from the problem for a day?*

Box 10. *Keeping the pool clean*

process. Carelessly chosen controls can increase the boundaries of the process and lead to more disorderly behavior rather than more orderly behavior.

Consider what would happen if a manager, early in a development cycle, were to impose a full change control discipline on a project; the learning experiences of the change control team would cause much larger variations in the effort and time required to fix problems than would the comparable learning experiences of the individual developer. This is another example of increased disorder resulting from attempts to exert control.

Consider also what would happen if no change control discipline were ever incorporated into a software development effort. In that case, changing requirements and code "improvements" could continue unabated long past the scheduled end date of the project.

The level and extent of the control has to be appropriate to the level of refinement and definition of the design. No matter how well intentioned the control, an inappropriate choice will extend the boundaries of the process behavior. We have to establish and enforce the right controls for the state of the process—controls that work in practice—if we expect the process to work.

The length of a feedback loop has a lot to do with the chaotic bounds of the process. Consider what this means for customer involvement.

If customers see only finished products and give feedback only on problems they encounter, the feedback loop with development will be extremely long. It's highly probable that the chaotic bounds of the process will be so large that the product will die before going through many cycles. Only the luck of the original product view can give it any hope for success.

If customers are closely involved with development efforts the feedback loop will be quite short. This means that the chaotic bounds of the process, too, will be quite short, and the product can be on target in a correspondingly short time. On target means happy customers and more demand for the product, so the life and profitability of the product will be long relative to the chaotic bounds. Missed success in early versions can be turned to real success in later versions.

Closure question:

  Why do software development organizations believe that they can satisfy unknown customers?

Box 11. *Customer involvement*

The risks we have to take come from the fact that we can't know what effect any particular change will have on a process. Still, our experiences tell us that certain things tend to produce good results and other things tend to produce bad results. Whatever actions we take, whatever controls we attempt to incorporate within a process, we need to temper our decisions with our knowledge of our experiences and with the awareness that the results are ultimately unpredictable. In practical terms, this means two things.

First, we needn't wait (indeed, we shouldn't wait) for full information on every decision we will make. All we need is a reasonable certainty that is consistent with the risks associated with the decision. Then we should make the decision. If the risk in a decision involves a threat to human life, we will be more careful than if the only risk is the loss of a pencil. The range of the risks we know about will determine what "reasonable certainty" means.

Second, we should follow every decision with observation of the results to see if they are desirable. Here, again, we shouldn't rush to change the decision, but should allow time for any disorderly reaction to die down of its own accord. If the results remain disorderly, the boundaries of the disorderly behavior are too large, or the results remain counterproductive for an unreasonable length of time, then we must act. We should accept that the risk didn't work out, adjust our knowledge based on that new understanding, and proceed to a new decision (possibly one that reverses the first one).

So the question of boundaries on chaotic behavior really leads us to several questions about making decisions. How much control do we want or need in a process? When are the controls appropriate? How well can we predict what results will come from particular decisions? Who should make the decisions about the control of a particular process?

Closure Questions:

> How might you know where the bounds for your processes are?
> As you take your risks, do you care whether your feedback information is direct or indirect?

THE STOCK MARKET

It's fascinating to watch the action around the stock market as people try to guess what stocks will do in the future. Stock market analysts thrive on reporting all the indicators they can find and telling how the market has "responded to those indicators" in the past. The number and magnitude of the fallacies inherent in this kind of reporting is impressive—we'll look at them after a few paragraphs of background information.

The stock market is an excellent and highly visible example of chaotic behavior derived from feedback. People evaluate all the known information about a company, decide what they think the company will do in the future based on that information, and then place some money on the line to gain some benefit from the predicted future. Other people evaluate all the known information about how other people have viewed that company in the past, decide what they think the other investors will do in the future based on that information, and then place some money on the line to gain some benefit from the predicted behavior of those other investors. We have to wonder what the stock market is really about.

Notice that the philosophies and techniques used by people who play the market have changed over the years. People have always used the stock market to make money, but the details changed.

Companies needed to raise capital, so they offered stock to investors who were convinced that the company would make or deliver good products or services. Companies still use the stock market for raising capital, and some investors still buy on this original basis.

Investors began to focus on stock trends, and bought or sold stock based not on the value of the company but on the trends of the company's stock. Note the feedback—this tactic is based on the perception of "the perception of the company's value."

Some investors don't understand how to evaluate a company's value, and can't understand the trends, so they look for significance in an even more indirect set of information: market indicators. Now we have feedback on feedback. Some market indicators measure factors that might bear on the performance of individual stocks, but others measure trends to try to predict trends.

Next some investors decide that everyone and his favorite sibling can evaluate the available information and will come to common conclusions based on that information. Also, stock recommendations often result in hordes of people buying or selling particular stock issues. Because an excess in buy orders drives a price up, and an excess in sell orders drives a price down, these mass actions force market results that are contrary to their expectations. So contrarians hope to make money by doing the opposite of what everyone else is doing. This is yet another level of feedback, watching the watchers and doing the opposite of what they do.

Finally, we see the feedback between the market and a company when the company takes internal actions to please the stock market. One example is where market analysts decide that a company has too many people, and the company engages in several people-shedding actions "to respond to the needs of stockholders." This kind of action should make even the strongest investors quake in their boots. It's bad enough to invest in a chaotic market using multilayered feedback, but the management team that closes the feedback loop makes it even worse.

With all of these tactics active at every moment of the trading day on the stock market, we should not be surprised at the market's chaotic performance. Indeed, we should wonder why it does not appear to be even more disorderly than it is.

Someone who wants to make a living on the stock market has several choices, based on the layers of reality of the situation. (Refer back to "Layers of Reality" on page 23.) For real value, one choice would be to get back to the basics of evaluating and investing in companies rather than in trends or indicators. We might even go so far as to recommend against investing in a company that publicly announces actions taken "to please the stockholders." But that is a very individual decision, and I don't want to tell you where your money should go.

The stock market is a bastion of people who are interested in outcomes (stock performance, getting a good position, making money). In a similar way, software development is populated by people who are interested in outcomes. Customers want products, developers want paychecks, and everybody wants a profit. All of these are reasonable things. But a focus on outcomes can backfire in software development just as it can in the stock market. Consider the push for zero defects in software development. In his paper on the "Fallacies of Zero Defects," IBM's Ken deLavigne says "By concentrating on outcomes rather than processes, Zero Defects obscures and postpones knowing where to act and what to do, and thus opposes its own function."

Not only do many players in the stock market measure their performances by outcomes, they establish their investment plans based on those measurements. Yet chaos downstream is not predictable and it is not reversible. That is, as you get further downstream of the change, it becomes harder to reliably predict a desired outcome. Eventually, you can't do it. This makes it multiply difficult to adjust a course based only on results. Think about the exercise you did with the stream of water on your car in the section on Chaos in Water and Wax; it was not possible, except in a gross fashion, to adjust the downstream flow of water by any movement of the immediate flow. Getting the right outcome in software development requires an experimental approach to the development effort and a focus on the work being done. The parallel with the stock market goes like this: Profit and financial value (just like low software error rates) are byproducts of substantial and effective business practices (development processes). Trying to manage directly for profit and financial value (low error rates) will probably make that goal unachievable.

It is often tempting to believe that correlations in information show cause and effect. In the stock market, an example of correlation might be the movement of market indicators and the prices of stocks. Yet information that moves together can often do so as a result of common causes or coincidence. We can see two things clearly in this kind of situation, and get glimmerings of other things less clearly.

One clear thing we can see is that coincidence is not a good basis for prediction. If this kind of information becomes part of a feedback cycle, any natural chaos will be greatly exaggerated by expanding the boundaries.

A second thing that we can see, slightly less clearly, is that common causes do not necessarily lead to correlation. Even if two outcomes in the stock market are the result of common causes, they need not correlate or help us with our investments. For example, airline and trucking company stocks will respond similarly to an increase or decrease in taxes on fuel. However, they will respond differently to legislation that affects just one of the industries. Whatever changes we make, we must watch the results, not take them as a matter of faith.

Now, you've been patient enough. Here are some of the fallacies in common stock market reporting.

Predicting futures from outcomes: We've seen how effectively we can predict futures from outcomes. All of the leading (and other) market indicators are results of various market conditions; they are outcomes.

Predicting details from aggregates: Though the stock market is measured as something that moves as a whole creature, all stock transactions involve individual companies and stocks. Even aggregate stocks, those which are tied to specific collections of stocks, are simply larger examples of the same thing; they approximate the performance indicators, but still they are individual purchases made at unique points in time.

Predicting one set of outcomes from other outcomes: As with the transportation stocks we discussed earlier, making even simple correlations of outcomes can be difficult. With something as complex as the stock market, we should recognize the difficulty of doing so. For example, having management that is good by all known measures does not mean that a company will make good products. The evaluation of a company has to be based on more than any simple, single set of information.

Making projections with inadequate, unverified, and uncorrelated samples: You might hear "The stock market has gone up for 15 of the last 20 Februaries following a January 31 when the market closed higher than it opened the previous January 2." There is no statistical significance in this information, yet people clutch at these straws in the vain hope that they will gain some slight edge over "the market." Then contrarians play the game, assuming that everyone else will follow the "trend" and drive the results in the opposite direction.

The stock market is a chaotic place, and investors seek mightily for information, views, and clues that will show areas of order in that magnificent chaos. Yet all the traditional stock market indicators suffer from chaotic and statistical flaws.

Similarly, software development is a chaotic endeavor, and many people attempt to pursue software development with similar kinds of outcome indicators. If we pursue software development with these kinds of measurements and practices, we should expect to see the disorderly part of the natural chaos of software development magnified immensely.

Closure Questions:

What measurements in your software development environment reflect outcomes?

Does your organization attempt to manage to the numbers or to the process?

How might you get the benefits of using outcome numbers and process measurements?

CHAOS WITHIN ACCEPTABLE BOUNDARIES

W. Edwards Deming takes a process view of business, and carefully illustrates ways in which good intentions and seductive theories are at the heart of many problems in American business today. Many of his prescriptions are to encourage control for the stability of a process, with the stability of a product being a byproduct rather than the goal of directed effort.

"W. Edwards Deming is the internationally renowned consultant whose work led Japanese industry into new principles of management and revolutionized their quality and productivity. . . . In recognition of his contribution to the economy of Japan, the Union of Japanese Science and Engineering (JUSE) instituted the annual Deming Prizes for contributions to quality and dependability of product."

"Quality to the production worker means that his performance satisfies him, provides to him pride of workmanship."

"It would be a mistake to export American management to a friendly country."

In his book Out of the Crisis, *Dr. Deming describes events and actions that put American businesses in their current sorry state. He further prescribes actions to take and practices to adopt to get those same American businesses out of the crisis.*

Closure question:

> *If you see messages that feel like indictments coming from a figure with the success and stature of W. Edwards Deming, what would be a good business action for you to take?*

Box 12. *W. Edwards Deming:* Out of the Crisis

Deming exhorts businesses to abandon their quests for quick fixes and instant solutions. Adjusting for crises (customer trouble calls, broken equipment, periodic inspection results) leads to processes he describes as chaotic (those whose bounds are so broad that Deming considers them to be out of control). Product quality is determined by the capabilities of processes that are stable, in control, and within predictable bounds. Notice the difference, here, between asking that results be predictable and asking that results be within predictable bounds. The former is impossible in chaotic processes, but the latter is good business.

Deming also advocates the elimination of output measurements of the productivity of individuals. When the goal of a process is pieces, quality takes a back seat. Violating his advocation is an example of the pursuit of short-term goals at the expense of the long-term health of the organization.

Closure Questions:

> How do your measurements show how your processes help to produce your product?

> Do lines of code or person-months have anything to do with software product function or quality?

MULTIPLE AREAS OF ORDER

The view of software that exploits chaos must necessarily endorse multiple areas of order. This is common in business, but it is neither recognized as such nor exploited. In fact, it is most often viewed as a problem rather than an opportunity.

Consider an organization that is divided into departments or functions. Each department or function usually represents different job responsibilities. Each represents a different area of order. Occasionally you will see multiple departments that do the same things, but even these will have differences based on the leader, manager, or supervisor, and on the personalities of the group members. And, in groups of three or more people, you'll see cliques or sub-groups with varying responsibilities. Each of these represents a unique area of order.

So normal, everyday business exhibits the chaotic characteristic of having areas of order. Now that we're familiar with chaos, we expect to see areas of disorder between the areas of order, and we do. Moving a person from one group to another almost always involves thought and adjustment, no matter what role the person adopts in the new group or had in the old. Changing the responsibilities of a group—changing the characteristics of their area of order—always requires thought and adjustment. In every case, the thought and adjustment are part of the process of moving across areas of disorder to get from one area of order to another.

The conceptual leap here is a simple one. A software development process that exploits chaos must be one that integrates diverse world views. We often do this in practice, but our techniques leave much to be desired. We tend to magnify, not minimize, the areas of disorder between groups (or world views). The most common example is the group that tries to work by setting boundaries in responsibilities, thus increasing the impact of areas of disorder. (The discussion in the section on Task Oriented Group Management in Chapter 9 describes some of the phenomena seen in this kind of organization.)

Organizations that have achieved the integration of diverse world views have done so by the use of higher values. They have had visionary leaders, strong cultures, and responsibilities defined by concept rather than boundaries.

Closure Questions:

> How can you recognize an organization that smoothly supports multiple areas of order?
> What kinds of boundaries would you expect to see in such an organization?

IMPOSITION OF ARTIFICIAL BOUNDARIES

People love theories. When things go wrong, people invent theories to explain what happened. When things go well, people invent theories to explain what they did that made them work so well. The theories may be based on lifetimes of experience, years of training, degrees of learning, and the advice of multitudes of experts. The theories may be compelling because of their fit with reality, convenient because of their fit with limited circumstances, or scary because people use them in the face of obvious conflicts with reality. Still, theories all have one thing in common—they're theories.

In a sense, a very real sense, theories are artificial. They don't have any necessary relationship with reality. They are often adopted and used by common consent, but history is full of inadequate theories that had the full agreement of a community.

Software development is also a community that is full of theories. Behavioral theories compel managers to give assignments or empower developers to figure their jobs out for themselves. Theories of linear development compel development groups to compartmentalize their work. Theories of the advantages of specialization compel development organizations to isolate activities in specialized sub-groups. And theories of the structure of software development compel organizations to adopt particular tools (for example, CASE, application generators, languages) and disciplines (among them Software Engineering, hierarchical management, chief programmer teams) as the "right" ways to accomplish their missions.

The fascinating thing that all these theories do is to impose artificial limits on a situation. Theories put bounds on what is allowed to be seen and done. The parallel with paradigms is clear, but we want to look at a different aspect of things here, the impact of artificial boundaries.

The phrase "artificial boundaries" calls up mental images of restrictions, of limitations on what can be done, and particularly of curtailing creativity. After all, how creative can we be if we're put in little boxes and not allowed to look beyond assumed limitations?

That question, the one about creativity and limitations, is a symptom of a linear (or at least pre-chaotic) way of thinking. As we discover in every chapter of *Exploiting Chaos: Cashing in on the Realities of Software Development*, there are right and wrong places for everything. I'll rephrase that. There are workable ways to use everything, and unworkable ways to use everything. And artificial boundaries are no exception.

Software development has applied its theories for as long as it has been recognized as a legitimate occupation (probably even longer). These theories have placed artificial boundaries on what developers could do and what they couldn't do. We've already established that these boundaries will be productive if they match the situation and counterproductive if they fail to match the situation. But what do they do to creativity?

If you read texts on creativity and problem solving, you'll find that they advocate looking beyond the problem and beyond the obvious solution space. They call for looking at problems from a variety of perspectives. This would seem to be in direct conflict with establishing artificial boundaries. But it doesn't have to be so. Two factors lead us to an understanding that artificial boundaries can enhance creativity.

The first factor is people's responses to challenges. Nothing will make some people work harder at something than to tell them that it can't be done. William H. Danforth tells about the light that comes into people's eyes when they're challenged in his book, *I Dare You*. Software developers have always found ways to do the impossible, in spite of boundaries. And it doesn't make much difference if the boundaries are imposed by hardware (memory limitations, processor speed), software (languages to be used, database technology available), or people (schedule constraints, numbers of people available to help).

The second factor comes from what falls within the boundaries.

Consider the differences between the programming languages COBOL and PROLOG. COBOL is procedural—programmers specify explicitly how to do everything that has to be done to arrive at a solution. PROLOG is declarative— programmers specify relationships and constraints that must be satisfied by a solution. Because the COBOL program performs the sequence of operations specified by the programmer, completion of the program should deliver the problem's solution. The PROLOG program explores possibilities until it finds all solutions that satisfy the specified relationships and constraints.

The boundaries of what the two languages can do are different. COBOL shines when the problem to be solved is inherently procedural, a situation that is unnatural for PROLOG. PROLOG shines when the problem involves searching complex possibilities for possible solutions, a situation that is unnatural for COBOL. The programmer who knows COBOL and who would master PROLOG must learn some different ways of thinking, adopting new perspectives and approaches to problems. The reverse is true as well. But notice what we've just said. Moving from one set of boundaries to another not only closes off some options, it opens up other options. With new sets of options, we almost always get opportunities to enhance creativity.

Right now, some readers are ready to do battle. They know that restrictive management can make it impossible to complete some projects. They know that full-color, high-resolution animated graphics require lots of memory. They know that transaction processing requires some level of database support. They can easily cite many examples where artificial boundaries have suppressed creativity and caused the failure of projects. And they're right.

But let's not do battle, let's look at what can happen without artificial boundaries.

What happens when a software developer has no habits of conserving computer memory and believes that memory is unlimited? That developer designs and writes programs that exceed available memory.

What happens when a software developer feels no time pressure for the completion of a project (whether the time pressure comes from imposed schedules or from a personal desire to see final results)? That developer never completes a project.

We could look at more examples, but let's not. We can easily give examples where artificial boundaries have caused problems. We can just as easily give examples where the lack of boundaries has caused problems. We can give examples in between where problems came from boundaries of the wrong shape and size. But more importantly, we can give examples where artificial boundaries, of the right shape and scope, have helped to focus and direct efforts that ended in the achievement of outstanding final results.

The concept of artificial boundaries is another tool for us to use. We can be so restrictive that nothing can be done within the boundaries, we can be so unrestricted that we flounder in a sea of choices, or we can explore a variety of boundaries to find sets that help us to do what we want to do. What we don't have to do, indeed shouldn't even consider doing, is to suffer within artificial boundaries that are counterproductive.

Closure Questions:

> Where have you seen "just a little wrong" theories that caused problems in software development?
>
> How might you intentionally set up productive boundaries for your projects?

PATTERNS AND PERSPECTIVES

People tend to work in patterns. They learn how to do some things well, then learn to carry that knowledge and those skills to other areas. This is highly productive for people, and leads to opportunities in software design.

When large software systems are being designed, the complexity of the system can often grow much faster than the number of components to be implemented, particularly if the interfaces between components are designed for the specific interaction. If the designer were to use patterns of interfaces (sometimes known as standards or common interfaces), this complexity could be significantly reduced. Then the complexity of the system would not grow as fast as the number of components.

Both of these factors are examples of the reasons why it is highly productive to look for patterns in application needs, and to define patterns in the design of a system. Other factors include productivity (patterns can be automated), quality (automated patterns allow no opportunities for human-induced errors, but do allow patterns of errors to be eliminated as a class), consistency (should be obvious), ease of validation (complex combinations are reduced), and many more.

Applications can often be designed and implemented in such a way that they support a general class of applications that includes the target application as a subset. Such applications are therefore useful in handling not only the immediate application, but any similar application need that may arise later. An implementation package designed in this manner can have a simple user interface while providing the functional richness required by the application. It is extendible, flexible, uniformly friendly to users, and provides a highly productive implementation vehicle for related applications.

The current state of the art in program design offers benefits that are not being realized in many application programming shops. These benefits come with the use of various programming tools and techniques that reduce the repetitive aspects of implementing applications. Common module techniques, macro languages, decision tables, language interpreters, high-level programming languages, and application generators are all tools or techniques that can help application implementers be more productive and produce application packages that are easy to use and maintain. Proponents of these techniques and tools all claim (and most demonstrate) productivity gains and other benefits for programmers, users, and managers.

We've just built a mind-picture, a way of looking at things. We've described application world views. We've described areas of order. In dealing with chaos, the use of patterns is a way to identify productive areas of order. Let's look at some of the concepts that are useful in applying patterns to software development.

These concepts describe a way of thinking, a road map, that can lead developers to the same benefits that are provided by the tools and techniques mentioned above.

Adopt a unifying vision. Using a simple and robust model for how applications will function, the developer, the application specialist, and the user will find it easy to communicate and identify a worthwhile functional packaging scheme. A working model can sometimes be chosen early, but may only emerge after several alternatives have been evaluated.

Make it adjustable. The user's world changes too rapidly for the developer ever to hope to provide a "once and for all" solution. The developer who wishes to have some career other than application maintenance must provide someone else (maybe even the user) with the necessary tools to keep the user happy.

Make it extendable. Two kinds of extensions will be necessary—base function extension and specific function extension. Base functions will be added to the provided set, so the implementation should support future developers as they add function in response to expanding user needs. Specific functions that are beyond the capabilities of the set of base functions will almost always exist. These specific functions probably will be hard-coded in some language and invoked within the framework of the base functions.

Provide abstracted capabilities, not concrete implementations. Work with the application specialist to isolate and identify those functions that are meaningful to the user, and implement the functions as flexible units within a consistent framework.

Give control to the user and/or the application specialist. The application

These are the generations of programming languages. In the beginning, there was hardware; engineers built the hardware for specific tasks.

The first generation was direct machine programming at the bit level. This was easier than wiring machines for specific tasks.

The second generation was assembler languages. Their symbolic capabilities released programmers from address computations and bit level entry to the machine.

The third generation was the higher level languages like PL/1, COBOL, and FORTRAN. Their logical capabilities released programmers from particular machine instructions, allowing work at a higher conceptual level and removing some machine dependencies.

The fourth generation was the application generators. Their structural support released programmers from much detailed logic, allowing work at the application level.

The fifth generation may be either object-oriented programming or expert systems and artificial intelligence. Whichever set wins, their conceptual bases will release programmers from many concerns with complex interrelations between specifications, allowing work on what must happen rather than how it will happen.

Closure question:

How can you turn the generation idea to your use in your work?

Box 13. *Generations of programming languages*

developer is too far removed to productively build what the user needs. The knowledgeable user or application specialist can use the functions as building blocks to customize the user's application.

Keep it simple. If the user needs complex functions with simple interfaces, build them. If the application specialist needs a nonprocedural language compiler, provide it. The developer must provide mechanisms that are robust, easy to understand, and simple to use, and he or she may have to be extremely creative to do so. But it's worth it.

Separate the application and the implementation. No direct application function should be built into the code, and no application values should be hard-coded or compiled into what the developer develops. This forces the developer to change paradigms and opens the way for the use of the other concepts.

These concepts and their application can help application implementers by showing how to achieve and cash in on benefits. The concepts lead to the benefits because an application is actually implemented in two steps. The first step is creating application-enabling tools. It is much simpler than creating an application from scratch. The second step is using the enabling tools to create

In Thriving on Chaos: Handbook for a Management Revolution, *Tom Peters presents prescriptions to be followed by companies that want to survive and thrive in the future. The prescriptions are organized into categories of:*

- *Creating total customer responsiveness*
- *Pursuing fast-paced innovation*
- *Achieving flexibility by empowering people*
- *Learning to love change: a new view of leadership at all levels*
- *Building systems in a world turned upside down*

The prescriptions are based on Peters' observations as a consultant and on analysis of successes of many companies in areas where such success was judged by the common wisdom to be impossible. Credibility of the prescriptions may be a personal thing, but the formula corresponds to changes that have been made in several companies prior to 1988 and that should be expected to continue into the future.

Peters is a self-professed extremist. He knows that not everyone is motivated and empowered by the dynamic pursuit of change and variety he espouses. However, the weight of our culture is so much for stability and things as they were that Peters is an essential force for drawing us toward a more balanced view of business and endeavor.

Closure questions:

Is your organization stagnant or constantly changing?

How can you create and exploit stable forces for change in your organization?

Box 14. *Tom Peters:* Thriving on Chaos

the application, and this is also much simpler than creating an application from scratch. The simplifications in the steps are so significant that the total effort required to build both the tools and the application is often much less than the effort required to build a single equivalent hard-coded application.

From 1966 to the present, experience with systems that use these concepts has consistently shown that when an application package is user-oriented, and it has been designed using the concepts, it will:

- Be implemented quickly,
- Function at a level that users need and understand,
- Require little maintenance effort,
- Require little translation between the languages of programmers and users,
- Be responsive to changes in the user's needs, and
- Allow specific applications to be implemented faster and with much less effort than what is required for other techniques.

This last point is fascinating. Using the patterned implementation concepts, applications have greater function, greater flexibility, and are completely implemented with less code and less cost than hard-coded applications.

The unifying vision noted in the first of the concepts is the synopsis of the world view represented by the enabling tool. In terms of chaos, the unifying vision is simply a device that brings out the order in a bounded area of application possibilities. It takes much less code to handle an orderly area than it does a disorderly area, so the productivity shouldn't surprise us. The means to extend the application by adding basic function is no more than a technique for broadening the orderly area beyond what had been originally supported. The means to extend the application with hard code is a technique to extend the coverage of the application into areas that are disorderly according to the vision.

Now the gentle reader should have a question or two to offer as a challenge for me. Look at Tom Peter's prescriptions in addition to the responses I've provided.

One question is "If pattern-based development is so great, why don't people do more of it?" One answer I've encountered with distressing regularity is the tendency of many developers to treat requirements as being explicit and complete rather than as examples of a more general need. If an application solution is designed for specific requirements, the resultant product will be very specific and inflexible. Another answer comes from what we've learned about people and areas of order; people tend to stay in known areas of order (programming as usual) until forces for change become overwhelming. (Remember the catastrophe theory we discussed on page 13.)

A second challenge is the question "If pattern-based products are so great, why aren't they more in evidence in the marketplace?" Again, there's a dual answer. The first part is again people's tendency to use what they've used before and to adopt new things only when there is clear and present need (and possibly danger from a current practice). The second part is that pattern-based products are very much in evidence in the marketplace. Spreadsheet products, word processors, database systems, and operating systems are all common examples of pattern-based products.

Pattern-based products are perceived as being just the same as inventions. Before the problem is solved, people are mystified and can't figure out how to solve the problem. After the problem is solved, the solution is so obvious that everyone wants to build one and people quickly forget that they were mystified.

Closure Questions:

> What common practices do you know of that prevent the use of patterned techniques?
> Other than decision tables, operating systems, and spreadsheets, how many examples of pattern-based tools can you name?

Do you have views of your application needs (or anyone else's, for that matter) that could be used as the basis for pattern-based tools?

IMPLEMENTING A PHILOSOPHY

I've been amazed, over the years, at the number of people who believe that organizations work because people follow orders, teams function well simply because the team members are determined to get the job done, and people are totally motivated by money.

None of these beliefs are totally mistaken, but, just the same, not one of them is even close to being completely true.

Organizations in which people simply follow orders tend to be very orderly organizations (pun intended, as usual), but they have only as many brains functioning as there are people making decisions. The old saw, "Too many cooks spoil the broth," is about having everyone independently making decisions at the same level and about the same problems. That typically doesn't apply in a software development environment, where a variety of people are working on a variety of needs. In a competitive situation, having all possible brain power focused on the job (and focussed appropriately) is much more productive than having only a few brains making decisions. But it takes confidence, mutual respect, and trust to empower more people to make decisions.

It takes more for people to develop mutual respect and trust than a simple awareness that each person has credentials suitable for the job. It requires some socialization, an understanding of priorities, personal knowledge, some experience together in a working environment, and a confidence in the absence of personality conflicts. None of this is found in credentials, none of it happens because people are thrown into a group together, and none of it survives without a nurturing environment.

Even beyond the nurturing environment, some direction is required. Who ever heard of an athletic team with no goal? Where would the NASA team have been without President John F. Kennedy's vision of putting a man on the moon within ten years? Good working teams are groups of people with a common purpose, the expertise necessary to get the job done, and mutual respect and trust. Team members know they can count on each other, so they don't have to worry about whether other members are pulling their weight.

Given guidance, some kind of framework for their decisions, and the authority to make those decisions, most people will make excellent decisions. The organization that provides that guidance and empowers its people to do their best will quickly leap ahead of its competitors who fail to do so. The guidance, framework, and authority together amount to a philosophy for the organization, a common philosophy within which the team functions exceptionally well. This is far more, and far more effective, than following orders or having high determination. The philosophy defines the team's high level area of order.

"Money as a universal motivator" is the remaining part of the first paragraph of this section. I'll agree that a very small number of people would continue to

In the midst of the debate on whether menu structures are good or bad, people tend to forget the human heart of the issue.

Menu structures are composed of categories of categories. In his paper "The Magical Number Seven, Plus or Minus Two: Some Limits on our Capacity for Processing Information", George A. Miller explained that people don't categorize things very well if there are too many categories. Things tend to get lost or mixed up with other things. So, menu structures have natural barriers to overcome.

The fascinating thing is that menu structures work well if they have a good, associated philosophy for categorizing things. They work poorly if users can't make sense of the categories.

This may not be a welcome message to people who have been intimidated by the word "philosophy," but the truth is here. Applications are made better by the common, ordinary, everyday application of good philosophies.

Closure questions:

> *What other common aspects of software development depend on having well-thought-out designs?*
>
> *How would you describe a working, coherent interface between software and users?*

Box 15. *Menuing philosophy*

do their jobs if their paychecks stopped. But look at Abraham Maslow's hierarchy of needs. Money is a satisfier, pride in accomplishment a motivator. Studies going at least as far back as Elton Mayo's work at the Western Electric Plant in Hawthorne, Illinois, show that while the impact of a raise is quite short-lived, buy-in is an immense productivity magnifier. However, buy-in is based on an identity of purpose between the individual and the organization. When leadership establishes the path and the rest of the organization buys in, there are very few things that the organization can't accomplish.

And guess what! Money fails because it is philosophically too weak to work. Pride, direction, and buy-in are philosophically strong and transfer that strength to the organization.

What does this have to do with implementing a philosophy? The strongest forms of guidance you can give people are an inspiring vision, a clear mission with understandable goals, and a set of values that they can identify with and pursue. This is the philosophy of the organization. It effects the shape and operation of the organization significantly, clearly setting it apart from its competitors. If you look at the outstandingly successful companies of this century, you'll find that they were all visionary, culturally coherent, and based on a clearly expressed philosophy.

My observation of successful software development over those same years shows a similar phenomenon: Successful software products are based on sound, robust world views and design principles. A product's success is correlated much more strongly with a development team's implementation of a philosophy for a product than with the development process used.

Think of it in terms of areas of order and areas of disorder. Products with clear, unifying conceptual foundations will have more comprehensive and robust world views than products without such a philosophical base. In terms of user interfaces, a clear world view guides the user much more effectively than an ad hoc and fragmented world view.

Closure Questions:

> What conceptually fragmented products have you enjoyed using?
> How would you expect your customers to respond to your product if you could not describe its purpose, use, and structure in a straightforward, concise way?

4

What Chaos We See in Software Development

METHODS AND TECHNOLOGIES

Many software development methods and technologies have assumptions of order, regularity, and serialism at their hearts. The standard software development process is a clear example, as are structured programming and software engineering. Each of these examples assumes (and almost states) an underlying concept of what software development really is, then builds a development process around it. Each has had clear cases in which people followed the discipline and built successful products. Unfortunately, each has also had clear cases in which people followed the discipline and failed to build successful products.

There's a term you should be comfortable with before you proceed. The term is "linear development process." A linear development process is one in which you perform a sequence of necessary tasks, one at a time; each must be completed before the next is begun. Another name for this kind of process is "waterfall process." One standard sequence is shown in Figure 4–1.

Programmers know that highly detailed linear development processes don't match the way real programming is done, but plans and schedules are laid out using the idea, anyway.

Proponents of each discipline will argue that the successful cases prove the validity of the discipline while the failed cases were the results of its improper application. That is, they claim that the disciplines should always lead to success and so any failure must come from not using them correctly. I agree that

Gather requirements
Design product at high level
Refine design to detailed level
Code the design
Test components
Test entire product
Ship product
Maintain product

Figure 4–1. *Waterfall development process*

the successes did, in fact, prove the validity of the disciplines. But I generally disagree about the failures.

The failures in software development are the result of applying valid and significant disciplines in areas where the base assumptions of the disciplines don't match the problems that are to be solved or the organizations that are involved.

There's a subtle difference between my claim and the claims of the proponents of specific disciplines. They say, "Use the discipline properly and it will work in all cases." The chaotic approach says, "Use the discipline properly and in the right circumstances, and it will work." They say, "Only this discipline (or a specific set of disciplines) will work." The chaotic approach says, "There's always another way. You should achieve a fit between the discipline, the problem, the people, and the organization."

So in this chapter we look at existing areas of software development and expose them for the chaotic things they are. We don't look at all areas, but we examine enough to give you the idea. Maybe you'll generate your own closure questions to determine if significant areas of your environment are chaotic although you hadn't realized that before.

We'll use two methods to expose the chaotic nature of the various areas. The first is a direct exploration of the feedback involved there. We look at related activities, show the feedback, and sometimes even point directly at chaotic examples. The second method is an indirect look at the characteristics of chaotic things. Chaotic things generally share the following features:

Areas of order—There are parts of the thing that have locally well-defined structures. There is a high degree of order and pattern in these parts. Program coding structures are clear examples. The list of checkpoints used to track a standard software development process is orderly and it is used for project after project. Further, the steps and approvals required for each phase in the project follow standard patterns of definitions.

Areas of disorder—Between the areas of order, there are areas where no overall pattern or order is visible. The boundary between one area of order and another is usually disorderly. In programs, this is often isolated in housekeeping code, even though the housekeeping code itself will follow a pattern and be its own area of order. In a standard software development process, disorder becomes apparent as the end of a phase looms closer than a normal schedule can accommodate and the project jumps into a war room approach to meet its deadlines.

Self-similarity—Chaotic phenomena are self-similar in that the view of the whole is similar to a magnified view of a part. Thus, a spine on a feather is similar to the whole feather, and you see the same characteristics in snowflakes, ferns, and coastlines. We see the effect in software development in top-down structured design, in the layering of abstract data types, and in project management where the management focus depends on the level of management. If you look at the structure of the whole, then look inside the whole, you will also find sub-structures that look "the same."

Self-dissimilarity—Looking at any particular areas of order, you will be able to find other areas of order that are drastically different. Indeed, some areas of order will be retrograde to other areas of order, apparently undoing each other. We can see this quite clearly in parameter passing, where a calling program sets up a parameter list only to have it torn down by the called program. Likewise, software development is full of pairs of activities that are retrograde to each other. Analysis (breaking down) and design (synthesis or building up) is one such pair. Planning (applying guesses from the past to a hoped-for future) and development (striving to keep present realities in synch with past guesses) is another pair.

Response to changes—As pressures change, so does the process, but not necessarily predictably. In a complex feedback (chaotic) system, we can't reliably predict which changes will lead to desired results. Remember that nearly every human system is a complex system that involves feedback. Often, relatively small changes will cause a process to become wildly erratic. Project reviews (a relatively small activity) close to project due dates have been known to trigger erratic responses in a project. Similarly, the entry of a competitive product into the marketplace can trigger some unforeseen changes in product direction.

Closure Questions:

> What parts of software development can you think of that depend on feedback but seem inherently orderly?
> What parts of software development can you think of that appear disorderly but don't have obvious feedback?

PROBLEM SOLVING IS CHAOTIC

Problem solving usually starts with a problem. Then someone comes up with a solution. That's simple, right? But in a very short period of time, people will lose track of the distinction between the problem and the solution. The two together become a new situation. If there are any problems in the new situation—if some bugs still lurk or if parts of the initial problem still haven't been addressed—their solutions will be framed in terms of the problem/solution pair, not just the initial problem. Even if the initial solution is officially abandoned, its effects will be felt in most subsequent solutions, a potentially undesirable legacy. (See page 88.)

The new situation, composed of the initial problem and the initial solution, is more complex than the original situation. It contains complexities derived from mistakes about what the original problem really was, errors in the solution, and changes in the environment. In short, the new situation contains both new problems and some version of the initial problems that must be resolved.

SWAT teams are the ultimate in trouble-shooting. The term is derived from the police units formed to deal with special problem situations using Special Weapons And Tactics.

In software development, we often see situations that were not predicted, are not predictable, and require quick and effective attention if the project is to succeed. Highly experienced and effective developers are put on SWAT teams to identify the causes of the problems and to invent the solutions that can get the project back on track.

Practical software developers are always ready to form SWAT teams to attack problems. When a project starts, they will insist that SWAT teams will be necessary even though they can't predict exactly what situation will require the team.

Inexperienced software developers and theoreticians are more likely to claim that SWAT teams are unnecessary and that just a little more care in planning will make them superfluous.

The student of chaos understands the chaotic nature of software development and can tie that chaotic nature to the need for (and danger of) SWAT teams on a project of any size.

Closure questions:

    Have you seen a project of any size that did not require SWAT teams at some time?

    Have you seen SWAT teams abused?

    How have they been abused?

Box 16. *SWAT teams*

Now when we have a new problem, we need a new solution. Solving this secondary problem leads to a secondary solution, making a third problem. The third problem leads to a tertiary solution, and so on. This cycle will continue until the whole set of problems and solutions is tolerable (good enough), money runs out, time runs out, or the environment is abandoned.

Just because we have a cascading series of problems (which the careful observer will identify as a chaotic situation), we don't have to give up and say that everything is hopeless. Look at the ways we solve the various problems.

Each solution to anything other than the primary problem will be built as patches for specific failures, redesigned parts for a subset of the problem/solution environment, or a total redesign that gives another primary solution.

Patches for specific failures lead to uncontrollable solutions in which it's difficult to tell what parts are solution, what parts are problem, what identifiable solution parts will handle any particular part of the problem, and whether or not the processing for the next encountered problem part will be accurate.

This is the general condition of solutions to problems. It is part of the reason why people have commented that solutions produce new problems. If patching is allowed to happen in an undisciplined way, the results include a classic definition of a kludge (grown rather than planned, with unknown processing paths and unknown results for specific cases), and a description of a business process that has accumulated rather than being carefully determined. Remember this description and notice that it is associated with the minimal application of development or business discipline.

Total redesign of the solution is the theoretically correct application of good discipline, giving a solution whose shape matches that of the problem. "Everyone" agrees that this is the right way to work, but "everyone" quickly points out that (except in a small number of exceptional cases) they are not allowed to do so and that there are trade-offs with other concerns. For example, some small problems are implementation problems; correcting the implementation really makes the whole thing work the way it was supposed to work in the first place. And we don't really expect total redesign of a solution mere days before it is to be shipped or installed. Still, total redesign is theoretically the correct thing to do.

Redesign for a subset of the problem/solution environment is a spectrum in between the first two cases, any particular example of which is a balance between expediency (minimize immediate cost, hold to the scheduled dates, redesign only the affected parts. . . .) and ideal discipline. Practically, the decision satisfies the question, "How good is good enough?" If the choice is closer to patches, the solution will become a kludge. If the solution correctly identifies and redesigns affected parts, it will be of higher quality. If the choice is total redesign, the good parts of the original solution will be discarded.

The cost and quality of the shipped solution will actually be dependent on many factors in addition to the design approach. Therefore, for the mix of skills found in a development group, I lean toward the middle solution, redesigning for an appropriately chosen subset but using what the circumstances call for.

Closure Questions:

> How would you know if a particular problem fits with a particular problem-solving technique?
>
> Should we expect any particular problem-solving technique to be applicable and productive for all problems?

REQUIREMENTS GATHERING IS CHAOTIC

Requirements are statements of what a product is supposed to do. (See page 8.) They can describe user interfaces, hardware, compatibility with other products, functions to be supported, or whatever is important to both the customer (if the customer is involved in defining the requirements) and the developer (if the developer is involved in defining the requirements). They can be precise or imprecise, since they are the result of human attempts at communication. They frequently are taken to be the definitive measurement of the success of a development effort; if the product matches the requirements, it's successful. Philip B. Crosby has spread the word that the essence of quality is meeting requirements; many groups have taken his word to heart and produced higher-quality products as a result.

But look at the process of gathering requirements. Once in a rare while, the user (or user representative) will know exactly what is needed and will be able to compose a set of requirements that can be encapsulated in a contract and be the right measure for what the project is to do. More often, however, the requirements are not well defined by what either users or developers know. (See page 26.) When the requirements are not well defined, the process of defining them is a feedback kind of process.

Defining requirements involves an interaction or cycle of interaction between developers and users. Because people understand by forming mental models to explain their observations, we can expect users to form mental models of what the developers have to work with (machines, languages, programs, and instructions for their use) and we can expect developers to form mental models of what the users want (functions, interfaces, data, and evaluations). The feedback process allows users and developers to evaluate the others' models and suggest observations and formulations that will work better. From your own experience, you know just how well such mental models usually fit together.

Since people seldom jump from a partial understanding to a complete understanding all at once, it is reasonable to expect that a full requirements definition (to an acceptable level) will take several such cycles. Further, each cycle is itself heavily dependent on considerable interaction between users and developers, another level of feedback.

At this time, it should be easy to see the parallel between the drops of water we looked at in Chapter 1 and sequences of mental models. In each case, there is change over time (added water, added information and understanding), dynamics within cycles (adding water to a forming drop, holding discussions between users and developers), and feedback between cycles (rebound effects from the prior drop, concepts inherited from prior mental models or concepts proven wrong).

The parallels suggest that there is chaos in the requirements gathering process; or, more accurately, that the gathering of requirements is a chaotic activity that should be carefully and thoughtfully pursued according to its nature. We should expect productive results from allowing degrees of freedom in the formulation of successive mental models, and we should expect productive results from intentionally fostered feedback between customers, requirements definers, and developers.

Closure Questions:

> What can you say about the relationship between the effectiveness of requirements and how happy the customer will be with the resultant product?
>
> Who should be involved in defining the requirements for a product?

DESIGN IS CHAOTIC

Design is another activity that involves feedback. In this case, the feedback is between the designer's knowledge of implementation technologies, the designer's understanding of the problem to be solved, the designer's imagination, the new information in the first two categories that the designer learns as the project progresses, and the expansion of the designer's imagination as the store of information and examples expands. The results of this feedback will be a sequence of mental models of the problem, the implementation technology, and the implementation to be used to realize the solution. We even know that the progress from model to model will not be a smooth progression but will occur in fits and starts as designers study and worry about problems, then realize new solutions, then discover new problems. Again, the models behave like drops of water, with change over time, internal dynamics, and feedback between cycles; so we should expect chaotic behavior in the design process.

Software development processes can work in several different (and conflicting) directions. We must accept the fact that no single approach can possibly produce "best answers" in response to all needs and problems. Frederick P. Brooks talks about this in his "No Silver Bullets" article. (See box 18 on page 72.)

When the problem to be solved is well known and is to be built on a well-known base, a specification-based approach is productive. In this approach, you write full specifications, hold reviews and inspections, prove the design before coding anything, then code, review, correct, test, correct, test, and ship the resultant product.

When the problem to be solved is not well known and is to be built on a base that also must be created, a chaotic approach is productive. In this approach you:

- design quick and dirty solutions to pieces of the problem,
- review (sanity check) the designs,
- code prototypes from the designs that might be sane,
- have user representatives play with the resulting prototypes for further sanity checks, and then

- iteratively compose a product prototype from successive functional prototypes until the problem is understood.

At this time, it's possible to gather pieces and "glue" them together to make them work. Eventually, the problem may become known well enough to allow the specification-based approach to be productive.

Note that each of these two processes fails miserably in the environment in which the other is highly successful. That is, the chaotic approach leads to kludges when used to make enhancements to existing, sizable products. Likewise, the specifications approach fails completely when applied to initial development of products for unknown environments. Even worse for the unknown environment is the collection of requirements that have no real meaning because there is no base upon which to build.

In reality, most projects will call for a combination approach. Parts of a project will be suitable for the specification-based approach, while other parts will be suitable for the chaotic approach.

In software application development the balance between control and flexibility is elusive. Sometimes control is overdone, with the result that the development group produces an unimaginative and cumbersome product. In extreme cases, tightly controlled projects are managed by change control, where a first design is chosen (possibly with no more thought than to have a place to start from) and improved upon only by tightly controlled changes. (A fallacy associated with design by change control is discussed on page 88). At other times flexibility is overdone to the point that no product is ever produced.

Closure questions:

> Experienced developers can point both to projects that produced high-quality and imaginative products when the design was tightly controlled, and to projects that produced good results when the design group retained considerable flexibility.
> Can you identify a common factor that makes both work?
> Is it possible to predict the success or failure of a project by looking only at the process or processes that are supposed to be used?

FORECASTING IS CHAOTIC

Chaotic phenomena occur more often in software development than you might expect and in ways that people often don't even associate with software development. Forecasting is just such an area—it's highly chaotic and is not normally thought of as part of software development. Notice that it is not even mentioned in the waterfall process described in the opening of this chapter. While most parts of software development go from low to high levels of chaotic behavior, forecasting goes from moderately high levels of chaotic behavior to fictitious behavior.

In being careful about the business of developing software, it's common to try to understand the balance between the cost of developing software and the potential revenues from the product. Forecasting and pricing go hand in hand to derive estimates of the potential marketplace, determine the market share that can reasonably be expected of the product, decide on the prices to be charged, and then to compute the balance of the revenues and costs for the product.

For examples of one kind of forecasting, consider software products that are useful but not essential parts of common ways of doing business. Such products might include a hard disk maintenance program or a spreadsheet conversion program. Neither program generates a marketplace for hardware or other software, but depends on an existing marketplace. Forecasters for the hard disk maintenance program can thus start with base numbers of systems sold with hard disks and compute potential sales based on a percentage market penetration of that number of systems. Forecasters for the conversion program can start with the number of copies of the spreadsheet that have been sold and the number of those sales that also have the second program served by the conversion program. Again, the application of an estimated penetration percentage leads to a reasonable forecast of the number of sales of the product.

The feedback is in the mind of the forecaster, as successive refinements of the forecast model and estimates lead to further understanding of the product and the marketplace. Feedback is involved in the larger environment because of the potential for increased sales due to an increased marketing emphasis or other reactions to the forecast itself. Any such effect is increased because of the fact that the forecast is an estimate, no matter how carefully the computations are made.

For a second kind of forecasting, consider a major application product that could itself justify the purchase of a computer system. Forecasting can look at industry projections of sales of system units, estimate that a certain percentage of those units will be sold for this particular kind of application, and then compute potential sales based on market share. But then the reasonable forecaster would have to estimate the numbers of units that would be sold specifically for this product, beyond those that would be used on existing units. Note that the difference between this kind of product and the other is that this one can have a significant impact on the size of the marketplace. That is, if this product is sufficiently useful, of high enough quality, and captures the imagination of the buying public thoroughly enough, the revenues can be significantly higher than would be expected from the projected sale of system units for other purposes. On the other side of the coin, a low forecast can lead the development team to cut corners and produce a less attractive, lower-quality product. This would lead to lower sales than forecast.

Third, consider a product unlike anything that has been produced before. No one knows what percentage of computer systems will run this product and there is no way to make any kind of estimate of whether people will buy systems specifically to use it. Now, forecasting becomes something akin to crystal ball gazing. Estimates, in this case, will depend on ranges of criteria from the knowledge the forecaster has of the computer business, to the forecaster's work load (or overload), to the quality of the first cup of coffee the forecaster has consumed that morning. This forecast will be a work of fiction, but it can range from a good guess based on usage scenarios to pure fantasy.

We need to look at one more kind of forecasting example before proceeding. In this case, a developer has come up with a super idea for a program that will count toothpicks. Being totally awed by the idea, the developer wants to build the product. However, the forecaster can look at the business environment and demonstrate that only toothpick manufacturers and government regulators are interested in counting toothpicks. Further, the toothpick manufacturers already have highly effective ways of counting toothpicks and will be unlikely to buy enough of the programs to cover the development expenses. Therefore, the super idea probably will not be profitable when applied to counting toothpicks, but may need to be applied to a more profitable endeavor. This is a sanity check level of forecasting.

There are many more styles of forecasting. These styles are indicative of some of them. Given the entire range of forecasting, the software development community should remain aware of how their products are viewed and what style of forecasting is used. In some cases, the forecasts should be taken very seriously. In other cases, the forecasts should never even be pursued beyond a simple sanity check level. In still other cases, a poor forecast should be ignored because the developer has as much or more knowledge of the marketplace as the forecaster.

One of the dangers of forecasting, particularly in established companies, is the institutionalization of the function. That is, the estimates of the forecasters can take on credibility beyond what is due, as though the forecasts were divinely inscribed on golden tablets. As with the topics in other sections in this book, the choice of how to do forecasting and how seriously to take the resultant forecasts depends on the needs of the project. In an already chaotic environment, the choice of an inappropriate use of forecasting can lead to disorderly behavior on a company-busting scale.

Closure Questions:

> What other business aspects of software development cross from chaotic to fictitious behavior?
> Are your forecasters accountable for the accuracy of their forecasts?
> When you start up a software development effort or propose one, how will you specify the role that forecasting will take in the effort?

OVERLOAD MAKES IT ALL WORSE

Various feedback systems affect software development, but one particular feedback factor is worth noting as a magnifier of disorderly behaviors in software development efforts. This factor is an overload in information to be handled and work to be done.

> *When faced with having too much to do, many people assert that they just need to work a little harder. But there's a boundary and a perspective indicating that simply working harder is often not the right answer.*
>
> *It's like being under water. If you're inches under the surface, just a little extra effort can get you up for a breath of air. But if you're hundreds of feet beneath the surface, major efforts on your part will just expend your energy and oxygen and leave you in worse shape.*
>
> *Closure questions:*
>
> > *How do you know when an overload situation can be resolved by working harder and when it requires working smarter?*
> >
> > *What balance between working harder and working smarter would be most productive in your organization?*

Box 17. *Working harder*

Information overload is the phrase used when people have an overwhelming amount of information being presented to them, and all the information appears to be too important to ignore.

With information overload, people either skim the surface of the information they receive or they only pay attention to selected parts of it. When they skim, they make decisions based on a shallow understanding of the information, so their designs and implementations are also shallow and not as robust as they could be. When they skip, entire areas of knowledge will be absent from the deliberations for decisions, and the resultant products can be expected to have gaps in function and usability.

Work overload is the phrase used when people have more work than they can complete with the time and resources available.

With work overload people will do the best they can, but some work will slip, undone or poorly done, through their fingers. Depending on the person, the resultant work will appear to be of poor quality, missing function, or exhibiting weak design. Many times, we respond to overload by simply trying harder. With minor overload this may be enough, but this response has limited value. In software development, major overload requires working much smarter, not much harder. Brooks' Law tells us about this about as clearly as we can be told. (See box 20 on page 77.)

The defense against information overload requires a combination of teamwork, the use of abstracting services, customer contact, work reduction, and noise reduction.

Teamwork helps by having team members keep current on information of interest to them and allowing them to review each other's work so that everyone gets the benefit of each individual's information.

The use of abstracting services allows people to identify information sources of probable interest quickly.

Customer contact keeps all developers on track toward the real goals of the project and the information the customer will use to evaluate the product.

Work reduction gives people time to breath and to gather the information necessary to actually get the work done.

Noise reduction is the elimination of unnecessary information that is passed around for a defensive combination of CYA (An old Air Force term, Cover Your Afterburner) and FYI (For Your Information) purposes.

All these techniques need to be used carefully and intelligently; the boundary between noise and useful information is never precise. We might even say it's chaotic. And there is a point of diminishing returns, where the cost of getting and using more information exceeds the value of the information.

The defense against work overload requires teamwork, innovation, pattern exploitation, function borrowing, and work reduction.

Teamwork helps by allowing people to do what they do best, thus maximizing the productivity of the organization, and by helping the entire team to become get more productive through the sharing of expertise.

Innovation helps by finding ways to do things more simply and with less effort, and by completely eliminating the need to do some things.

Pattern exploitation helps by solving recurring problems just once, so that wheels don't need to be reinvented and the same problem solved time after time.

Function borrowing is reuse, a partner to pattern exploitation that relies on people searching out others who may have already solved particular problems or classes of problems.

Work reduction helps by relieving the pressure for people to function without looking around; people who don't look around are unable to use any of the other techniques for overcoming work overload.

Notice that the successful techniques for overcoming overbearing feedback situations (work and information overload) are themselves feedback techniques.

Closure Questions:

> How do you react in an overload situation—by working harder, by overlooking quality or details, or by finding ways to simplify, eliminate, or reduce the overload?
>
> Which of the overload handling techniques have you mastered?

CHAOTIC USER INTERFACE

If any guiding principle is used to design user interfaces, the results will (and should) show self-similarity. This is the intent of such guidelines, and guidelines do, indeed, work. Further, if the application is sufficiently complex, rules of simplicity will force several layers of user interface and the self-similarity will increase correspondingly.

This is usually part of the intent of such guidelines and allows people to learn the pattern of the user interface without exploring all of the complexity available in the application. With proper recognition of how this works, the application designer can take advantage of areas that are not known to the designer and/or the user to create an easily extended and easily learned application. (See page 26.)

However, it is highly unlikely that there are any universally proper guiding principles for user interface. Even the best ones we have are heuristic, based on our past (incomplete) experience and our guesses about what might be good (often proven wrong by usability testing or use by real customers). Therefore, we should not be surprised to find that adherence to particular guiding principles will often be retrograde, either by forcing the adoption of user interface choices that are contrary to application needs (the application suffers), or by being overridden to satisfy the immediate needs of the application (the guidelines suffer).

An excellent example of the contrary (retrograde) nature of application user interface in the face of guiding principles is in the choice that a user interface will be object-action or action-object oriented. Neither orientation is adequate to cover all the needs of a typical application; the 80—20 rule seems to hold. (See page 161.)

If you look more closely at the "which comes first, object or action" question, you'll notice that about 60 percent of the project choices could go either way, 20 percent of the choices will only be natural one way, and 20 percent of the choices will only be natural the other way. Where the choices are unnatural you'll see dramatic disorder, so it's well worth your while to try to discover if the most critical parts of the application belong in either of the 20 percent areas. If you've decided to make this question one of your key design points, this look at your critical function can help you decide on the answer.

It's fascinating to watch the results in a project in which the choice to behave in either a totally object-action or a totally action-object manner has been made. Some people will endorse the choice and perform unnatural acts to adhere to it. Others will disagree with the choice and build things as they wish, using the excuse that their responsibility falls within the known class of exceptional cases. Still others will find themselves fighting with both of these camps as they try to discover to which class each particular case should belong.

Closure questions:

> What would you expect of an application with no consistency or self-similarity in its user interface?
>
> Where an application (for example, a spreadsheet) requires function with another shape (for example, printing), would you expect the user interfaces of the parts to be completely consistent with each other?
>
> (Does the printing user interface take formulas, or does the spreadsheet interface require single responses to queries for parameters?)

CHAOTIC CODE AND DATA STRUCTURES

From the advent of modular programming to the present, the self-similar nature of code structures has been clearly evident. As with user interface design, adherence to guiding principles leads to self-similarity. It also leads to the limits where the guiding principles are appropriately reversed. A classic example of this is in the GOTO-free programming work of Harlan Mills. When Mills first started his promotion of GOTO-free programming, he had all the evidence of mathematical equivalence and good feelings about program elegance to buoy his decision. However, several years later he moderated his stand and acknowledged that situations existed where it was better to use GOTOs than to blindly reject their use.

Similarly, relational data structures can be manipulated, through carefully defined rules, to create more and more pure organizations of the data. These rules, producing normal forms of data, eliminate redundancy and clarify relationships so that everything is "formally correct." However, performance and other practical requirements of real applications and systems dictate that the live application data be stored in a form that is less formally correct.

Coding structures show considerable self-similarity, far beyond the obvious entry-exit conventions followed in modular programming. Decision tables follow highly regimented structures. However, even where the programming or design language does not enforce such explicit structures, experienced and highly productive programmers evolve their styles of programming toward the same levels of self-similarity. This is simply the result of the successes these people have experienced. The patterns they use have worked for them and are familiar. Yet even as we notice these common structures and self-similarities, we should notice that there are boundaries on the patterns. Decision tables have boundaries where housekeeping code supports the neat and orderly patterns of the tables. The work of experienced designers and programmers shows less patterned areas, where they adjust their productive patterns to the immediate application. In the most productive techniques, we expect to see the boundaries hidden within compiler-generated code.

So, self-similarity and the boundaries of the use of the self-similar structures (code and data) are separated into layers of differing flavors. Each, in its own way, contributes to the productivity of the effort. Yet a view of the entire package clearly shows the self-similarities and the dissimilarities across boundaries that we've learned to recognize as symptoms of chaotic phenomena. Visual analogies to this include the Mandelbrot set and the convergence graph of the equation $i**4 = 1$. Figure 4–2 is an approximation of the Mandelbrot set. You can see both the Mandelbrot set and the noted convergence graph in James Gleick's book, in full color. In each of these visual examples, areas are defined and have drama because of the appearance of their boundaries.

Similarity even shows across traditional boundaries between data and code. Michael Jackson's Jackson Design—he's the British computer scientist, not the rock star—is based on data and the processing program sharing a similar

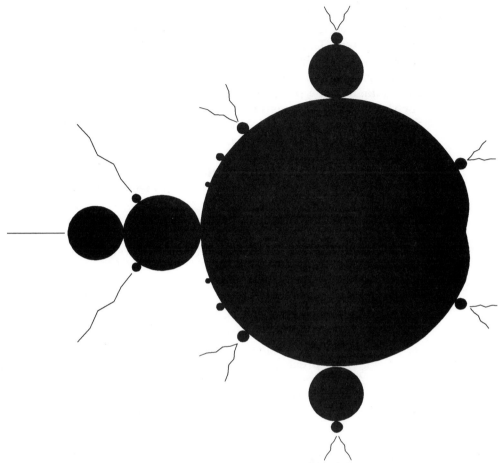

Figure 4–2. *An approximation of the Mandelbrot set*

structure. Jackson's technique starts with the data structure, defined according to particular precepts, and builds the program structure from that. Notice that Jackson Design shows areas of order where data structures are well defined, and areas of disorder on module boundaries where modules on each side have different views of the same data. Jackson provides coding and design techniques to handle the interfaces, which are the most difficult parts of the Jackson Design technique to master.

On a different level, IBM's Data Flow Development Manager (DFDM) system uses the flow of data as the primary organizing feature of an application. (See box 24 on page 87.) In one of the fascinating twists of chaotic software development, these two data-oriented views are not in competition, they're compatible. Jackson Design deals with the structure of data within a processing unit (program) and helps to identify where different processing views of the data require data flows. DFDM supports flows of data and helps to link together the various programs (now called data transforms) in a complete application.

You can observe the same structural correspondence in many applications developed without the explicit use of the Jackson Design technique or the DFDM system. The correlation suggests that we could productively and intentionally use self-similarity in various parts of our designs. This would lead a designer to use coherent mental models for the user's interaction, the application data, and the program structure.

One of the guidelines in a good definition of data is that the definition be flexible and extendible. A balancing guideline is that the data definition enhance good performance in applications that use it. The first guideline has led, several times, to data definitions that are (or approach being) self-describing, with special reserved definitional codes for use as extensions. The result has been a layered definition with each layer looking structurally like each other layer.

Similarly, good programs are also flexible and extendible. Good designers recognize that requirements are never fixed or right, and that well-designed programs will be easily adapted to changes in requirements (data or function).

Closure questions:

> Given the similarities we've noticed between user interface guidelines, design principles, coding structures, and data structures, should we expect that consideration for any of these should always take precedence over any of the others?
>
> Are we wearing blinders if we try to believe that any particular part of an application can be fully completed (functionally, structurally, or by interface) before the rest of the application can be begun?

STRANGE SOFTWARE DEVELOPMENT

We know what feedback is. Output of a system is fed back into the system and has some effect on the future of the system. We've talked about lots of places where we see feedback and chaos, both inside software development and outside it. We've talked about catastrophic transitions and how things can change drastically because of very minor changes in simple controls. But we've looked at our examples as though they had single stable points or areas.

Strange attractors are feedback systems that don't have single stable points. Rather, they have several points, called meta-stable points, because their behavior tends to remain close to these points but also jumps between them. Successive states of such systems will cluster around one meta-stable point for a while, then jump to the vicinity of another, then possibly jump to a third, or back to the first, or on to other meta-stable states. Possibly the most notable strange attractor (for us) is the global climate of the Earth; weather simulations show that our current livable climate is one possible meta-stable state but that there is another probable meta-stable state that corresponds to an ice age.

Software development is more strange than a strange attractor. When requirements gathering is isolated from development, the resultant product is universally found to be something other than what the customer wanted or needed. When developers become intimately involved with a customer, the day-to-day interaction with the customer is nonlinear, wandering all over the possibilities of the application design, never revisiting the same point, always changing, but tending to get very close to one or more visions of what the customer wanted and needed.

Closure Questions:

> Assuming that your development processes have multiple stable states, how might you identify variables in the environment that might influence the processes toward more desirable states?
> What tendencies within an organization might make the organization cycle around if the tendencies were unchecked?

5

How Software Development
Tried to Avoid Disorder

This is a good news, bad news chapter. People in software development have tried a variety of things to make software development more businesslike, more orderly, more predictable, more disciplined, more palatable, more profitable, and more fun. Some of these things have worked, some haven't. Nearly all of them have worked in some cases, but none has worked in every case.

The first sections in this chapter are about the things that have the highest potential for success, the ones that can help to exploit the chaos in software development if we use them appropriately. The last sections in this chapter are about the things that have little or no potential in helping us to exploit chaos.

One thing you'll notice in this chapter is that not one of the listed things is adequate, on its own, to resolve the chaotic software development dilemma. Each, within its area of order, may look wonderful. But step even a little way outside of that area of order and the result will be entirely different. You've had clues about this all the way through *Exploiting Chaos: Cashing in on the Realities of Software Development*, but now we really rub it in. There are no silver bullets in this chapter.

Closure Question:

> Although some of your favorite techniques aren't in this chapter, will you evaluate them from the chaotic point of view?

In "No Silver Bullets," Frederick P. Brooks makes the point that no single design technique or development process is going to magically solve the problems of software development productivity and quality. The title alludes to the magical properties of silver bullets in killing werewolves; the paper suggests that the most difficult problems in software development are those that change shape, appearance, and behavior.

Closure questions:

Do you have a favorite "silver bullet" that would solve all software development problems if people would just wake up and use it?

If so, how drastically will the software development industry have to change to exploit the benefits of your particular "silver bullet?"

Box 18. *Frederick P. Brooks, Jr.: "No Silver Bullets"*

SOFTWARE ENGINEERING

Software engineering is one of the most visible attempts to squeeze the chaos out of software development. At the least, it is applicable to those projects that are already able to use the standard software development process. The added rigor in software engineering makes it further applicable to some applications outside of that set, where the rigor pulls the application within bounds. However, the prerequirements for software engineering often exclude it from proper use with other applications.

Software engineering has several aspects that make it quite a useful tool even in disorderly development processes.

The concept of the "abstract data type" says that a top-down design should be accomplished by using an abstract view of the kinds of operations that should be used with particular data. For example, the designer should design using abstract list operations rather than a specific implementation of a list. When the next level of design is explored—but not before—the list constructs can be translated into more detailed operations. The designer is thus freed from detailed considerations about the support of data structures in the application. Further, the use of common abstractions leads to simpler designs and more reusable code. This concept, incorporated into software engineering, is one of the most powerful and simple concepts to hit the computer industry in recent years. Even if the remainder of software engineering is not rigorously adopted, this concept will promote simpler, more maintainable designs than what has been previously produced.

Among the disciplines associated with proofs of correctness is the practice of explicitly stating entry conditions, exit conditions, and transformations expected in sections of code (or design, for that matter). Rigorously followed and checked, this practice leads to a significant reduction in the time required to validate and test code. It tends to prevent the most troublesome of programming problems, mismatched interfaces and improper variable contents. When the practice is followed with discipline, the errors that slip through tend to be misspellings of variable names.

Software engineering, being a structured and rigorous discipline, provides an essential counterbalance to less structured and innovative explorations of the unknown. Exploratory efforts can be used productively to determine the feasibility of implementations and the value of certain requirements. Then software engineering techniques can be used to produce high-quality results with fully disciplined efforts.

Software engineering does have some problems that now act as inhibitors to a full realization of the potential of the discipline. The precision and rigor that are required for the full application of software engineering are beyond what the average programmer is trained or willing to apply. Until current research in software engineering has fulfilled its promise, software engineering will remain a discipline that is used mainly by its cognoscenti or on projects where extreme reliability and quality are required.

Consider a group of highly talented, successful, inventive, and individualistic research programmers who decide that they would like to get into maintenance work on medical applications. (Don't ask me why, I have trouble imagining researchers making such a move myself.)

In their research environment these people had been rewarded for building all of their own components, hoping that several of them would involve new ways of doing things and would lead to advances in the field. Their very success in the research environment will get in the way of possible success in their new environment.

As problems are reported in the medical applications, the natural tendency of these programmers is to discover new ways of performing the existing functions. With their practice of replacing standard support, their fixes eventually make the application incompatible with changes to the system on which it is to run.

Coming from an environment where they exploit disorder, these people fail in an environment that require a more orderly approach.

Closure questions:

> *What would you expect to happen if you formed a team of people who are not suited to the jobs involved?*
>
> *Do you want heavy-duty innovators on a straight coding job?*
>
> *Do you want coders (no matter how experienced) performing an innovative design job?*

Box 19. *A need for order and a chaotic organization—a broken team*

As noted elsewhere in this book, software engineering enforces an essentially linear process, which limits its applicability to particular kinds of problems.

Closure Questions:

> How do you keep in touch with theoretical and practical work in the area of software engineering?
>
> What kind of partnership can you form with the software engineering community so that they can look for methods and techniques that would be applicable to your environment?
>
> How closely does your environment match the environment required for successful use of software engineering techniques?

PILLARS AND FOUNDATIONS OF SOFTWARE ENGINEERING

Successful software engineering projects—indeed most of the successful software development efforts in the software development industry today—are found in a very restricted set of circumstances. (The most famous successes in software development are not found in these circumstances, but the largest numbers of successes are.)

The circumstances surrounding a viable project for software engineering involve three constraints (or necessities) that are easily summarized:

1. There is an existing base of technology and product.
2. Requirements are well-defined and well-bounded.
3. The project is staffed by expert practitioners, knowledgeable in their technology and (probably) in the product base.

The reasons for these constraints are found both in the attitudes of the practitioners of the software engineering trade and in the tools of the trade.

Software engineering practitioners begin with the presumption that a project will succeed if it is approached with sufficient engineering discipline and conscientious application of proven transforms. If you'd like that in English, it goes like this, "We'll succeed if we try hard enough and follow the rules carefully enough." A diehard software engineer who wanted to guarantee the success of a project would try to satisfy the three constraints before making any promises for the project. The project would be in deep trouble if any of the constraints were allowed to be relaxed.

Without the base of technology and product, an unknown amount of development would be required before work could begin on the project at hand.

Without well-defined, well-bounded requirements, there would not be a stable finishing line to use for estimates. It's interesting to note that the state of the art in requirements dealt with the organization (not the gathering) of requirements until very recent times.

Without knowledgeable practitioners, there would justifiably be little confidence in either the estimates of the work to be done or in the learning curves of the people who would be working on the project.

We find the same thing in the tools of the trade. Proofs of correctness are easy examples, with the base of the specifications, the goal of the coding to be

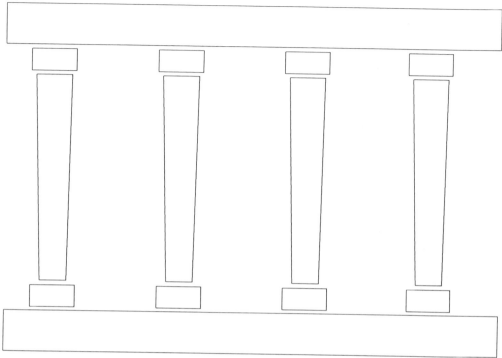

Figure 5–1. *The Pillars of Software Engineering*

proven, the rules to be followed in the proof, and the expert practitioner who is to devise the proof. Even specification languages are carefully constructed to eliminate as much ambiguity as possible, to specify the tools and languages to be used, and in assuming that they will be used by people who know how to use them.

Lest you think that these examples are contrived, consider this: These three constraints are so much a part of the world view of software engineers that it is seldom (if ever) necessary to express them. Indeed, the diehard software engineer will consider it a triviality to even *consider* mentioning them.

The Pillars of Software Engineering, these three constraints, define yet another world view that can be productive in software development. The software engineering view defines an area of order in the chaos of the software development environment. The clear definition of the area allows the software developer to identify software engineering as one of the applicable techniques for appropriate software development efforts.

Some readers will have looked at this section and wondered why there are four rather than three pillars in Figure 5–1.

One view of the figure is that each pillar in the figure should correspond to each of the three pillars mentioned in this section. This follows what you've read so far. For this view, the figure is wrong. But you have more than enough imagination to view the figure as if it had only three pillars.

Another view of the figure is that the base represents the technology base and current release of a product, each of the pillars represents a unique and separate set of requirements, and the cap represents the new technology base and next release. In this case, the number of pillars isn't significant, but it is representative of having several sets of bounded requirements.

The figure actually corresponds to several of the thoughts mentioned in this section and the reader should feel free to pick any of them as a favorite.

Closure Questions:

> What kinds of preproject activities could you use to ensure that your project could use existing software engineering techniques?
> Are there other ways to expand the bounds of the applicability of software engineering?
> Can software engineering help to build software right the first time?

DO IT RIGHT THE FIRST TIME

"Do it right the first time" is one of the funniest lines in the software development business. It's funny because at the same time it's both impossible and necessary.

The line comes from valid observations about products that have to be fixed and corrected for several releases before they are acceptable to customers. Customers have been trained never to trust the first release or model of anything because they know that the first release will have the wrong features, low quality, and untrained support. But they want better. They say, "Do it right the first time!"

From a delivered product point of view, "do it right the first time" is a wonderful thing to do. So why is it funny?

Seeing the validity of the line from the customer's point of view, some development organizations have taken the message to heart and pushed it into the very heart of the development process, to the most detailed level. Think about that a bit. What kind of chaotic congruence would you expect when a "one chance to get it right" idea is pushed into an area where learning curves, sequences of mental models, and multiple kinds of feedback are rampant? Carry the idea further and think of what you would expect if the "do it right the first time" idea were coupled with cost-cutting measures so severe that developers were not allowed to talk with customers.

None of what you read in the previous paragraph is fiction. It represents a reality that is all too common. The reality is at least silly, but it is common none the less. Of course, having brought up the idea, I'd like to suggest something better to you.

"Do it right the first time" is an achievable goal, if you identify the chaotic parts of your efforts properly. You know that the development group has lots to learn, otherwise this would not be "the first time." You know that you want the final arbiter of your results to be involved very early so that your results can be "right." You know that you don't want the feedback and learning to be

This is the classic collection of essays on pitfalls to be found and avoided in software development. Famous ideas from the book include:

Brooks' Law—"Adding manpower to a late software project makes it later."

"Plan to throw one away, you will anyway." First efforts in a project are to learn the requirements. Subsequent efforts are more productive in actually building the product. Ignoring this, you'll do it anyway.

The second system syndrome is the unfortunate result of designers getting carried away with the successes of their first efforts and trying to put all their dreams into the next ones.

The chief surgical team is a mixed metaphor for having the right mix of skills available for getting the job done.

Closure question:

> *If you haven't read* The Mythical Man-Month *recently, why do you think you are immune to the mistakes and oversights that are preventable based on the knowledge contained in this classic?*

Box 20. *Frederick P. Brooks, Jr.:* The Mythical Man-Month

at the delivered product level, otherwise it wouldn't be "right the first time." And you know that you want your mistakes, corrections, and adjustments to be completed before your product ships.

Stating things this way, we can easily formulate the kind of organization that will deliver things "right the first time." The organization will have intimate customer involvement throughout the development effort. The organization intentionally will do prototyping and evaluation of multiple ideas, but the organization will also work to polish the delivered product so that it pleases the customers who were not involved in the development effort. In other words, the organization will intentionally allow areas of disorder in the middle of the development effort, then carefully extract the best results from that effort and feed them through areas of order to produce a polished product, "right the first time."

Closure Questions:

> Does your organization have a balanced mix of people that will enable it to handle the disorder of learning and invention while gaining the benefits of order?
>
> Is it possible to develop a new product in a totally orderly fashion, perhaps by using a well-defined set of requirements?

REQUIREMENTS

Standard software development processes include early efforts to gather all the requirements that are necessary for producing the product. Philip W. Metzger gives specific guidance on the importance of getting accurate requirements and tells how to get the right people doing the right requirements-gathering job. In the academic community, considerable research is directed toward getting and organizing requirements to ease the rest of the development process. Also, contract programming organizations are heavily dependent on acquiring and mastering the correct requirements for their projects so that they can have measurable success in the fulfillment of their contracts. Finally, the Philip B. Crosby definition of quality is "meets requirements."

Many software development efforts begin, shortly after starting as a gleam in someone's eye, with the accumulation of a set of requirements for the resultant product. Indeed, many successful software development efforts were never undertaken until the requirements were fully and formally defined in a contract. The apparent correlation between well-defined requirements and project success has led many people to think of requirements gathering as the most significant factor in the success of software development.

So requirements are a necessary prerequisite for software development and should be gathered before anything else happens, right?

Philip Metzger relies on something much like the traditional software development process as the framework for some highly useful comments on managing programming people. Most of those comments are worthwhile far beyond that development process. Of course, you'll want to look for chaotic congruence between his descriptions and your project.

Metzger tells about specific management practices that help to develop discipline in people. Metzger's clarity of thought and obviously productive experience, along with the readability of his book, contribute to making Managing Programming People *required reading for successful software developers.*

Closure questions:

How often do we succumb to the arrogant tendency to define our development processes solely based on our own experience?

Why might you think that you could successfully define a process or build a product without looking at the wisdom and experience of people like Frederick P. Brooks and Philip W. Metzger?

Box 21. *Philip W. Metzger:* Managing Programming People

Would you believe "maybe"?

Requirements gathering and adherence are critical to lots of development projects. Further, efforts directed toward better handling and use of requirements are important. However, there are circumstances in which requirements are difficult or impossible to obtain and there are projects that must proceed without well-defined requirements.

The best way to get outstanding requirements is to have the requirements defined by one person; where that person understands the application need, is knowledgeable in solution technologies, is well-respected for his or her knowledge of requirements, and who can communicate effectively enough to lead (not manage, but *lead*) the implementation effort to a successful conclusion. Everything else we've seen is second best.

This winning combination has six key parts. A failure in any of the six has to be covered by some other requirements gathering, coordinating, or managing technique.

Let me emphasize that point. All six of the following points are key: The single person, understanding the application need, knowledge of solution technologies, respect, communication, and leadership.

Every software developer builds products for someone. The label for this "someone" is the customer surrogate who lives in the developer's head. This customer surrogate whispers requirements more compelling than any found in requirements documents. This customer surrogate colors every development decision made.

But what does this customer surrogate look like? In the absence of any other influence, the customer surrogate looks just like the developer. You've probably heard statements like, "Our customers won't want to do that, I never do!"

The best software developers have customer surrogates in their heads who look just like real, knowledgeable customers. But these customer surrogates don't grow there by accident. They grow out of contact with real application users, out of knowledge of the business associated with the application, and out of an understanding of the differing perceptions and desires of many people.

Closure questions:

What customer surrogates drive your projects?

How might you ensure that you have the best set of customer surrogates for your work?

Box 22. *Customer surrogates*

If the requirements must be gathered from or through more than *one person*, differing points of view will automatically creep in, and they will have to be resolved. Failing resolution, the implemented solution will have flaws derived from a variety of inconsistencies and the side effects of the inconsistencies. Any clear requirements statement, whether it comes from one person or from more than one person, will read as though it came from one person with one comprehensive point of view.

If the requirements are not based on an *understanding of the needs of the application*, clearly they are not useful. This is one of the most often neglected aspects of software development. Projects fail when they are out of touch with their customers or if their developers don't know what competitive products they're up against. Often people will attempt to substitute function lists for an understanding of application needs, as though an accumulation of function were good enough. Unfortunately, a truly useful application is useful as much because of the synergy between the provided functions as because of the provided set of functions.

If the people defining the requirements don't understand the application need, typically they work with experts in the application both to establish the correct (workable) requirements and to get the solution validated. Although this sounds obvious when it is stated this way, it is not always so in a development group. Developers often argue about the application needs without having any real idea or experience with the actual application or the kinds of users who will ultimately determine the success or failure of the product.

An unfortunate reality is worth noting at this point. By definition and demonstration, software developers have little knowledge of user requirements unless they have some contact with those users. In large development organizations, developers are actively insulated from contact with users, and learned their trade in that vacuum. For the requirements to be defined by such developers to have any relationship with the needs of real users is such a remote possibility that only the most foolhardy venture capitalist would even think of investing in such a project.

Defining a working set of requirements for implementation of a solution depends heavily on whether it is practical to satisfy the requirements. For example, a requirement to support a database of all United States citizens is not practical if the solution is to run on a standalone PC with 640K of memory and two 360KB floppy disk drives; it can be done, but it's not practical.

If the person(s) defining the requirements don't have the *knowledge of solution technologies*, typically they work with experts in solution technologies both to establish the correct (workable) requirements and to get the solution implemented.

Respect and credibility tend to go hand in hand, at least where requirements are concerned. This is such a basic fact that it is often missed. That is, without credibility, there might as well be no requirements. Without respect, all requirements are challenged, possibly changed, and continuously re-evaluated. The result in either case is wasted time and a product that clearly differs from what should have been built.

If the people presenting the requirements aren't respected, their options are to take a second-rate product or to ensure that respect and credibility are established. This can be done through a hired intermediary, through a management change in the implementation group, or through the replacement of one implementation group with another.

Again, having an accepted project direction is one of the most basic of considerations. A change in project direction, through lack of acceptance or intentional diversion, is the same as a change in requirements. When the requirements are well enough defined to determine the success or failure of the project, acceptance of direction is essential.

Communication and *leadership* are so basic that we tend to take them for granted, but without them there would be no realistic project. This leads to a couple of choices. If the people implementing the requirements don't accept the direction, a management change in the implementing organization normally is called for. If that can't be done successfully, then get another implementation group. The alternative is the implementation of the wrong requirements.

Now, it's clear that failures in the last three categories can be fixed by management action or contracting practices. What happens if there is a drastic failure in one of the first three categories? That is, what do you do if you can't get a requirements agreement, if you don't understand the application need, and/or if you're not knowledgeable in and aren't allowed to hire knowledge in the available solution technologies?

The answer is that you don't use a requirements-driven process. Potential alternatives for all of the cases involve rapid prototyping, application studies, exploratory partnerships between customers and implementers, application education, implementation-oriented education, and lots of elbow grease and inspiration. This is an acknowledgedly chaotic process, with everyone involved having a different set of needs for information and understanding. When all of the churning is done, the most significant accomplishments will be

- The common base of understanding that allows discussion between people with different specialties and interests
- Enough exploration of the application need to allow you to decide what is important enough to include in the product
- Enough education on the solution technology to allow requirements to be defined in terms that allow them to be implemented practically.

In going through this chaotic development, it's highly probable that the intellectual property of the entire group will differ from what it would have been if the project had started with a known, firm, and understood set of requirements. That is, there will be prototypes, models, procedures, and designs that can contribute directly to the more expeditious development of the product than would have been available otherwise. This fact leads to a different continuing process than the standard software development process.

It's more typical for a project to try to use a standard process in the absence of good requirements than to step into the more appropriate exploratory process. The result is that, as Frederick P. Brooks suggests, you "throw one away." In this case, the first "implementation" determines the requirements and the second implements the requirements. The developers prove that they understand the problem with the first implementation, and then actually solve the problem with the second.

As a side note, there's a circumstance that makes requirements gathering more difficult than most people care to admit. That is, it's often extremely difficult to tell the difference between problems and solutions; this fact lends its own chaotic influence where none is expected. (See page 55.) To illustrate the point, consider an application that is defined to coordinate information

This programming pool is intended to provide application support for an entire nonprogramming organization. Most of the people in the pool came from the same research group that provided the people for the organization in Box 19. However, the management and senior staff came from a NASA software development organization, where they were immensely successful.

The team serves several kinds of internal customers. Most of them have customized tools for their private use. However, several common tools are used throughout the organization, tools that tie the enterprise together and which are directly involved in the final production of the organization's product.

The team's management and senior staff apply all of the project management skills and software development disciplines to all requests for team assistance. This is true whether the request is for a minor modification to a customized one-user tool or to one of the common tools. All requests are evaluated, sized, prioritized, and scheduled for optimal use of the team's resources. Part of the priority computation involves the number of people who will be impacted by the change, so customized tools never get quite the attention given to the common tools.

This team needs a very orderly approach to its work with the common tools. Yet it experiences problems here because of the research orientation of most of the staff. Of course, the managers and senior staff are mystified. They can't understand the failure of all the techniques that worked so well for them in their other organization. Similarly, the middle and junior staff are mystified by the responses to their wonderfully creative endeavors and feel that it would be entirely reasonable for each user group to have more customized tools to replace the common tools.

This team needs a very responsive approach to its work with the customized tools. However, it experiences problems here because of the control orientation of the management and senior staff. Of course, the middle and junior staff are mystified by their lack of opportunity to work productively on those fun things. The requesters don't understand why it takes two weeks of evaluation and six months on a queue to accomplish a one-week modification to a program. And the managers and senior staff have no concept of software that does not require the full use of NASA disciplines.

Both of these conflicts are the result of trying to impose incompatible world views on particular situations. As you can see, the more conflicts you can find between world views and situations, the more disorderly and unsuccessful the results will be.

Closure questions:

> *Are the world views represented in your organization conformable?*
> *Do you have a vision, mission, goals, and a set of guiding values to help to keep your organization on track?*
> *How many chaotic failures in organizations can be traced back to incompatible assumptions that lead to conflicting responses to feedback?*

Box 23. *Mixed organization with flexible needs—a broken team* from several locations in a company. In an ideal world, every location would use the same kinds of data in the same ways, using the same formats, and meaning the same things. In fact, none of these are true; the new application not only has to coordinate the information, it has to get it, convert it, interpret it, and hand the undefinable residue to a person for resolution.

Part of the problem of this application is part of the solution for previous applications. Now the question is whether the previous applications can be fixed as part of the solution or whether they have to remain part of the problem. I claim, without further examples or proof, that this is one of the most common difficulties in requirements definition and application design.

Closure questions:

> Consider requirements listed in a document, stated as a simple point by point list of requirements, gathered by people with widely diverse backgrounds. What is the value of this document?
>
> If your product requirements show signs of being put together without having one or more of the six categories covered, how will you proceed with the project?
>
> What tools might you acquire that might help you to do your whole project better?

COMPUTER AIDED SOFTWARE ENGINEERING

Computer Aided Software Engineering (CASE) is a fine case in point for the thesis of this book—exploiting chaos. This is so true, and the examples and cross-references are so frequent in the discussion, that I'll add a list of references to the end of the section rather than making you stumble over all of them.

The field of CASE tools is much more broad than the graphic-based box-drawing structuring tools that appeared in the mid-1980s. It includes advanced versions of those kinds of products, plus editors that support structured languages, requirements-gathering tools, cross-reference and reference-checking tools in recent compilers, visually interpretive executors, and others.

Each of these tools shares a common set of attributes. First, each is based on a world view that keeps things orderly. Second, whether this environment is established by its own supporting code or by de facto or architected standards, it is necessarily well defined. Third, it forces its users to adopt a set of practices that would not be required without the tool.

Some folks would assume that the third attribute is bad while the other two are good. But this is not true. Each of the attributes is essential to the success of the CASE tool. The thoughtful reader might consider these three attributes relative to the Pillars of Software Engineering.

For the first attribute, no tools can function effectively if they have no structure to work with. All CASE tools assume that the software task conforms to certain structural concepts. (Which concepts depends on which tools.) The more the project at hand conforms to the structural concepts of the tool, the more the tool will aid in the project.

For the second attribute, CASE tools depend on having some combination of supporting code (as with the execution environments of Fourth Generation Languages: 4GLs), stored data formats (as with the underlying data structures of the box-drawing CASE tools), and interface standards (as with the linkage architectures of compilers and program linkers). With these things being predictable, the tool can derive its required data, retain and propagate appropriate information related to the associated structures, and resolve implications that would otherwise have been considered "too much work" for manual efforts.

For the third attribute, truly generalized programming languages and environments allow programmer/designers to do just about anything they would like to do. However, to do so would make the world view associated with the tool too unpredictable. Therefore, CASE tools (in self defense, if you'll forgive the anthropomorphication) only allow the use of constructs and specifications that fit within their world view. In some cases, this is all that is allowed because the CASE tool controls the specifications. In other cases, the user is cautioned that deviations from the standards will result in unpredictable results.

In terms of chaos, CASE tools are wonderful examples of adopting a world view that forms an orderly area in what might otherwise be a disorderly and overly complex environment. Where that is true, the CASE tools provide excellent leverage for quality and productivity. Where the world view of CASE tools disagree with the attributes of the project, the CASE tools actually make the situation worse, introducing complexity and lowering quality and productivity.

Note that a CASE tool doesn't eliminate chaos, it just exploits chaos. Within the area of order for a tool, we still find lots of feedback (learning the tool, creating a good design, establishing and using requirements, and so forth). So the area of order is useful for us if we "get in tune" with it. We can have a chaotic mismatch within the area of order if we don't learn the tool or if we don't apply appropriate disciplines. Further, even if we adopt a tool, we may have a chaotic mismatch by being outside of the area of order.

Now that we've heard the theory, what does all of this mean?

First, you need to ask yourself the question, "What would happen if my project structure and needs were not compatible with the structure and capabilities of my CASE tools?" Phrased this way, it should be clear that it would be a drastic mistake to adopt a set of CASE tools for a project just because they're called CASE tools and given rave reviews in the trade press.

Second, you should ask yourself, "Is the world view of the CASE tool all-encompassing or does it depend on standards that exist within my project?" If you're thinking about using a CASE tool with an all-encompassing world view, you will only adopt the tool through a major upheaval of an existing project (which may be good, depending on what kind of trouble the project is in) or through starting from the absolute beginning of the project with the tool.

Third, you should ask yourself, "Does the CASE tool have interfaces that will allow me to use other tools both within the area of order (within the world view) of the tool and outside of that area of order?" You need to select sets of CASE tools that are consistent and compatible within the set. Individual tools may impose requirements on your project that prevent the use of other tools. Since we are still working with the first generations of CASE tools it is quite likely that individual tools will not cover all your needs, and so having tools with well-defined interfaces and repositories is essential if you are to select a complete working set of tools.

Now, here are some of the references pertinent to this section:

- World view—See Paradigms and World Views on page 21.
- Using differing views—See Layers of Reality on page 23.
- Order within bounds—See Bounds of Chaos on page 34.
- Recognizing and exploiting patterns—See Patterns and perspectives on page 45.
- All-encompassing solutions—See box 18 on page 72.
- Software Engineering—See Software Engineering on page 72.
- The pillars of software engineering—See Pillars and Foundations of Software Engineering on page 74.
- Bureaucracy—See The Purpose of Bureaucracy on page 158.

Closure Questions:

Have you heard CASE advocates claim that their favorite tools can solve all software development problems?

Did they explain the associated world view so you could understand the area where you could believe the claims?

Do your criteria for selecting or rejecting CASE tools include procedural, declarative, or object-oriented considerations?

OBJECT-ORIENTED PROCESSING, ET AL

Object-oriented things, including programming, design, user interface, and computer architecture, are all the rage these days. The attributes usually given to object-oriented things include encapsulation, information hiding, inheritance, polymorphism, and methods, all of which are explained in following paragraphs.

Encapsulation packages the code and data for an object within a single unit. This is to keep everything simple. In practice, the code and data aren't really kept together, but an instance of an object has the data and object class information, and the code resides with the definition of the object class.

Hiding keeps object data so that no programming construct other than the object code can see the data for the object. If object data is required outside of the object, the object is to provide an interface to make that happen. Because implementations actually keep code and data separate, this often becomes a convention rather than an enforceable reality. However, it can be a reality with appropriate hardware architecture and related support.

Inheritance allows objects to be defined as "like" other objects, so that the new object doesn't require replication of the code associated with the other object. The new object has code for its special cases, and passes all other interactions on to the other object. This is a construct usually associated with software objects, not hardware architecture objects, because indirect memory references are associated with poor hardware performance.

Polymorphism ensures that objects with similar operations use the same interfaces for them. This is to make inheritance work more smoothly, but leaves something of an open question about what operations are "similar." Polymorphism is a little less obvious than the other attributes, but a few examples might help to make things more clear.

For objects such as numbers, matrices, and vectors, addition is a well-defined operation. Polymorphism says that the same interfaces should be used to make addition happen for these objects. The problem with polymorphism is that all operations don't apply to all objects. For example, addition doesn't seem like a natural thing to do with a sentence, multiplication and division really seem strange for things other than numbers and matrices, and the "check spelling" operation on a sentence doesn't seem to have any obvious parallel for use with numbers.

Still, polymorphism requires a common interface technique for all operations that can somehow be fit into a common conceptual framework between objects.

Methods, as defined by the object-oriented view, are what any other project would call action subroutines. Each method corresponds to an action that can be requested of an object.

Object-oriented design and programming are supposed to keep programming simple and highly productive because of the ways in which objects behave. That is, any particular object has only a limited amount of data and a limited set of behaviors (methods) associated with it. Further, the objects should be defined so that they are "natural" to the user and programmer. Thus, object-oriented programming is supposed to have optimally sized sets of code and data, and interactions between objects are simple and easily understood.

Object-oriented approaches provide excellent examples of a world view that provides an area of order. Now consider other views, the "et al" of the section heading.

If you consider the total domain of processing that is possible in an unstructured programming environment, you can see how various disciplines establish views of the domain. For example, functional decomposition of a required set of processing for an application gives an "operation" view of the domain, where data flow is dictated by the necessities of the operations. Similarly, data decomposition of the processing gives an "operand" view of the domain, where procedural details are associated with the requirements of the data structure. (An excellent example of the data flow view of applications is noted in box 24 on page 87.) Finally, object-oriented design gives an "entity" view of the domain, with both data and code being associated with the requirements of the entities that are defined.

Notice that each of these disciplines defines an area of order where the discipline will be highly productive. Notice further that there are areas where each discipline is disorderly while one or more of the other disciplines will be orderly.

Overall, the implicit constraints of each view (discipline) eliminates some processing from reasonableness. Once you select a view, your choices are to:

> Ignore the unreasonable processing.
>
> Kludge your support so that the unreasonable processing kind of works if you don't look too closely at it (obviously chaotic in the common, derogatory sense).
>
> Provide an interface so that another view (discipline) can be used.

IBM's Paul Morrison, from Toronto, Canada, was instrumental in inventing DFDM (Data Flow Development Manager), a support platform that makes applications easy to build and maintain with a data flow view.

DFDM provides certain building block transforms that will be needed by most applications, including file storage, file retrieval, file copy, printing, and user interaction. It also provides a systems framework so that an application can be defined in terms of its data flows and transforms; the framework handles scheduling, concurrency, and data transfers (queues) between application components (transforms).

To use DFDM, you first define the data requirements of the application, defining how the data flows and is transformed during the application process. Then you create transform modules for the places in the flow where data must be merged, split, transformed, or reported. The full application definition consists of the data definitions and data flows, defined to DFDM, and the transform modules that are invoked by the platform.

Productivity and reuse are inherently increased with the data flow world view, because many of the transforms are handled by utility functions, and programmers are able to focus more on what has to be done for other transforms than on how the whole system is hooked together.

Closure question:

> *If you don't know the flow of data in your organization, what confidence do you have in the mutual support of your processes?*

Box 24. *Data flow processing view*

In the software development world, all three of these approaches are used. The first is common to first releases of products that fully endorse a discipline but haven't yet felt the boot of reality. The second is common to subsequent releases of products that must satisfy customer requirements but where development groups haven't yet realized the limitations of their technologies. The third should be found in mature products, but often isn't. Generally, the third choice is only found in products with primary requirements to be extendable or to have multilingual interfaces.

Closure Questions:

Do you have enough experience with object-oriented techniques to evaluate their use in your project's disciplines?

How might you demonstrate that the area of order for your favorite implementation and design disciplines is adequate to the needs of the application you're building?

TRANSITION

Just in case it isn't obvious, this shortest section in *Exploiting Chaos: Cashing in on the Realities of Software Development* is here to separate the good news from the bad news. Earlier sections in this chapter dealt with potential successes in software development. Subsequent sections deal with things that are so unlikely to contribute to success that you should only consider their use in extreme circumstances.

STAKE-IN-THE-GROUND DESIGN

"It's easier to change something than to invent something, so the most practical and expeditious way to design is to pick an approach, document it, then fuss with it and change it until it works. This approach will result in a good design that we know we can work with."

Thus saith the popular wisdom. Its appeal is so seductive that those who are least well served by it agree to follow it. Even as we agree, we wonder at the disquieting feeling that there's something subtly wrong with it, but there's not enough time to pursue the problems and so we follow the popular wisdom.

It's time to stop! The popular wisdom is wrong!

While it might work in a small number of cases, the "stake in the ground" approach to software development is a variant of rapid prototyping that is too likely to get out of hand in a large organization. If that happens, the result will be a mediocre or inadequate product.

Look at the statement of the popular wisdom. The problems with it are in the qualifiers.

- "most practical"—What is "most practical" changes as your resources change. The stake in the ground approach may be practical if your designers are mediocre. However, if your designers have significant talent (and you'll have good designers in a group of any significant size), the approach is a straitjacket to their capabilities.
- "expeditious"—The only "expeditious" aspect of this approach is that it makes it look like results are being achieved when they really aren't. That is, a stake in the ground is no substitute for a good design decision, but an outsider can't tell the difference.
- "good"—The judgement that the design will be "good" is the most rash of all. As a matter of fact, the design resulting from the stake in the ground approach will usually be mediocre or worse.

Removing all those qualifiers from the statement of the approach and substituting simple, neutral articles in their places, as appropriate, we arrive at a more correct statement.

"It's easier to change something than to invent something, so one way to design is to pick an approach, document it, then fuss with it and change it until it works. This approach will result in a design that we know we can work with." Notice that this is a statement of safety, low risk, and acceptability. It is not a statement involving excitement, customer delight, high quality, or progress in the state of the art.

Having taken issue with the statement of the approach, let's take a look at the reasons why the approach is not suited to good design and desirable products. Further, not to throw the baby out with the bath water, let's look at the areas of business where the approach can be highly productive and explore the qualifying attitudes that help it to be so.

A stake in the ground is an early design decision, based on acknowledged ignorance, that is intended to allow people to progress toward an understanding of a complex situation. It is an early solution to a hypothetical problem; the hypothetical problem is assumed to have something in common with the actual (probably unknown) problem to be solved. It is the (idealistic) intent of the designer to carry the design forward, based on the stake in the ground, until a better solution is found, then to replace the stake in the ground with the better solution. This idealistic intent can get lost in a large organization because the weight of the organization gets behind the stake and makes it part of the fabric of the organization's world view. Also, the hypothetical problem can itself get lost so that few people, if any, understand where the stake came from. Those who don't understand will be afraid of changing it. The less understanding a person has of the stake the more likely he or she is to defend it as a "given of the world view," leading directly to firm management support of a wild guess as a required design decision.

However, incorporating the stake into the organization's world view has even worse consequences. People in the organization now try to view the problem as though the stake were a required part of any solution. Any formulation of the problem that is not amenable to the incorporation of the stake in its solution is automatically rejected. Thus, the stake blinds developers to possible valid understandings of the real problem. Once this has happened, a change in the organization's world view is required before this simple stake can be replaced with anything else.

This last broken team is involved in a project with nearly unknown requirements, but it is staffed with people who have always been successful in enhancing products that have known users and known requirements. Their natural response when a project gets into trouble is to tighten controls (change controls, freeze requirements, increase emphasis on regression testing, and so on), which is exactly the wrong thing to do when requirements must be discovered as the product is being developed.

The team's natural responses make the situation worse. Formalizing customer contacts isolates the developers from their only reliable source for product requirements. Bringing the project to full staffing levels very early and beginning implementation without design guidance creates barriers to future flexibility. A final death knell would be sounded if significant project resources were put into testing cycles rather than into requirements and design efforts.

The conflict should be clear. When the project calls for dynamic and highly flexible work in determining product requirements and the designs that can satisfy customer needs, it will be a disaster to adopt a highly structured, isolated, and firmly controlled approach to software development.

Closure questions:

What kinds of mind sets would lead people to form teams like those broken teams?

Is there something you can do to ensure that you don't do that to any of your people, and nobody does it to you?

Box 25. *Orderly organization with unknown requirements—a broken team*

Notice that the "expeditious" decision has now become a drain on effort and resources, as it requires major organizational upheaval to get it changed. The fascinating part of this phenomenon is that a formal change control process, one in which everything can be challenged, can, in some cases, cause the removal of a stake in the ground faster than would be possible in a less tightly controlled process where the stake becomes part of the culture. However, the word "expeditious" should be used with this approach only with its overtones of "quick, dirty, and wrong," rather than with its more positive meaning, "quick and effective."

When you look at the capabilities of designers, you see that the stake in the ground approach has a significant impact on the utilization of the available design skills. Imagination is restrained, the reasons for the stakes are lost in the organization, and organizational inertia impedes the progress of the very changes that were initially assumed to be the salvation of the stake in the ground design approach.

So, three phrases were picked out of the statement of the popular wisdom: "most practical," "expeditious," and "good." Expeditious clearly is not a positive trait of the approach. Most practical has to be seriously in question when the approach places so many pitfalls in the path of progress and inhibits the production of good design. Thus, claiming that the approach is the most practical and expeditious falls in the realm of wishful thinking. Finally, claiming that the approach will lead to "good" design can only be the attempt to make it so by claiming it, a verbal clutching at straws rather than a statement of a result that can be reasonably expected.

Focus, for a moment, on the feedback and chaos here. Feedback on the stake itself is key. The pressures to fix problems will correspond with the significance of the mismatch between the stake and the needs of the application. If we see high levels of feedback (change request activity), high disorder, and strong pressure for control, we have all the requirements for a catastrophic transition. In many situations, we should expect the catastrophic transition to be breakage—the project will fail.

Finally, let's not lose sight of the fact that there is value in the stake in the ground approach; look at what can happen in a small group. As long as the group can retain its grip on the hypothetical problem formulation that the stake in the ground helps to solve, the stake is an evaluation technique for measuring the formulation. Each stake represents a solution paradigm, and a sequence of such stakes helps the designers to understand both the problem and possible solutions. This suggests two things for the approach.

First, the approach should be used on a short-term basis to minimize the possibility that the group might lose its grip on the hypothetical formulation. This focuses attention on the problem formulation rather than on the design possibility represented by the stake.

Second, the approach should be used in a small group so that the inevitable communication problems in a larger group don't mask the source of the stake and allow it to achieve some permanence.

These points, in turn, suggest that the stake in the ground approach should be a part of rapid prototyping and requirements gathering, but only in the most carefully controlled circumstances.

Closure Questions:

> How could you use several stakes to offer some comfort and security to your peers who prefer the stake in the ground approach?
>
> If your development group is large, how could you clearly identify stakes so that you could reap their benefits while avoiding their traps?
>
> What management style would be the most dangerous in a group using stakes?

MICROMANAGEMENT

When people see situations moving beyond their control the natural and intuitive response is to clamp down, as most parents of teenagers know all too well. Micromanagement is the software development manifestation of this response. The desire to make software development into a full engineering discipline (like hardware development or, even better, like construction of bridges and buildings) reinforces the response. Unfortunately, as with the stake in the ground design, the intuitive response is the wrong response. This is one of many areas where software development is counterintuitive.

Early airplanes were somewhat unstable, so pilots had to keep them under control constantly. As people understood better how to design airplanes, they made them more stable, comfortable, and easy to fly. Well, that's true for some airplanes—cargo, passenger, and personal airplanes. But fighter planes had different requirements.

Fighter planes have to be aerodynamically unstable to achieve their required performance. Over the years, airplanes' higher performance outstripped their pilots' ability to control them. To balance the needs, computers were added to the airplanes' support systems to keep them stable while delivering the required high performance.

Of course, this caused a problem for the pilots, who were used to controlling everything. When the pilot and the computers both used feedback to achieve the same stability, the combination made things worse and caused violent oscillation. Pilots lost control. Airplanes crashed. This was chaos beyond acceptable bounds.

To survive, pilots had to learn to stop their efforts to stabilize the airplane. Pilots had to learn to signal their larger intentions and let the computers maintain the airplane's stability. Micromanagement is deadly to pilots.

Closure questions:

How would you know if your attempts to control were causing problems?
What micromanagement techniques are deadly to software development organizations?

Box 26. *Pilot induced oscillation*

You see micromanagement when project leaders try to assign tasks at the most detailed level. (See page 163.) You see micromanagement when the plans for a project are kept at the most detailed levels and not allowed to change. You see micromanagement when success measurements (profit, customer acceptances) are applied to the everyday activities of the organization. (See page 167.) Micromanagement is based on the idea that it is possible to know and direct the smallest details of an effort, and on the idea that the manager is not part of the system being managed.

Look at the inherent conflicts between micromanagement and a feedback (chaotic) system.

Micromanagement works at the most detailed levels. It pushes attention to those levels of detail very early in the process. Then, it requires approvals and explanations for any changes in those details, should any be necessary.

In a feedback system, the most detailed levels of the system tend to be the most dynamic and changing. Thus, early guesses about the details are likely to be wrong and the required approvals and explanations will slow the changes when they are necessary.

Micromanagement is particularly greedy for measurements at all levels. There is a tendency to use adjustment and success measurements indiscriminately, more as a result of a common cause than as a necessary part of micromanagement. The measurements are, however, viewed as being immensely important parts for understanding the effort.

In a feedback system, the magnitude of variations is often determined by the scope of the feedback. When micromanagement uses success measurements as part of the feedback, the resultant variations will be quite large. The almost exhaustive use of measurements leads to two other phenomena that also degrade the effort. One involves the pertinence of the measurements, since the use of irrelevant measurements leads to process changes that have no bearing on what is desired. The other is that the measurements are often pursued at the expense of productive process work.

The common causes of both micromanagement and the improper use of measurements are the lack of a balanced understanding of what software development is and does, and the assumption that there is no need to consider chaos in software development. In a very real sense, micromanagement is a symptom of those common causes. The good news here is that there is hope that the micromanager may learn better, over time.

Closure Questions:

> Do you see the micromanagement symptoms in your organization?
> What education and experience might you pursue if you discovered that you were a micromanager and wanted to learn better habits?

FIRE FIGHTING IN THE MIDST OF CHAOS

A firefighting organization, which has to respond constantly to crises rather than real fires, is one of the worst examples of chaos abuse known to the software development industry. If you ever wanted to see an organization that had the worst possible response to chaos, the firefighting organization is it. It's the abuse of the SWAT team concept. (See box 16 page 56.)

However, this section isn't really here to help you point at firefighting organizations and yell, "Stupid!" There's something more significant to be learned. We'll get to that in a few paragraphs.

In the firefighting organization, there is one overriding priority, "Take care of the latest problem!" It doesn't make any difference whether the problem is a rumor, a real problem, or something that just came to the boss's attention. What makes a difference is that somebody noticed a problem, and it's a high priority to take care of known problems immediately.

Look at what firefighters really do. First, they don't spend all of their time fighting fires. Between fires, they maintain their equipment, learn about and practice better firefighting techniques, and, in many cases, perform other civic duties. They also learn that their primary business is protecting people and property, not just putting out fires. So when they are called to fight a fire, they will do so in such a way as to minimize the damage to the victim's property.

Firefighting has a bad reputation in the software development community. That's because of the characteristic of dropping everything to fight the fires, then doing the same thing again and again. The flaw in this comparison is the fact that while firefighters are in the business of fighting fires, software developers shouldn't be.

If software developers were to follow the pattern of professional firefighters, they would have (or take) time between projects to learn about and practice better software development techniques. They would maintain their tools and equipment so that they were well prepared for the next development effort to come along. They would not be totally immersed in software development all the time, and they would develop software with more than just the immediate product in mind.

Closure question:

What might you conclude about any software development organization that focussed on one single point of view, one single approach to business, or one single method for solving problems?

Box 27. *Real fire fighting*

Look at this in terms of feedback, and think of my friend with the swimming pool. (See box 10 on page 35.) When we see a problem we might respond to it immediately, in a knee-jerk fashion. If we respond immediately and with vigor, we give the system a kick. Then, like jelly, the system will bounce around. If we respond immediately to lots of problems, we give the system lots of kicks. Then, our jelly system really bounces around. If we kick hard enough and often enough, we may splatter the system all over the place.

With our instant response to the problem, we may have solved it, not solved it, created a new problem in solving the old one, or responded to something that wasn't even a problem. In the best world, we were the Rambo of the problem world and we took out a threat before it became a real problem. But that doesn't happen very often in software development. The most likely thing is that we attacked a perceived problem and implemented a solution that caused even more problems.

Given that perceived problems vary from the real and immediately solvable to the unreal and not worthy of attention, we can expect several things if we treat all perceived problems as real and requiring immediate attention. First, the real problems we solve will lead us to believe that all things we attack are also real. This will give us a false sense of security about our approach. Second, we'll almost always create more problems than we solve. Partial solutions leave the original problem and create secondary problems; solutions to nonproblems are most often problems in their own rights. This is an example of continued feedback leading to almost violent disorder.

As the final factor, notice that unnecessary problem-solving takes time and resources away from the primary work of the organization. In the degrading cycle of creating more and more problems, the firefighting organization ultimately ends up churning, looking busy and productive in solving problems that are really not problems, and producing none of what it is supposed to produce.

Now we have the picture. Pure firefighting is bad for an organization, leading to zero productivity. But lots of folks already knew that. So what's the big deal?

The big deal is in using our awareness of this to help us detect disorder in our organizations. Remember that feedback leads both to areas of order and areas of disorder. We'd like to use whatever tools and concepts we have to create productive areas of order. We'd like to learn to detect and avoid areas of disorder. We'd like to use our time to take care of business and make sure our skills are aligned with the work we need to do. We'd like to be well prepared for emergencies so that we can handle them in a professional and orderly manner.

That's what we learn from firefighting organizations.

Once we've formulated the view, its use is obvious. We can look at our discovered problems to see if we're in an area of disorder. If we are "strongly encouraged" to deal with every problem as soon as it appears, we're in an area that will soon become disorderly if it isn't already. If we deal with each problem as a special case, we're already in an area of disorder. If we are so besieged with problems that they interfere with our work, we're in a dominant area of disorder.

If we continue the practices that got us into firefighting mode, no matter how effective we think we are at solving problems, we know that we'll continue in that mode.

Closure Questions:

> What can you say about organizations that receive reports of trouble and respond either in knee-jerk fashion or by ignoring the reports?
> What can you learn from all the things in this chapter that might help you with your work?

6

What Software Development Should Do

CHAOS, GOOD AND BAD

In a large working group, chaos is evident when competing factions have contradictory ideas and are unable to resolve them into robust designs; instead, they compromise on weaker solutions. Chaos is evident when discussions get dragged into side alleys, a situation that becomes more likely to occur and more difficult to control as the group gets larger or remote sites get involved. Chaos is evident as a sub-group adopts a goal and pursues it consistently, even though that goal is actually contrary to the larger goal of the development effort.

Given the kinds of communications that go on and the kinds of communication problems that exist within large, multigroup projects, it's almost inevitable that sub-groups will evolve countercultures. Since it is so easy to justify the goals of a counterculture as being necessary for the associated components, and because of the communications blockages found in multigroup projects, these countercultures are highly likely to become embedded within the organization and to get the ego involvement of members of the sub-group involved. To make the news even worse, notice that *Exploiting Chaos: Cashing in on the Realities of Software Development* proposes that some retrograde areas are necessary to the smooth functioning of the overall project in the user's eye. So, what's to keep every sub-group from running off with its own culture, its own user interface, and its own vision of the future?

The answer has several parts, none of which are universal or totally natural in human endeavor. First is the pervasive self-discipline in a project that members of the group use to direct their efforts toward the project goals, subordinating their desires for individual stardom while pursuing the best possible support for the user. Second is the management propagation and support of the project vision, so that sub-groups are not subverted by seductive provincial views while the project founders. This relies on the self-discipline of the managers who might be tempted to use project divisions to further their individual careers. Third is a strong set of efforts to keep the end user as the final arbiter in decisions about what the project is to do. The user/customer will be the final arbiter in any case, but having that happen during development is far less expensive and far better for product quality than waiting until the product hits the marketplace. Fourth is a fresh point of view that keeps the project from becoming a development toy instead of a user tool.

In balance, what is good in one sense may be not so good in another. There are times when the best progress is made by retrograde motion—efforts contrary to the goals. This is the basis for simulated annealing. (See page 29.) The concept of simulated annealing suggests that dogged pursuit of a goal is sometimes less productive than a more broad-based (but still disciplined) exploration of alternatives. Apparent steps backward actually lead to more optimal results. The techniques have been demonstrated with metallurgy (whence the name) and with Artificial Intelligence applications.

All of this suggests that there are disadvantages to large groups, advantages to personal discipline, and significant advantages in less-than-dogged pursuit of development goals. These are the premises of the fractal development process. (See page 115.)

No particular defined process will achieve success in all cases. However, defining a process that allows disciplined people to select the right tool for the right job will lead to more successes than if people are required to use one tool for all jobs. This will work even better if the process itself is flexible; the process will support work styles consistent with the immediate job to be performed, as well as supporting the use of tools appropriate to the job. If this is done, the percentage of successes will be higher than with the existing development processes, the quality of the results will be higher than with the existing development processes, the resulting products will be more successful in technological and customer acceptance terms, and the cost of successful and unsuccessful development efforts will be lower.

Closure Questions:

> Have you experienced situations in which the lack of a "devil's advocate" allowed a disaster to happen?
> Have you been on a project that was scuttled because no two people could pull in the same direction?
> How would you steer a course between these two extremes to produce the best possible results?
> Can your current process deal with multisite development?

Is it flexible enough to allow different people, groups, and goals to contribute positively to your product?

This team maintains a newly released product. The team is committed to timely response to customer problems. Maintenance people are experienced but not fully trained on the product, relying heavily on the expertise of the product developers.

The development team is relatively small, and there's a good rapport between the development and maintenance teams. The development team has begun the next version of the product but has incomplete requirements; they want to incorporate requirements given by new customers who are still figuring out what the product does.

When a problem report comes in, the maintenance people work up a fix. If the base documentation is clear and the fix is straightforward, they code the fix, send it to the customers, and send the problem and fix to the developers. Developers cover the need in the requirements and design for the next version. Developers also evaluate the fix and warn the maintenance group if the fix might cause secondary problems.

When a problem report comes in that the maintenance people can't figure out, that has unclear choices for fixes, or that might be a future requirement, the maintenance team calls in the development team. Developers and maintainers jointly build two solutions—the short term solution for the customer and the long term solution for future versions of the product.

Part of the chaos here comes from customer feedback. Another part comes from the learning experiences of both the developers (requirements and real customer experiences) and the maintainers (product expertise and considerations for future designs). A key point in the chaos of the environment is the timely response to the customer. It's not always possible for the effects of the feedback (learning, conflict resolution, and so on) to stabilize before a fix is sent to customers.

Closure questions:

> *Would this situation (and the product) be less or more stable, over the long run, if developers and maintainers were isolated from each other?*
> *How might more formal control and rigor help or hinder the efforts of this team?*

Box 28. *Flexible maintenance team*

CONTROLS VERSUS ENABLERS IN SOFTWARE DEVELOPMENT

The Harvard Law found in Arthur Bloch's *Murphy's Law* states, "Under the most rigorously controlled conditions of pressure, temperature, volume, humidity, and other variables, the organism will do as it damn well pleases."

To practicing computer scientists, this applies as well to software development as it does to the living organisms envisioned by the framers of the Harvard Law. In software development we attempt to control projects by the use of plans and schedules, requirements, tools, processes, visions, management, resource allocations, and other methods. Yet each of these is more properly an enabler rather than a control. First, look at each as if it were a control.

A project without a plan will seldom show any signs of progress, other than the participants' vague feelings that they must be moving ahead. Projects that are forced to follow a plan to its utmost detail often founder when the realities of the implementation demonstrate that some of the assumptions found there were impossible. Still, nearly all of us have seen projects that had neither formal plans nor formal schedules, yet were truly amazing because they resulted in a product that was high in function, high in quality, and went out the door in an astonishingly short time.

A project without requirements will often be fragmentary, as various subgroups adopt their own "customer surrogate" to support. Further, the implementations of each of the views will show differing levels of capabilities and inconsistent user interfaces. As with plans and schedules, projects that are forced to follow the requirements will fail if those requirements prove impossible during the implementation effort. Still, most of us can point to projects that were implemented successfully for happy customers with no formalized requirements of any kind.

Some projects have failed because of the lack of good tools, while other projects have succeeded in spite of such a lack. The selection of improper tools can set a project back more than providing no tools, yet it should be recognized that development and testing tools are the white-collar equivalent of capital investments in blue-collar productivity.

Processes, visions, management, and resource allocations all follow the same patterns. Theoretically good examples have led to the demise of projects, while theoretically bad examples have failed to kill the projects to which they were applied.

As you can see from the previous examples, as from the Harvard Law and from the experiences of those who have practiced Bonsai, vital and chaotic things will grow and flourish according to their natures, not according to the theories and wishes of those who believe that they are in control. Strongly controlled things may flourish in spite of the controls, or may die because of them. Even those things that flourish may have to be stopped because of the directions they take, if they become wonderful things with no useful purpose or no redeeming value. In software development cases like these, we hope that the authors would document and publish the results so that other groups with different needs and visions can exploit them.

Now look at these things as enablers.

When a project is moving strongly in a desired direction, solid planning and scheduling can help to ensure that the project continues in that direction and arrives at a closure point in good shape. Where the project takes a turn that

This team is developing a new product. The functional requirements are known, in terms of the industry to be supported and the particular areas of expertise represented by eventual users. However, the user interface is not defined, detailed algorithms are unknown, and the development group has incomplete knowledge of the systems that are to be replaced by the new product.

Members of the development team represent a mix of experience and expertise. The variety is in dimensions of design, coding, base systems, and customer knowledge.

The development team has sub-teams working on both the known and unknown aspects of the development effort. Knowledgeable representatives of the end user community are involved in designing the user interface, designing the functional details, designing the data base, and exploring the capabilities of systems to be replaced. A consultant on the design of 4GLs has been hired to help the team in identifying and exploiting patterns in the end user environment.

The entire team of 200 people meets each Friday afternoon to share the latest information on requirements, user interfaces, internal interfaces, function, and project status. After a more formal information exchange, team members remain in the meeting hall. The company provides refreshments, and the team members have a relaxed atmosphere in which to discuss topics of their choice and to demonstrate their current work to each other using support machines and terminals scattered around the edge of the meeting hall.

This is not a small team, yet it retains a small-team flavor. Individuals have jobs to do, some assigned and some adopted, yet none are isolated by overly formal reporting structures. At the Friday sessions, team members have the opportunity to show off their work and are encouraged to do so from time to time.

Chaos in this team is clearly identifiable because of the dynamic of refining incomplete requirements; keeping up with product ideas, people, and tools; and developing product components with immediate customer feedback. Still, the experienced hands and the known areas of the product requirements, together with company support for team interactions, provide a secure foundation to keep the chaos from getting out of hand. In addition, the product itself is designed to exploit areas of order in the user environment.

Closure question:

> *What companies can you think of that already use some of the techniques mentioned for this team?*

Box 29. *Dynamic development team*

was not expected in the plan, the best new combination of plan and project should be chosen.

When a project is growing from a well-established base, has a known customer set, and has a cadre of expert developers to implement it, solid and well-defined requirements will help it to stay on course, satisfy the existing customer base, and attract a larger customer base than was enjoyed by previous versions. Where some of the requirements prove to be impossible to implement in the required time frame, the existing customer base is there to negotiate replacement requirements or to modify the rest of the requirements to satisfy the needs.

When a project is to be implemented with a particular technology, existing tools can be purchased or new tools developed that will enhance the productivity of the development group and the quality of the resultant product. If some of the selected/developed tools prove not to be supportive of the group's needs, they should be discarded or modified, rather than used as a standard to force the development group to perform unnatural acts.

Looking at all of these, we can exploit the chaotic nature of software development in the following ways, using the characteristics of chaos as our guide:

> Areas of order—You can define tasks that need to be done, including requirements gathering, designing, coding, testing, and so on. For each of these, it's possible to put them together in clumps so that there is some benefit from concentration. Use the most productive and compatible theories you can to organize and pursue your work, and they will be very likely to deliver good results.
>
> Areas of disorder—Remember that areas of disorder make most people uncomfortable. Remember that areas of disorder also tend to take lots more code than areas of order. And remember that areas of disorder are highly likely between areas of order. Try to generalize the patterns in areas of order so that the areas of disorder shrink to more manageable sizes. Banish the areas of disorder into new areas of order (housekeeping code, standard interfaces . . .). Or, redesign (take a new world view) so that the disorder disappears or becomes insignificant.
>
> Self-similarity—Designing and coding are similar tasks, even though their outputs are different. Actually, if you look at the entire process of developing software, it looks very much like the process of designing a smaller part. Tools and common notations can help with areas of self-similarity, both in detecting inconsistencies and in improving productivity.
>
> Self-dissimilarity—Testing is not the same kind of ordered process as design. As a matter of fact, testing and design are retrograde to each other since designing is a process of composing and building logical actions while testing is a process of determining and breaking down logical actions. So, you should allow the flexibility for different groups and different portions of the implementation to work according to their natures.

Response to changes—Take a development effort that follows a specific development process and change the schedule; if the new schedule varies too much from the original, the whole effort will break down. If the time is too short, the process will get in the way of the essentials of the job; if the time is too long, the requirements will change and Parkinson's Law will administer the coup de grace as every individual part of the process expands to consume all of the new time. Orderly theories are only guidelines when you're involved in chaotic activities. So watch carefully for anomalous results (both people and implementation results). You don't want to overwhelm the effort with tracking but you do want to detect unexpected results and respond to them in the most effective way possible. When you see things that aren't as expected, you look more closely to see what happened. Then you adjust your efforts accordingly.

Programmers have known these things for years, but they haven't had the right words, theories, or examples to convince very many other people. The concept of chaotic processes may prove to be more persuasive.

As a side observation on chaotic behaviors, note that you can see them not only in the software development process but also in the business process, in the structure and code in a system of programs, and in the structure of the company.

Closure Questions:

How would you know if you had a good balance of controls and enablers in your projects?

What relationships do you need between your people to make the enablers work most effectively?

TEAMWORK

An excellent parallel to the use of various techniques in a fractal development process is a team of people working together.

- Each team member brings a different world view to the project.
- Each member's talents represent areas of stability where those talents can be used very productively.
- Each member's limitations represent areas of instability where the team member might be less than productive.
- The areas of stability are complementary and provide the team with an overall set of capabilities that far exceed the capabilities of any individual member.

This view of a team helps to clarify the role of management in getting the best work from the team. There are actually three project-related things management must do.

First, provide the vision, values, mission, and goals that the team will pursue for the project. These provide a rallying direction for the team so that they can work together more effectively. Without this guidance, each team member will pursue individual needs as the most important direction for the team to take. The effort of communicating this guidance includes keeping the team fully aware of the importance of the team's efforts and of the changes in the larger organization that bear on the project or the futures of the team members.

Second, enable or empower team members to best exploit individual talents. The manager who wants all of the team members to be interchangeable cogs is ignoring the unique capabilities of each team member and thus is wasting them. The manager who wants explicitly to control all the work of the team will restrict the team to do only work that the manager can do, thus wasting all the talents on the team that differ from the manager's own.

Third, fill in the gaps in the team capabilities. The manager has the ultimate responsibility for the team's work, and will work to have the right skills and capabilities represented in the team. The manager can grow team members to fulfil the needs (the first choice), recruit additional team members with the right skills, or adopt portions of the work and act as a team member to complete them him or herself.

In addition to these skill and communication questions, the manager must watch over the team interactions to ensure that they remain healthy. The manager must also protect the team from disruptive outside interference while encouraging productive outside contact.

Closure Questions:

> How do you know your effectiveness when you are trying to take care of these teamwork issues *and* make technical decisions on a project at the same time?
>
> What ideas can you extract from the parallel between a team and a collection of technologies for organizations that might exploit multiple technologies in a single project?

PRESCRIPTIONS FOR EXPLOITING DEVELOPMENT'S FRACTAL NATURE

The following sections describe some basic decisions that must be made to exploit our knowledge of alternative development processes in the most productive ways possible. Our decisions must account for any fractal characteristics or situations we expect to encounter, or we will quickly run afoul on the shoals of reality. Our successes in using the tools we select will follow directly from their suitability for the tasks at hand. Where we used to view every problem as a nail (all we had for a tool was a hammer) we now can be more discerning. We can look at the jobs to be done (software to be developed for the customer) and select the right tools (languages, processes, components, and marketing focuses, for example) to get those jobs done with high quality and profits.

This team maintains applications that must be available all the time. Members are on call 24 hours a day, with designated responsibilities for particular applications. During normal business hours, team members are developers for additional applications within their areas of responsibility, depending on their maintenance load.

When a problem is found, the appropriate team member is called. The team member is responsible for diagnosing the problem and implementing an immediate fix that will get the application back on-line. Then, during normal business hours, the team member corrects, tests, and installs the updated application, ensuring that the problem will not recur.

Team members have high levels of expertise with their applications. Their mature responses to situations keep them from running up a backlog of ever more complex problems. With their knowledge and expertise, they are adept at making both quick fixes and robust incremental improvements.

We see feedback between the team member and the running application here. With restricted time, some of the immediate fixes will reflect guesses about causes rather than fully validated diagnoses. The team member relies heavily on an ability to learn and adjust quickly.

We see feedback between the fix levels. Some of the immediate fixes will be incorrect, so the longer-term actions have to fix both the original problem and the short-term fix.

Closure questions:

> *If your situation calls for time-critical maintenance, do you want to have team members who thrive on putting out fires?*
>
> *Or would you prefer to have team members who prefer to prevent problems?*
>
> *Could you productively compose your team of members from each camp?*

Box 30. *Time-critical maintenance*

Closure Questions:

> When can you most productively select the tools you will use in support of your project?
>
> What balance can you achieve in your selection of tools and processes

between absolute knowledge (which comes too late to be useful), and theoretical guesswork (which comes too early)?

Separate the Processes According to Their Goals

Current development processes frequently are codifications of both the business needs of the enterprise and the organizational needs of the software developers. In such comprehensive processes, the needs of one group typically dominate the needs of any other involved group. Further, there are more than two groups involved in a software development effort of any size. These simple observations lead to conclusions on boundedness and on task-oriented management.

Having more groups involved in a process increases the bounds of the process, implying uncontrollable disorder as the number of groups gets large.

Supporting the needs of the separate groups with separate processes will enhance the clarity of the individual processes and the productivity of the work efforts for the respective groups. This allows the bounds of the individual processes to be kept as tight as possible.

There is a limit to how much the base process can be broken apart productively, particularly since the resultant processes are interdependent and it is counterproductive to allow the groups to get out of touch with each other.

Project coordination involves a careful balancing act, using enough processes to keep each one nicely bounded, while not using so many that the interdependencies cause another unmanageably disorderly process.

It is impossible to keep the individual groups and their processes focused on the overall goal by using task management. (See page 163.) The groups must see and pursue the common goal as part of their basic structure and focus. W. Edwards Deming calls this leadership, Tom Peters calls it vision.

Closure Questions:

Can we expect different groups to have identical goals for their respective processes?
If so, why do they have separate processes?
If not, how would you keep them working toward the common project goal?

Business Process

The business process is the dominant part of some standard software development processes. A challenge facing management is to determine how much of such a process contributes to the timeliness and quality of software products and how much is distracting formality instead. It's highly likely that the business process will have to be streamlined, even as it monitors the quality and suitability of the associated product. Further, the business process must enhance partnership between developers and customers, instead of the current insulation it often enforces between those two groups.

Business processes usually start with an idea of how the technological process should be controlled, then grow through the addition of fixes to perceived problems. They are often and repeatedly reviewed with the intent of streamlining them.

Programmers don't much like business processes; they see too many reports, too many plans, and too much work that doesn't directly contribute to the production of products. However, for an interesting exercise, try to reduce a business process by the elimination of any particular part. Better yet, ask management to remove parts of a business process and replace them with simpler mechanisms to accomplish the same purposes; the odds are that management will decide that there is no simpler mechanism that will do the job. While the entire process appears cumbersome and excessive, each of the individual parts is judged to be an essential step in assuring good business decisions and high-quality products. The flaw in the exercise is that you can't simplify a process that has grown as a collection of fixes; such a process calls for redesign and replacement, not fine tuning.

All of this is not to say that business processes are perfect, but that the processes will be improved only through the application of considerable effort and with careful analysis of the needs of software development and marketing. Because of the continuing attempts to streamline the process by simplification or direct replacement of individual parts, it's highly likely that a business process can be improved only by stepping back from the process itself to look at the entire business at hand. In the press of daily crises, this is a difficult thing to do.

As you have undoubtedly gathered from reading this section, designing a good business process is just like designing a good software solution to a difficult problem.

Closure Questions:

> What parts of a good business process require knowledge of the technology being used?
> How could you demonstrate that a business process enhanced or degraded a development project?
> What kind of person could design a good business process and what would she or he need to know?

Implementation Process

The programming process is the subordinate and most suspect part of some software development processes. As noted in the sections describing alternative development processes, the wide variety of development needs can not be satisfied by a single, simplistic process. Notice that the scopes of the alternative processes differ because it's not always clear what aspects of the entire product cycle are appropriately part of the business process and what aspects are part of the programming process. However, the choice of a suitable programming development process is critical to the actual production of working code, and should occupy a significant part of the attention of project management.

Closure Questions:

>   If this section deals with a topic that is so critical, why is it so short?

Management Process

Too often, people believe that software development is only a matter of technical and business considerations. Yet an effort of any size also requires a mature management team if it is to be successful. Peter Drucker, in *Innovation and Entrepreneuring*, comments on the need for mature management in all entrepreneurial organizations if they are to have more than one success.

Also too often, people believe that management is invisible and outside any technical and business concerns. With all that we now understand about chaos and fractal behaviors, we know that this can't possibly be true. For management to be effective, it must respond to the business and technical situation to direct the business and technical approaches to be taken by the organization. Since the organization is part of the situation, feedback is clearly involved and the results will be fractal.

Management will always have a process to follow. The process may be well defined in a book of management guidelines, policies, and practices, or it may be something that is understood and passed on by example and word of mouth. Neither style of definition is inherently good or bad; the key point to be noted is that the management process is often the most significant barometer of the overall culture of the organization. Because it embodies the culture, the management process is often difficult to pin down and quantify. Similarly, it is often difficult to change or redirect. There are a few managers who reshape the cultures of their organizations, but they tend to be the exceptions rather than the norms.

Since the management process is the process that is the most resistant to change, it is necessary to ensure that the organization either must have some managers who are able to change the culture to support the business and technical processes, or the business and technical processes must be defined to survive and thrive with the existent management process. This is the prime point of this section and it is worth reinforcing.

An attempt to use new business and technical processes will fail if the new processes are incompatible with the culture of the organization.

Closure Question:

>   What signs can you look for that might indicate conflict between a management process and either a business or a technical process?

Select Workable Processes According to the Situation

At this point, the existence of several alternative ways to do business should cause the gentle reader automatically to understand that it is necessary to make a choice.

Evaluate your project and situation, looking at possible processes that can be useful, then select the set of processes that will best help you to achieve your desired goals.

Closure Question:

> What parts of typical projects and situations are considered in selecting processes?

Business Process

Factors for selecting the business process include:

> Schedule requirements—Can the business process be followed within the desired schedule? Does the business process fit appropriately with the schedule?
>
> Requirements complexity—If requirements gathering is significant and part of the schedule, then the business process should monitor the completion of the effort. If the requirements are known, a simple check-off would be appropriate.
>
> Existence of base implementation technology—Business processes are not normally sensitive to levels of technology. However, the business process must fit with the overall development. Further, the technology base will have an impact on both the sequence of events and the amount of time it takes to get the job done.
>
> Well-defined marketplace and knowledge of the intended customer— The marketplace may be defined by specific customers, by the needs of a class of customers, or by the technology provided by your solution. These will be reflected in the vision, mission, and goals of the organization, which provide the fundamental basis for the business process.

Closure Questions:

> What indications should you expect to see if your chosen business process is incompatible with the selection factors discussed above?
> Does your process address all of the factors that apply to your customers and products?

Implementation Process

Factors for selecting the implementation process include:

> Requirements complexity—Understanding complex requirements has much in common with learning and is a nontrivial effort. Nei-

This team is assigned the mission of developing a product to support efforts in marginally understood areas of application need. The mission requires the invention of the expertise necessary to build the product, as well as a close partnership among those who are involved in the target application.

The software developers are expert in both developing software and learning diverse subjects. They and the ultimate users of the application view themselves as a single collective team.

The user group looks for the kinds of patterns they think might be useful in the application. The software developers watch the patterns and play with various implementations that might support the users' needs, including data structures and functions that might enhance the use of the result. The user group explores the impact of the evolving application, keeping the effort practical and useful. Frequent free-for-all meetings expose problems to be solved and areas where breakthroughs are needed. Periodic outside evaluations help to prevent hardening of the attitudes that might block the project from productive areas.

The chaos in this team is nearly pervasive. Requirements change from day to day. Implementation technologies fade into and out of fashion. The whole effort is one of inventing, shaping, searching, and sorting through possibilities to find sets of choices that are productive. Previously understood areas of order are sources (but not the only sources) for concepts, structures, and implementations that can contribute to the resultant application.

One big benefit of this chaotic development is that it covers lots of possibilities very quickly. Another is that it encourages the use of possibilities that didn't exist before. Pay dirt can appear in many different forms. It would be counterproductive for the development team to start with any particular assumptions when the unknowns in the project are so predominant.

Mutual respect among the team members is absolutely critical for this approach to work. The intense work on problems and changing points of view would cause a disaster if it were allowed to reflect on the participants rather than the problem.

Closure question:

> *What business areas can you think of where a broad, highly varied exploration would be productive?*

Box 31. *Breakthrough development*

ther learning curves nor mastery of requirements can be assumed to be trivial in a development process. Selecting a process with no provision for mastery of requirements is betting with a high probability of losing.

Projected product size—Small projects tend to have fewer communication problems than larger projects. Where possible, larger projects should be organized as collections of smaller projects.

Existence of base technology—A base technology implies lower reliance on invention for the successful completion of the project. A more traditional process is possible if there is a well-defined and comprehensive base technology. A fractal process is needed if invention is required or if requirements are complex and unknown.

Customer knowledge base—Absence of a customer knowledge base leaves development somewhat adrift (which may be a comfortable state for some developers, but it places the product's sales potential at greater risk). The selected process should incorporate customer feedback according to the customer knowledge base.

Available programming expertise—Again, the process must account for required learning time. This learning will be fractal in nature, occurring by leaps and bounds, and the process must tolerate or support this.

Expected product lifetime—Just as you don't use a long-haul truck to move a sofa across the street, you must design a development process to be appropriate for the amount of work to be done and the length of time it is to survive.

Closure Questions:

What indications would you expect to see if your chosen implementation process were incompatible with the selection factors listed above?

Does your process address all of the factors that apply to your technology and people?

Management Process

Factors for selecting the management process include:

Management maturity—Peter Drucker speaks of the requirement for mature management for long term success in a company. If the management team does not have enough experience, the management process will need to provide guidance and support to carry the entire team while the managers accumulate experience leading to success. This is a chicken and egg problem in a small company but a realistic (if somewhat undesirable) formulation for a group in a large company.

Project management expertise—It's true for all projects, but particularly for larger projects, that a project is unlikely to succeed if no one manages where it is and where it is going. If the management team does not have project management expertise, project management education or project management consultants will be needed immediately to allow management to see where the project is and to make the decisions required to keep things moving properly.

Degree and level of innovation required—Innovation is a key ingredient in any productive, improving organization. However, different degrees of nurturing for the people and support for invention are required in advanced development organizations than in the more stable environments of release-to-release software enhancement.

Culture of the larger organization—If the project is a sub-group of a larger organization, it will be necessary for the project's management to communicate with the larger organization. Further, the people on the project will seek advancement within the larger organization. Thus, the management process of the project needs to have ties with the process and culture of the larger organization to ensure the survival and advancement of both the people and the project.

The organization's vision—The management process must be compatible with the vision of the organization. If the vision is for innovation in customer support, the management process cannot restrict customer awareness or require approvals for every new idea before it is tried.

Closure Questions:

If the management process is out of synch with the needs of the project, which is most likely to suffer?

What indications should you expect to see if your chosen management process is incompatible with the selection factors discussed above?

Ensure That the Processes are Compatible

Even if the processes they use have been carefully selected for a group's specific purposes, no useful software development process exists in complete isolation. That is, every useful process performs some beneficial actions or produces some beneficial results. Further, some input is required for the process to work.

This is another self-similarity within the larger world of software development. That is, the relationships between processes are much like the relationships between modules or objects in the software that is being developed. Each has its set of outputs and results. Each has its set of required and optional inputs. Each has its internal ways of doing things that no one cares about if the results are effective, efficient, and reliable. And each relies on the reliability of interfaces to the others.

Therefore, simply selecting or defining appropriate processes for the various software development needs is not sufficient. You must ensure that the various processes work together, provide the required results, use the appropriate input information, and give people enough flexibility both inside the process and at the process interfaces to ensure that things work right.

Closure Questions:

> How would you know whether your candidate processes would work well together?
>
> How can you gain the benefits of specialization while avoiding communication blockages?

Measure Your Results

Not all measurements are numerical or quantifiable. Indeed, W. Edwards Deming says that the most important things aren't measurable. Still, if you're looking for certain values or indicators, you probably won't have to find hard measures for them to know whether or not they are there.

You can expect to see certain kinds of results from each development process that you select.

The traditional process will have requirements completed, specifications written, functions designed, code written, and so forth, on a mostly predictable schedule. Failure to meet that schedule with credible results is an indication that the selected process may be a wrong one for the project or that the project estimates are bad.

The Skinner extension process will have requirements finalized with individual extensions identified and sized in a fairly short period of time. (See page 147.) After that time, you can expect to see specifications, prototypes, and unit-tested functions (as well as a number of failed prototyping attempts) at predictable intervals (according to the sizings and what the people/teams sign up for). You will also be able to measure the progress toward the goal according to the completed (unit-tested and integrated functions) enhancements from the list, measured against the yardstick of the estimated sizings.

A fractal process will always appear chaotic, but it will be measurable by requirements gathered from customers and added to the list, prototypes demonstrated, efforts attempted and dropped as failures, interface disagreements between implementation teams, and functions accumulated beyond the prior release of the product. Remember that the goal of the more disorderly portion of that particular process is the accumulation of functions in response to customer requirements, not necessarily a fully integrated and smoothly functioning product. That final integration and smoothing is the job of the release and announce team. (See page 115.)

Measure your project results according to the expectations for the process you've selected. If any measure of successes, achievements, or failures is out of the expected range, either the estimates were bad or there is a mismatch between the needs and the processes selected to meet those needs. Exposing a mismatch, you can then adjust or replace the process, the expectations, the measurements, or all three.

Measurement also helps you to learn about your processes. When you start using multiple processes, much of what you decide to do will be educated guesswork. Measuring what happens can not only help to catch a mismatch between a process and a need, it can also help to improve the value of your subsequent guesswork and allow you to better select an appropriate process for subsequent work.

Closure Question:

> What can you predict for a project when its people twist their measurements to agree with the estimates or the plans?

Verify/Challenge the Selected Processes Constantly

Whatever processes you've chosen to use, consider that your initial choices were based on inadequate information and might well be contrary to the need. If you've chosen a traditional development process and the problem is overly complex, the effort will fail. If you've chosen a fully fractal process and the problem is extremely simple, some effort will be wasted.

Closure Question:

> If you suspect that your project or process isn't working properly and your process measurements look normal, how would you decide what action might be necessary?

7

A Process that Exploits Chaos

This chapter describes a fractal software development process, one that is intentionally nonlinear. It relies on and attempts to enhance feedback, the basic cause of nonlinearity and chaos. By having a process that explicitly deals with feedback, software developers can remain aware of and exploit the resulting chaos. The process is designed to achieve:

- Periodic and probably frequent emission of a product
- Quick ramp-up for the first product
- Intimate customer involvement
- Supportive environment for nonlinear efforts
- Exploitation of existing strengths of standard software development
- Improved innovation and response to market needs

Work flow in this fractal process differs from the work flow in other software development processes. (See page 129.) There is some similarity to other projects as a project starts up, but the similarities diminish before the shipment of the first release of the product. After going through its initialization, the process becomes a steady state process with different kinds of work being done in different parts of the organization. Instead of being time phased, the process is organizationally phased. The process is characterized more by the things going on in parallel than by sequences of activities.

The following sequence looks like the way products ought to be developed and handled, and any particular piece of a product might go through this sequence. But individual pieces don't have to do that, and the organization performs all of the following activities in parallel:

- Exploring new ideas
- Exploring the application of new ideas to the business
- Fully implementing the ideas to be incorporated
- Preparing the product for marketing
- Selling and supporting the product
- Helping customers to migrate to other products

In a fractal development group, people will migrate through the entire organization, possibly to follow a component, possibly to gain experience in all the aspects of development. Management must support this and cheerfully assign people work that matches their current interests, talents, and expertise. Some people will settle into a particular type of department and call it home, some will cycle forever. This is not an assembly-line process, with each group performing an assigned kind of task. Instead, each group is doing full problem solving and development with the techniques that are most appropriate to their problems and situations.

Because of this organization, management guides the project by defining the organization's vision, values, mission, and goals, by enabling productive customer partnerships, by matching people and work within the appropriate parts of the organization, and by supporting the necessary communication and team attitudes in the group.

The fractal process has a small group flavor. It exploits the talents of many developers who have not previously been able to contribute directly to the product line. It provides for recognition and advancement of people with a wide variety of talents and interests. Lest anyone think that this panacea is some kind of free ride to success, it must also be recognized as requiring the full support and commitment of management and employees alike.

If the project is large enough, five kinds of departments emerge from this. Watch what happens in each of these groups, as this process has both potential benefits *and* potential traps for the unwary. And if you're wondering about what it takes to start up an organization like this, be patient. That is covered later in this chapter, beginning on page 125.

Splinter Department

This is the nursery for new ideas. As the larger organization progresses with its development work, it will spin off ideas that might or might not work. People are assigned to the splinter department to explore the fledgling ideas, to see if they should be pursued or dropped. But the ideas don't have to prove their worth immediately after they are conceived. The splinter department explores their potential until they can stand on their own.

This is an ad-tech, creative development from an exploratory department and may or may not result in success on every idea. It will, however, provide

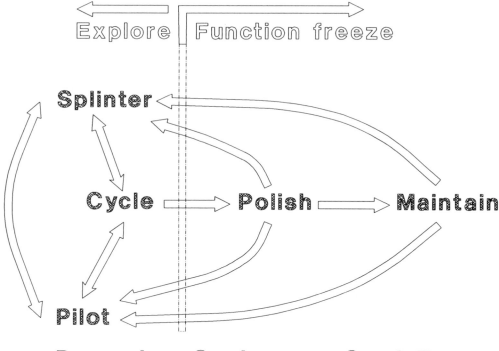

Figure 7-1. *Structure of one fractal process*

the arena for suitably motivated (and enfranchised) people to get lots of ideas into the process with minimal cost. Some of the ideas explored here may be related to specific existing products (how an unproven idea can enhance the product) or to the business of the organization.

In an ideal world, no splinter department would be necessary for these explorations. The explorations would simply be done as potential ideas came along. However, new ideas are often distractions in a more goal-directed environment. If it is a department, it is the last of the five groups to be formed into a department. The splinter department is one of the sources for new product ideas.

People may be directly assigned to the splinter department, but it is more likely that they will have rotating assignments there. A typical exploration there would have one person full time, with a variety of others consulting. Consultants would include customers, other software developers, information developers, representatives of marketing, management, and so on.

When it is presented with a particular idea, the splinter department will explore and evaluate it. If the evaluation is positive, the department's output might also include a proposal, a set of specifications for the application of the idea, and a prototype of how it should be used.

Customer involvement in every group but the splinter department should be a given, and it should be encouraged for the splinter department as well.

Customers will look at the ideas and help to decide whether the ideas will be desirable when integrated with the product. Still, customer involvement has to be handled carefully in the splinter department. Some ideas that look wonderful will not work in practice, and other ideas that look marginal (too trivial for attention) in the splinter group will turn out to be key product features when they are fully implemented. Customers' views are needed for the balance and short feedback loop they provide, but no one should believe that a splinter idea can be injected easily into the product in a short period of time.

Every idea in the splinter department will ultimately come to a decision point. The decision will be either to kill the idea or to pass it (and its associated output) to a pilot or cycle group.

Pilot Department

This is the growth arena for ideas that have definite promise but are not yet well enough understood to take their place in the mainstream efforts of the larger organization. An idea might move to a pilot department after getting a favorable recommendation from a splinter group. Actually, an idea could come to a pilot department from any place in the organization if it were clearly a good idea but still needed a substantial demonstration of its impact on the product.

Considerations high on the list of importance for the pilot department include performance and user interface. Many ideas look good on a small scale but suffer from poor performance when they're applied to real world processing loads. Likewise, user interface concepts that appear good in exploratory trials might hinder use or customer acceptance. The pilot group builds a working version of the idea, suitable for evaluation of the impacts of frequent use, high load, or other quantities of scale. Ideas and programs in the pilot departments are regularly shown to real, forward-looking customers for evaluation and feedback.

Business aspects of the product begin to be visible in pilot departments. Software developers and planners are involved in the effort. Planners will help with competitive evaluations, estimates of how the ideas will fit with the product, and projections of markets and new customers.

The output of a pilot project is a full-function model of the idea, possibly integrated with existing components or efforts. With a positive recommendation, the pilot group will also provide specifications for how the idea should be incorporated into the product.

Every idea in a pilot department will ultimately come to a decision point. The decision will be either to kill the idea or to pass it (and its associated output) to a cycle group.

Cycle Department

This is where ideas get their product-level muscle, but it is not the final development group for code that goes out the door.

Cycle departments are both interrelated and independent. Their primary responsibility is to provide robust function in a loose framework of components. As they work, members of cycle departments will present their current results to the rest of the organization and take feedback on their work and related work that is going on. The presentation and feedback sessions are key factors in keeping the organization on a meaningful track and building a coherent product while providing for use of the best possible component functions.

Customers will be heavily involved in cycle department efforts for functional evaluation, use testing, and making decisions about the disposition of particular functions.

This is also the beginning of complete group involvement, with versions of the work in process being exercised by secretaries and executives along with the normally involved developers and testers. The list of problems and recommended enhancements from customer partners and group members are not only fed back into the cycle departments, they are used to become the requirements for the structured development departments in the "next" stage of development, and may lead to new splinter or pilot efforts.

Cycle groups work in a "freeze to freeze" mode. That is, cycle groups strive to carry their current work to a solid, functional closure point. The reason is the decision point that is always at the end of cycle efforts.

The real purpose of the cycle groups is to accumulate product function that can be turned into a release of the product. To preserve freedom of action and development, cycle groups are not required to be synchronized with each other. However, eventually their work results have to fit together.

The decision at the end of cycle efforts is a decision about a functional level. When the available function reaches a desirable level, the decision to move that function into the product is made. Cycle group members who wish to see their work get into customer's hands will make sure that they have a version ready to go. Overall, cycle developers will ensure that their freeze level versions function properly within the collection of cycle group results. This discourages the phenomenon of function that is perpetually "almost ready."

Cycle groups document their work so that the function level decision can be made most effectively and so that those who inherit their work can deal with it effectively. It is the responsibility of cycle development groups to ensure full knowledge of what code is really good enough to move forward and what code is prototypical.

The decision at the end of the cycle department differs slightly from the ending decision for the splinter and pilot groups. Cycle efforts may be of short duration or take quite a long time. The decision here is to see what's currently available and decide how much of it is to go into the product. There is no guarantee that every individual cycle effort will be considered for injection into a product, but a small amount of tracking information can easily detect efforts that never get considered or selected.

Group members and customer partners periodically review the function that is available within the cycle groups. When the function would make a desirable release of the product, that function is captured and passed to the structured development group. In practice, there's a balance between the cycle time of the structured development group and the function reviews for results from cycle groups. The balance involves the time it takes the structured development group to move a product release out the door and the amount of function the cycle group produces.

The decision for the product is what function to include. The decision for individual efforts within the cycle group is whether to kill the effort, continue the effort, carry the current results into the product, or some combination of the three.

Structured Development Department (Polish)

Some software development groups have a tendency to take the "code that already works," including code produced by cycle departments, and ship it as a product. This is often foolish. Cycle department results are only loosely integrated and are not at the level of refinement required in high-quality products. This is not a failure on the part of cycle group members, but a result of the approach we use to get the best benefits of their efforts. Splinter and pilot group results are even more suspect for direct shipment as product code, yet the software development business has seen it happen time after time.

This process has a built-in feature to ensure that product-level code is of product-level quality. Results from cycle groups provide the base product technology for the new release. Members of the structured development group are expert in both the product technology and systems engineering. The requirements are well-defined, including user interface work, functional interface work, and work that verifies correctness of results. Documentation from the cycle groups, reports on evaluations from customer partners, and usage reports from the entire organization are used to define the work to be accomplished by the structured development group. Notice that this group and its work now satisfy the criteria we explored in the section titled Pillars of Software Engineering. This group will use the best applicable software engineering disciplines to transform the cycle group results into a high-quality product.

Many readers will have identified some seductive traps in the process. It's worth noting that this process can fall flat on its face if there is significant contention and disagreement between the cycle groups and the structured development group. It is absolutely essential to the process to have people in full and meaningful communication. To make this happen, people will probably need to move between groups frequently. Having cross-group teams for a variety of purposes will also help. (We'll discuss this a little on page 122.) It's very significant that problems found and changes made by the structured development group must be returned to the cycle, splinter, and pilot groups. Failure to make that feedback happen would lead to the most destructive and disorderly kind of chaos within the organization.

The structured development departments not only fill their primary roles in implementing the required extensions on the base provided by the cycle departments, but work closely with customers and the marketing group as well. As this effort progresses, all sales aids, pricing, marketing training, support training, and information needs have to be met. Training must be prepared for customers, and the groundwork laid for customer feedback to have its impact on future product functions.

In this group, as in each of the others we've discussed, there is a decision to be made. The decision here is whether to ship, delay, or kill the product. Fortunately, because the group satisfies the conditions of the Pillars of Software Engineering, the ship-or-kill choice will almost always be to ship the product. The question of delay is minimized, also because of the use of software engineering disciplines, and the final criteria for when to ship is the level of quality of a well-planned, well-executed effort.

Product Support Department (Maintain)

The product support group functions as customer heroes. People in product support are involved with customers, and they are consultants for all other groups. They produce code fixes, make sales calls, get excited and move the business, and communicate urgency back through the organization. Product support departments are integral parts of the marketing focus for the product and are key in both resolving customer problems and feeding requirements back to other departments. Heroes in product support must be recognized throughout the entire development organization.

Closure Questions:

> Does your most used development process consider the kinds of work to be done in a variety of situations?
> Can your process or processes support a variety and mixture of needs for innovation, discipline, rigor, and productivity?
> What do your processes look like?

LASER ANALOGY

The fractal process functions much like a laser. A laser consists of a resonance chamber (crystal, gas, liquid, or whatever), energy input, and emission controls. In early crystal lasers, the emission controls consisted of a fully mirrored surface on one end and a semi-mirrored surface on the other end. As energy is fed into the laser, it is retained in the resonance chamber by the mirrored ends. When more energy is added, the contained energy resonates until enough has built up to overcome the obstacle at the semi-mirrored end of the chamber. When that threshold is reached, the laser beam is emitted.

With this fractal process, the analog of the semi-mirrored end is a decision that there is enough function available to allow a product to be emitted. Ideas (energy) are injected into the organization from a variety of sources. Those

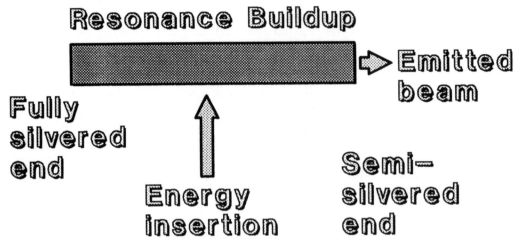

Figure 7–2. *Laser structure and function*

that prove themselves worthy (nothing is absolute) through evaluations in splinter and pilot organizations are added to the resonance chamber (functional development) so that the threshold of function can be achieved. When the decision to emit has been made, some final polish and focus are added to the selected functions, and the release is shipped. As with "out of resonance" energy that is injected into a laser, ideas injected into the fractal process may never be emitted, if they are "out of resonance" with the rest of the product.

Closure Question:

What other analogies might you use to devise productive processes?

PROJECT STAFFING

For initial staffing, the ramp-up should be based on the available knowledge and skills base. That is, if the people to be assigned need education and training, they should be brought on board early enough so that they can be trained and have some practice before the full demands of the project arrive. Note that training and practice are both part of the education process; project work will be likely to increase such that real project problems can be used to develop skills.

Migration to a fractal process (actually, to any process) depends on the correspondence between the old and the new. With a close correspondence, the migration would involve minor changes. With conflicting characteristics, the migration would involve drastic changes.

Overall, it will be possible to start the fractal process with a larger than normal initial staff, much closer to the level needed for steady state in the project. Education, toolsmithing, and culture growth are all parts of the start-up that should not be ignored or left to chance.

Using management as an example, you'll need to take some extra steps if your new process requires a management style that differs radically from your current management style. You can select a different process that is more suitable to the current style, select new managers who will support the process, or manage a transition from the existing style to the new process and style. (Some guidance for managing this transition can be found in *Organizational Transitions*, by Richard Beckhard and Reuben T. Harris.) Buy-in by all participants, management and nonmanagement alike, is critical if the process is to be successful.

Depending on the project, the first groups to be actively involved in project development work may be splinter, pilot, or cycle groups. People who are going to work in formal release groups obviously must be trained before the cycle groups reach a freeze point.

One of the key points in the fractal process is in the mobility of the involved people. Metzger has specific comments on this. According to him, every member of the organization should be respected, and should be expected to perform various jobs (including repetitions of some sequences of jobs) on the project. For example, one person reasonably could be expected to start work as a tester, become a toolsmith (programmer) when the need arises, move into a job as a developer, become a customer interface representative, become a tester to ensure that all that experience is reflected in the next version of the product, and then fulfil several other roles. This kind of mobility should be encouraged and associated with doing the best for the project.

Respect is the second key point Metzger raises and ties in with the mobility point. Testers are not second-class citizens, or some enemy to be fooled, but partners in quality—former developers, future developers, and customer representatives. Customers are not self-serving interlopers, but partners and representatives of the entire customer set. Secretaries are not telephone answering machines and bureaucrats, but communications partners and expediters. Managers are not gods and inquisitors, but leaders and expediters. Finally, mobile people should be viewed as moving through jobs and through learning experiences, not through status elevations and penalties.

Closure Questions:

Is your current management scheme up to the challenge of the people and idea movement required for this fractal process?

Does the culture of your organization show enough respect for everyone in the group to allow this process to work?

WORK FLOW

The fractal process can't be viewed productively as a linear process; to do so would be to strip it of some of its most productive features. To avoid this, look at ways that ideas and pieces of work can wend their ways through the organization.

In this fractal process, people are mobile. Some will want to remain in a particular group forever, but others will want to migrate with their products through several kinds of departments, and this should be encouraged. Those with the closest customer contacts may be in an ideal position to splinter off and try out new product ideas. Individual explorations may be carried into pilots and on into cycle departments by their advocates. Cycle developers may be best suited to put the final polish on their work in structured development departments. People movement and training are essential ingredients in maintaining the vigor and competitive aspects of the process.

A gleam in a cycle developer's eye can require some independent exploration. Management sends the developer to a splinter group to explore the idea. The developer quickly determines that the idea doesn't work, reports those results, and returns to the cycle department to pick up another assignment.

A resident splinter assignee takes an idea proposed by a customer, builds a user interface mock-up, and finds some technology that promises the kind of support that is required to make it work. Working over the mock-up with the customer representative to polish the description and user interface, the assignee then demonstrates the concept to management. Management agrees to do a pilot, and the splinter assignee heads a small team in a pilot department to build a working prototype. The prototype development is so successful and the supporting technology proves itself so well that the function is added to the next release cycle for the formal release department.

A tester detects a problem in the product, suggests a solution, and is given a splinter assignment to explore the proposed solution.

A formal release assignee notices a functional hole in a release of the product and proposes a well-thought-out solution. The solution is added to the to-do list for the cycle departments, picked up by a cycle assignee, and implemented in time for the next release of the product.

These examples show people and ideas wending their ways through the organization. This is as it should be in a full development organization, the best way in which the development effort can progress. Expertise and experience should be accumulated by people through their movement within the organization so they can better pursue their careers and provide the broadest perspectives to their work on the project.

We can observe that the migration of experience and expertise is much more rapid in a smaller organization than in a larger one. Based on the size and needs of a project, this can be enhanced by management in a larger organization or may even call for revisions of this fractal process where rapid migration is required.

Closure Questions:

> How might work flow and idea flow happen without people flow within a group?
>
> When the size of a group requires high formality in communications, how might you devise ways to continue the flows without jeopardizing that formality?

How does communications in the fractal process compare with communications in the surgical team as described by Frederick P. Brooks?

TIMES FOR VARIOUS PROJECTS

Times for projects using the fractal process will be relatively stable and predictable; that was one of the criteria for laying it out the way it is. We can look at the efforts by group, and describe the approximate times required.

SWAT teams are not represented by formal organizations in the fractal process, but they will be necessary. (See box 16 on page 56.) They attack and resolve particular problems immediately, and are formed and dissolved within days.

Splinter efforts will last from one month to about a year, with some special efforts (orphan or research assignments) taking up to two years. These longer assignments may be associated with work leading to results for the project or to an advanced degree for the assigned individual. The average or expected time for most splinter efforts is about three months.

Pilot group efforts will take from two to six months. They will usually be larger efforts than splinter groups, involve more people, and start out better defined. They will also have a higher (but not guaranteed) probability of success. The average or expected time for a pilot effort is about four months.

Cycle groups will be continuously functioning groups, with individual pieces of work taking from one month up to several years to complete. However, because of the absence of release and marketing work, cycle groups maintain high productivity rates and are able to deliver freeze levels of function every six months.

The formal development and release work of structured development groups is defined to take six months. Constraints forcing this are the results of both the business and the technical needs of the company. It's no accident that this is the same time required for the commitment checkpoint business process. When developers in the fractal process certify (assert?) that code has suitable function and quality, the work of the structured development groups and the business support groups fits together naturally, leading to a common conclusion: product shipment.

Thus, the ramp-up of a new product to the fractal process can be expected to take from twelve to eighteen months. The conversion of an existing product to the fractal process can be expected to take twelve to fifteen months (it takes three months to change how the requirements are fed into the group). At the end of this time, the groups and culture of the organization will be self-maintaining. Once the organization is built and the cycle groups are in full swing, subsequent product releases will be produced every six months. Responses to most unforeseen customer needs can be delivered within six months to a year from the time when they are perceived and accepted.

What are the times involved in various kinds of efforts in your existing process?

How well does your process work in crisis situations?

TERMINATING A PROJECT

Every once in a while, projects have to be stopped and groups have to be disbanded. When that happens, it's possible simply to fire everyone, lock the doors, and move to Brazil. But this is hardly a businesslike approach. Everyone involved has invested something in the project, and it is often possible to protect possible returns on the investment even if the project must go away.

The kinds of things to be protected include existing customers who depend on your products, the ideas you've devised (patent them so you can get royalties when other people need them), the designs you've created (document them for possible later use or for sale to others), the code you've written (document it for possible later use), and the other experiences you've gained on the project (write papers or books telling how to match your successes and avoid your failures).

Notice that each category of investment has associated ways to protect the investment. There are other categories—you'll have to determine them for yourself on your own projects. But the time associated with protecting your investment or continuing your business is associated as well with the circumstances of shutting down the process (yes, I meant process rather than project). Consider the following four circumstances.

Abandon the business area before any releases—The group continues its efforts long enough to document the results (for the shelf) and to write any papers and patent applications that are appropriate. All other efforts can be stopped or quickly wound down and the people assigned to other products. The orderly termination could be completed within two to three months.

Abandon the business area after one or more releases—Since there is a maintenance responsibility after the stabilization of a product, the splinter and pilot groups can be discontinued quickly and the people assigned to other projects. Cycle groups will terminate long-range development and close out current efforts toward a freeze. Formal release groups may go through one final release, leaving the support group (if that's not vended out) for the remaining life of the product. Depending on the urgency of the abandonment, one release can be expected after the decision to abandon. The orderly termination could be completed within two months for splinter and pilot groups, within two to four months for cycle groups, and within eight to ten months for the structured development group (assuming shipment of another release). The support group is special, so no generic time estimate is possible for them.

Product superseded by another product—In this case, the organization is retained longer than if the business area is abandoned. Long-range efforts in the cycle group are terminated, but splinter, pilot, and cycle efforts toward migration are started. One or two releases can be expected after the decision: one as an enhancement and stabilization release, the second as a migration aid to the superseding product.

Stop using the fractal process—The time to convert to another process would have to be associated with that other process and can't be estimated here.

Closure Questions:

Do you ever consider dropping a project or stopping the use of a process?

If a process is terminated too abruptly, what happens to the people who are involved?

8

More Possible Processes

There are clear indicators that the business processes have a fractal nature just as the technical processes do.

Documents produced to satisfy the business processes follow much the same structure, no matter what their purpose. Further, they come in pairs: plans and certifications. The artificiality of the phases and sequencing of the business processes are much like the artificiality seen in the technical software development processes. For example, estimates are built before anyone knows product content, adjustments are difficult once the schedules are established. The business processes are full of cycles that are not explicitly called for in the definition of the processes. (It's not called an approval cycle for nothing.) The business processes have retrograde parts, where plans must be undone in order to proceed, and so on.

Overall, the fractal nature of the business processes shows as responses to problems previously encountered. Programming error rates lead to the definition of quality plans and certifications, business tools intended to patch that particular technical problem. Product conflicts between divisions of a company lead to lengthy chains of required approvals across division boundaries. This is similar to attempts by programming organizations to modify their controls to prevent the failures of the past. The challenge is to make this happen without getting the organization bogged down in controls.

The development process is the documented attempt to impose some order and discipline on the development of software. Even when there is no defined process, there will be an operative process. This is much like a culture; you have one whether or not there are formal rules for it. In the normal pursuit of a goal over time, successes and failures lead to patterned ways to do things.

All processes are intended (designed or accumulated) to give some feeling of control and predictability where such is not always apparent. Various processes focus on different aspects of the need, from actual code production, to business justifications, to managers' needs to feel comfortably in control.

However, it is almost a universal characteristic of processes that they are based on simplifying assumptions or theories. While this is not necessarily bad, the quality and value of a development process will depend on three points:

1. How well do the assumptions and theories fit the most significant aspects of the development to be done? This is the conformance between the theory and the reality.
2. Can the process be subverted (will the developers subvert the process to try to make things work) when the realities of the situation clearly make the process unworkable?
3. Can the process be adjusted/improved to get back in step with reality? That is, can the subversions in point 2 be made positive parts of the process?

As an example, consider the standard software development process. It is based on valid observations about the sequence of tasks, starting with conception of a need, and going through requirements, specifications, design, coding, testing, and shipment. It is also strongly oriented to the business of producing software, rather than being limited to the more technical aspects of conceiving, building, and finishing programs.

The technical assumptions behind a standard development process are contrary to the general realities of software development. However, the process works because the assumptions are useful from a business point of view and because developers are able, for a particular class of development projects, to subvert the process and get the job done anyway. This has been the standard use of software development processes in the past. However, there are some indications in the early 1990s that the third point listed above will soon become more significant.

So attempts to codify a culture or process can and often do lead to artificial simplicity, which is theoretically pleasing but impractical. This has been the major problem with most processes we know, whether they are business processes, development processes, management processes, or whatever.

There are three additional factors that are worthy of note in all development processes—documentation, quality, and personal discipline.

First, look at documentation.

Hardware development has long been recognized as being a paper-producing process. That is, hardware development groups seldom build a prototype machine and then turn it over to a manufacturing operation for duplication. Rather, the engineers design a machine, build prototypes for testing and debugging, and finally give the manufacturing group a complete set of specifications for how the machine is to be built. Because of the communications problems, the obligation to turn the designs over to another group, and the need to get prototype parts built, the documentation associated with hardware tends to be fairly well-defined.

Aspects of software development are analogous to hardware development, but software developers are not as aware of the documentation needs associated with development. This lower level of awareness comes from the immediacy of the need for documentation. Hardware documentation is required when the product is turned over to manufacturing, while software documentation is required when bugs are reported or the product is to be extended. It's too easy for software developers to sacrifice documentation for the sake of immediate code development.

Some software development processes can be described as "roll your own" processes. With these processes, software developers simply "know" what they want to build, so they build it. With experience and use on several projects, roll your own processes are improved and codified. They retain their ad hoc flavor and carry along coincidental baggage that is not really pertinent to the success of the projects that use the processes. Tools in these processes consist of automated support for problems encountered in the current and previous projects.

Other software development processes are conceptually based. These processes are based on a conceptual model of how software development ought to work. Tools in these processes support the conceptual model of the process.

Both kinds of processes, the experientially based and the conceptually based, have strengths and weaknesses. However, the experientially based processes are grown almost totally from feedback and thus are highly suspect from a chaotic point of view. Conceptually based processes begin with an area of order and are useful if the area of order matches an area of need.

The best processes are both conceptually based and experientially based. They start with a conceptual area of order and are improved to practicality through use and experience.

Closure question:
   What are the origins of your processes?

Box 32. *Process origins*

The popular wisdom is that programmers hate documentation. The view is that documentation gets in the way, is wrong, is not as much fun as the rest of development, and is useless anyway. Yet documentation is critical for product support, user education, user reference, design of related components, approval of designs, quality, and management of the project. In each of these cases, significant product problems (in schedule, quality, and function, among others) are allowed to happen if developers fail to document their work and plans appropriately.

This push for documentation is not to say that documentation should be pursued at the expense of all else. Indeed, total and exhaustive documentation can scuttle a project as effectively as any other pursuit that neglects the real goals of the project. However, appropriate documentation actually smooths the development effort and provides opportunities to increase the quality and productivity of the effort.

Second, look at quality.

One of the strange facts of software development is that there's a set of disciplines that can be measured, proven productive, and demonstrated to increase the quality of products. Yet this set of disciplines is unpopular, viewed as a nuisance, and subverted as a matter of course. These disciplines include but are not limited to inspections, causal analysis, and reviews.

In each case, developers look for ways to remove defects in their designs, code, and documentation as early as possible. This is an uneasy effort, because many people are uncomfortable when there are problems in work they've done. Also, developers tend to be an optimistic lot, prone to the belief that the bug they just removed was the last one.

Quality measurements and statistics offer guidance to developers, being useful techniques to expose work where quality improvement techniques can be productively applied. In every development process, including the fractal one, we can derive significant quality improvements through the appropriate application of quality diagnostic and quality improvement techniques.

As with documentation, it is possible to work so hard at measuring quality that you sacrifice the goals of the project. (See box 35 on page 168.) However, the more common problem in software development is the inadequate or inappropriate use of quality improvement techniques.

Third, look at personal discipline.

Personal discipline is nothing more than the individual recognition of the goals of the project and the careful pursuit of those goals using the best available techniques.

- If requirements are well defined and the project is to use software engineering techniques, people with personal discipline use the techniques to satisfy the requirements.
- When working through a design, people with personal discipline will check their work (probably including some forms of peer reviews) to eliminate possible problems in the design.
- When designing a user function, people with personal discipline will find out what the user wants and needs.
- When internal conflicts jeopardize the goals of the project, people with personal discipline will do their best to re-emphasize and enforce the project goals.

Quite often, people on a project will not understand the goals of the project. The temptation, in such cases, is to follow the rules and hope that the rules will lead to the right result. This cookbook thinking looks like good personal discipline, but it is actually highly damaging to the project. Following the

Page	Process description and attributes
143	Traditional software development process Inflexible, task-oriented, experientially based. Low customer involvement, little attention to the future, insignificant prototyping.
149	Geographically distributed development process Inflexible, task-oriented, experientially based. Low customer involvement, little attention to the future, insignificant prototyping. Highly bureaucratic.
115	Fractal development process exploiting some existing strengths of software development groups Flexible, style-oriented, mix of experiential and theoretical base. High customer involvement, moderate attention to the future, significant prototyping. Moderately bureaucratic.
141	Japanese-style fractal development process Flexible, task-oriented, experientially based. High customer involvement, high attention to the future, significant prototyping. Bureaucracy not noted.
148	Evolutionary development process Moderately flexible, style-oriented, experientially based. Moderate customer involvement, moderate attention to the future, significant prototyping. Moderately bureaucratic.
147	Jack Skinner's enhanced development process Moderately flexible, task-oriented, experientially based. Customer involvement not addressed, moderate attention to the future, prototyping not addressed.
138	Mike Barnhouse's customer-involved development process Inflexible, task-oriented, mix of experiential and theoretical base. High customer involvement, moderate attention to the future, significant prototyping. Moderately bureaucratic.
134	The skunk works process (Kelly Johnson's "invention" at Lockheed Aircraft) Flexible, style-oriented, experientially based. Customer involvement not addressed, moderate attention to the future, significant prototyping. Anti-bureaucratic.
145	Top down and bottom up development processes Inflexible, task-oriented, mix of experiential and theoretical base. Low customer involvement, low attention to the future, prototyping not addressed. Moderately bureaucratic.
150	A standard phased business process Inflexible, task-oriented, experientially based. Low customer involvement, moderate attention to the future, prototyping not pertinent. Highly bureaucratic.
152	A modified and less bureaucratic business process Moderately flexible, task-oriented, experientially based. Low customer involvement, moderate attention to the future, prototyping not pertinent. Moderately bureaucratic.

rules for the sake of the rules is the same as managing for the form of a business process rather than its content. You can make plans and schedules forever, following the form, but with no code there's no deliverable software. You can give your people busy work, following the stated mission of your department, while depriving the project of critical skills and delaying the delivery of the product.

Business and management processes require corresponding involvement of the same three factors (and avoidance of the abusive use of the factors). Documentation has to be complete enough, must be done well enough that people can understand what is going on, and must not become an overwhelming obsession. Quality must be an important part of every result, and must be pursued rationally rather than through wishful thinking. Personal discipline is what keeps each person's efforts in balance with the goals of the organization and as productive as is possible.

Now, with those three concepts explored, the table on page 133 contains a list of some of the processes you can find in *Exploiting Chaos: Cashing in on the Realities of Software Development.*

Closure Questions:

> With all of these possible processes, how will you know it when "the right processes" for you come along?
> What will you get if your group doesn't decide explicitly on a process or set of processes?

SKUNK WORKS PROCESS

The skunk works process is one that has received much favorable press, and rightly so. The name "skunk works" was adopted for Kelly Johnson's development group at Lockheed that built such highly successful aircraft as the U2, the F104, and the C130. The most notable characteristics of the skunk works deal with interference, leadership, buy-in, group size, communication, and people.

Definite barriers to outside interference—The skunk works projects were all highly classified and the security requirements were used to prevent casual interference with the efforts.

Fanatical leadership—Leaders were determined to do the right job, not a safe job of acceptable compromise. Kelly Johnson's rules included "Do the best possible job in the simplest way, at the cheapest cost in the quickest time."

Motivating leadership—Leaders recognize the value and take the contributions of the employees. This is done intensely and visibly to lead to the next item.

Employee dedication and personal discipline—All employees in a skunk works are signed up to get the job done; those who don't sign up find themselves in different jobs. The right people are assigned to the right jobs; assignments are for the needs of the project and according to how the people buy in to the goals of the project, not to satisfy body count projections. Having the skunk works as a small part of a larger organization provides a safety net for those who could buy in to a project in a different area of the organization.

Small group size—This is a universal comment made about all of the successful skunk works kind of efforts; the groups were kept small enough that they didn't get bogged down in the kinds of communications problems that plague larger groups.

Effective communications—A wide variety of skills and capabilities are represented in even a small development group; keeping the people talking together about their problems is the only way to get the problems solved and to keep the project moving. Inappropriate formality is too expensive.

But so far you haven't seen any process in the skunk works process. That's a fascinating characteristic of skunk works projects. Skunk works projects are renowned as places where things get done by violating all the process rules of the larger organization. But how can that be, particularly when creating complex, state-of-the-art products? If you look at what happened at Lockheed and remember what we say here about chaos, you begin to catch a glimpse of some significant realities.

Consider the people in the Lockheed skunk works. They weren't novices brought in off the streets for a project, they were expert practitioners in their fields. They knew how to design, how to build, and how to document their work. They knew productive processes for doing their jobs.

They also knew the processes they were violating.

Now we have to grant the possibility that not all of the people involved in the Lockheed skunk works projects were absolute experts in their fields. But we do know that there were more than enough experts to lead the work and everyone worked together on productive teams.

The people joined the projects with full knowledge both of how to do their jobs and of the company processes usually used to get the company's work done. Once they got inside the skunk works, they practiced the parts (processes) that worked and discarded the parts (other processes) that didn't work. They matched their processes to their jobs and the project needs. They adjusted their processes for the needs of the situation. They worked together with the full knowledge and confidence that their teammates would also do the right things at the right times. In essence, the real process was embodied in the minds and interactions of the teams.

We can say the same things in almost zen-like terms. Skunk works projects work because the involved people know the existing processes, go beyond the processes, and become the process.

Closure Questions:

How would you recruit people for a skunk works project, considering the culture and politics of your current organization?

How could people in your current organization prepare themselves for skunk works opportunities?

RAPID PROTOTYPING

Rapid prototyping is one of the favorite "silver bullets" of the late 1980s. Proposals have been put forward with the full intention of doing all product requirements gathering, specifications, design, and some level of implementation through the use of rapid prototyping. Rapid prototyping has some highly significant benefits that allow many things to be accomplished in a highly productive manner. It does not, however, produce products.

Consider the following benefits of rapid prototyping:

Shortened design and implementation cycles—By not requiring all the rigor of the standard development process, a cycle of rapid prototyping can be very fast. This is a process of trying ideas to see how they work. While the success rate is lower, the number of trials can be so high that the number of successes produced is much higher than it would be with a more rigorous process.

Reduced effort—On the surface, a prototyping cycle involves the same kinds of work as a full development cycle. However, it includes no formal planning exercises, no formal estimating exercises, no preparation of educational material beyond the prototype, no formal testing, and no preparation of distribution channels.

Rapid response to user feedback—Rapid prototyping is an ideal process for getting customers involved in products, because the short cycle time allows the customers to repeatedly see results that respond to their needs and expressed wishes.

Expeditious gathering of requirements—The customer involvement in a series of prototypes leads to an early and clear statement of the product requirements. Continued customer interest leads the requirements to the leading edge of what is really needed and possible with the available technology.

Development group learning—If your project is short on some expertise, including knowledge of implementation technologies, rapid prototyping can help to adjust for that shortcoming. Prototype parts can and should include explorations of the technology to see how it works and to ensure that there is a match between the technology and the application need.

Now, before we get too excited, consider the down sides of rapid prototyping.

Implementation of kludges—Rapid prototyping is often a sequence of patches and adjustments to existing code, so that the result is pretty on the surface but ugly underneath. The standard description of a rapid prototyping effort should be recognized as nearly identical to the standard description of the growth of a kludge. This is not the kind of quality that belongs in products; prototypes should never be shipped as if they were finished products.

Loss of design discipline—Again, because the process of rapidly building a sequence of prototypes is approached expeditiously, rigorous design disciplines are seldom used. When the time comes to apply more rigorous disciplines to produce the final, shippable product, an intentional effort is required to ensure that people restrain themselves from taking the shortcuts they took when building prototypes.

Loss of requirements direction—Early and continued involvement with customers is a good thing, but the iterative nature of rapid prototyping opens the possibility that the sequence will wander from the intended direction originally established by the customer and software development groups. Since the new direction could be either wrong or right, the results should be carefully evaluated.

False feeling of substance—Looking at a prototype, you feel as if you are seeing a complete product. However, by their very nature, prototypes are thin. That is, prototypes are built on approximations of the supporting function they need, not on the full function required by a final product. Error checking is typically slighted, as are full database support and alternative operating system and device support. Prototypes seldom work on the full range of hardware, the required limits of memory sizes, and with the full spectrum of user responses that will be encountered in the real product.

The conclusion of this balance of good news and bad news is that rapid prototyping should be used to its best advantage, but not relied on to produce what it doesn't tend to produce. We should exploit the good features of rapid prototyping.

> Try lots of ideas, fast. Then carry the successes forward through more rigorous processes to get closer to product level quality and reliability.
> Check out product functions. Get customers involved early and often

to evaluate possible additions or changes to a product's function set.

Check out user interfaces. Get customers involved early and often to evaluate friendliness and functionality of alternative user interfaces.

Accumulate verified product requirements. Get customers involved early and often to establish product requirements and audience definitions.

Train developers in the latest technology. Rapid prototyping, with its quick cycle, provides lots of opportunities for spreading needed expertise among the people in the development community.

Try ideas quickly and fail early, when the cost of failure is less. In addition to the failures, at low cost you'll find some very profitable successes.

Closure Questions:

When you learn something, is it more often by incremental trial and error or by blinding insight?

What other approaches can be used in conjunction with rapid prototyping to further enhance the effectiveness of each?

MIKE BARNHOUSE'S CUSTOMER-INVOLVED DEVELOPMENT PROCESS

Mike Barnhouse is heavily oriented to customer involvement in making products right for customers. The standard software development process is not well suited to this, and Mike has independently defined a process that stresses customer involvement while exploiting the strengths of the standard process. As with the Skinner process, the initial parallels with the fractal process are both striking and coincidental; they are derived from common causes and observations, not from coordination of ideas. Still, responding to Mike's review of early work on *Exploiting Chaos: Cashing in on the Realities of Software Development*, I strengthened the emphasis on customer involvement in the fractal process.

Here are the phases of Mike's process.

Proposal submission and evaluation phase—You have to start somewhere, and starting with a proposal has several advantages. The unique thing about Mike's process is that you use the proposal both for deciding what to build and for recruiting customers to be involved in the process.

First prototyping and requirements gathering phase—Developers and customers (end use customers, not executives) work hand in hand to define what customers need in the business area and build prototypes of the solutions that

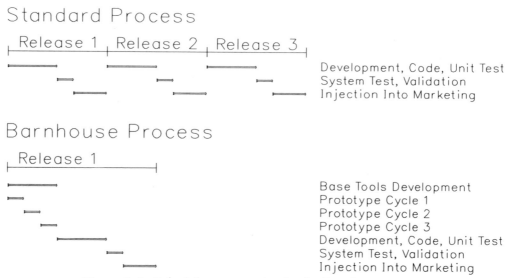

Figure 8–1. *Schedule compression in the Barnhouse process*

the developers think will provide customer solutions. Customers for the second prototyping and requirements phase are recruited.

Second prototyping and requirements gathering phase—Using the results from the first prototyping and requirements phase, work with an expanded set of customers to refine the requirements and build better prototypes. Customers for the third prototyping and requirements phase are recruited.

Final prototyping and requirements gathering phase—Using the results from the second prototyping and requirements phase, work with an even larger set of customers to further refine the requirements and build even better prototypes. Document the final requirements and write a high-level functional specification for product design.

Subsequent phases look much like the standard software development process, but they are completed faster because you already agree on requirements and you already have well-trained developers. (Remember the education involved in building the prototype.)

Product building phase—The requirements and functional specifications, now representing a product definition with which customers fully agree, is transformed into detailed design and code. The prototype code is available to ensure that the intent is clear but is probably not suitable for inclusion as product code. (There are only a few exceptions.) Various organizations will announce the product at various times, from those that will announce plans to those that will announce only when they have running code. As the product nears completion, the development group validates quality, educates the support group, and helps the marketing group prepare for product sales, all while keeping the customers involved in keeping things sane.

Product support phase—In this phase, development is no longer in the picture. Development's baby has been adopted by new parents who have no patience for errors or poor performance. The worm turns, however, and a product that bites its marketers is quickly abandoned if there is not another sibling in the development chute.

It's well worth noting the side effects and economies of the Barnhouse process. Mike has estimated that a standard three-release product cycle of one year per cycle could reach a level of quality and marketability that this process achieves in a year and a half. Given the low quality and maturity of early product releases, this is excellent news. The credibility of that estimate is supported by several factors (starting with a 36 month total: three release cycles of one year each).

Insertion into the marketing and distribution channels only needs to be done once, rather than three times. Since that insertion usually takes four months, the saving is eight months. The development time now nets out at 28 months.

Heads-down development, as usually practiced in the standard software development process, has little tolerance for adjustment or change. The use of three cycles of prototyping can thus be considered to replace about twelve months of development (two releases) with about six months (three cycles of two months each) of prototyping. The time for the development of the third release remains in the process for the shippable product. The development time now nets out at 22 months.

The integration of prototyping and education (hands-on, generally the best way to learn) saves an additional two months (conservatively) of project time. This time is usually assumed, erroneously, to be negligible, but many products have paid the price. The development time now nets out at 20 months.

The existence of agreeable requirements and design will reduce the change activity significantly as the actual product is developed, pulling out another month. The development time now nets out at 19 months.

Exercises that successively remove time from a process are always suspect, but the categories listed above are relatively independent. The other potential flaw in the example is that the assumed base process is one year in length. You should work through your own version of the Barnhouse process using your own base process and the amounts of time involved in the various stages. Then decide for yourself how much value you can derive from using the concept.

The Barnhouse process exploits (requires) rapid prototyping, customer involvement, and the strengths of the standard software development process to achieve a higher quality and more acceptable product than the standard software development process achieves alone.

The apparent delay in the delivery of a product is a specific point in the

Barnhouse process that is well worth examining. That is, the process used as an example turns out a product half a year later than the base process. But who is affected by the delay? Customers are—they don't get a product as early as they would like. But they do get several things in return for that delay: a higher quality first release, release 3-level function a year and a half earlier than it would otherwise be available, and enough involvement in product development to make the first release much more pertinent to their needs. Even for those customers who are not directly involved in the development process, the quality and functionality of the first release product are significant benefits that will be worth a six-month apparent delay in the delivery of the product.

In keeping with the entire tone of *Exploiting Chaos: Cashing in on the Realities of Software Development*, we'll now take the obligatory step to the side to achieve a balanced view. As with all good processes, there are times and situations where the Barnhouse process shouldn't be used. One of the key attributes of the Barnhouse process is customer involvement—what happens to the Barnhouse process when the described customer involvement isn't enough?

Recognize that even the close customer involvement of the Barnhouse process isn't as productive as a good customer surrogate in the heads of the developers. (See box 22 on page 79.) For example, good CASE tools require an expert knowledge of software development. Having expert software developers as helpers is no substitute for being an expert software developer and having a good knowledge of the theoretical foundations of software development. For good software development tools, the developers have to *be* the users. But for balance, the developers have to allow for differing development points of view so that the resultant tool can be used by more than the development group.

The business process for the Barnhouse process is quite similar to that for the fractal process. It uses the concepts of the commitment checkpoint process to ensure that the time from approved requirements and functional specifications to product shipment is as short as possible while satisfying the business needs that are handled so well by standard business processes.

Closure Question:

> In your existing processes, how do you negotiate the balance between the need for compressed schedules and customer demands for products with high function and high quality?

JAPANESE PROCESS

This fractal process is based on the model of Japanese software development. It should come as no surprise that we first want to look at the Japanese software development model to understand it a little bit.

In his thesis for his work at the Sloan School, Bob Arfman documented Japanese efforts to improve software development and described some of the actual software development techniques that form the basis for the future of Japanese software development. This section looks specifically at the factors directly affecting software development and ties them in with the operative Japanese approach to quality and productivity.

Japanese software development has the following characteristics:

- Software factory–Deming style
- User-oriented measurement of quality
- Life cycle tools
- Software reuse
- Rapid prototyping
- Investment in and intent to improve software development

To understand what the Japanese are really doing, we need to first look at the Japanese approach to a factory. (Yes, this is a step aside from a step aside.)

A Deming-style Japanese factory is a collection of processes within which people do their best. Poor quality in output is viewed as the result of a failure in the process, not in the people. Within this view, both managers and the production workers bend their efforts to tuning the process to produce the highest possible quality in the resultant product.

The first step in the tuning is to make the process consistent so that it can be measured. To this end, production workers are trained in the use of their equipment and educated about the goals of their organization and the uses of their products. This training and education, together with experience on the job, allows the production workers to achieve consistency in their work results within the defined process.

The second step is to examine the process for the causes of the kinds of quality problems that are found in the resultant product. The process is then adjusted to eliminate these causes.

Notice that both steps are highly significant. The process is not adjusted until its working is consistent. This avoids the disorder derived from adjusting for random and inconsistent variations, which leads to more randomness and inconsistency.

Now, let's go back to Japanese software development.

The Japanese approach is to create a software factory. Using the description of the Japanese factory, this means that the Japanese first define their processes following the best ones they can find or devise, and then make sure that everyone involved knows the organizational goals as well as the processes and tools.

The Japanese invest in the life cycle tools that are best to help make the process more productive and in producing higher quality. The quality is measured from the point of view of the user and in terms of support of the organizations goals. Thus, what they produce is not code for code's sake, but code to achieve particular purposes. The goals of the software developer are not just to produce working code within the process, but to produce reusable, working code within the process. Remember that this is part of the definition of quality, so that success in the current project automatically increases the leverage and productivity of future projects through reuse.

Finally, there is an emphasis on prototyping. Software developers try things to see if they work and to develop their expertise. When the results are usable (and reusable), they are incorporated and used. When the results are not usable, they are treated as learning experiences rather than as failures. The team ownership of the project, as opposed to individual ownership of programs, leads to the adoption of improved reusable modules when they are written.

Taken as a whole, the evolving Japanese software methodology promises to produce significantly competitive products. Japanese products will compete not only in the applications developed, but also in the libraries of reusable componentry. Key factors in this increased competition include the current investment in componentry for future products, the continuous improvement in the development process and tools, the elimination of entire categories of quality problems, the involvement of managers and employees alike in the improvements, and the inclusion of software development improvements in the working goals of the organization.

Closure Questions:

> How does your software development process enhance your organization's future?
>
> What areas of investment, other than reuse, can give you the kinds of leverage the Japanese hope to derive from their current software development efforts?

STANDARD SOFTWARE DEVELOPMENT PROCESS

This traditional software development process is based on the observations that field use comes after program completion, that program completion comes after testing, that testing comes after coding, that coding comes after design, and that design comes after conception of the need. However, for all the correctness of these observations, developers have long claimed that this software development process is a work of fiction.

The key fallacy in this process is that while the observations are correct in the detailed efforts of producing anything, they are not extendable to a broader picture. For a particular piece of code, the sequence holds. However, it does not necessarily hold true that all code for a project should be written before any testing is begun, or that all design should be completed before any code is written. The fractal nature of software development shows very clearly here.

In more common terms, development of software is highly interactive between the developers, the problem, and the solution. While sequences and observable order does exist in some areas of software development, there is considerable feedback involved in the interaction between developers, developers' knowledge of the underlying technology, their knowledge of the application to be developed, and their knowledge of related components of the project. This feedback and dependency is a basic part of software development and unavoidably leads to the fractal nature of such development.

Because of the fractal nature of real development, this standard process cannot be productively applied to any original development effort of large magnitude, of more than minimal complexity, or of a significantly innovative nature. (Remember the Pillars of Software Engineering on page 74.) These and other characteristics of software development must be absent from any development effort that is to successfully use the standard software development process.

Note that this process has not just been branded as worthless. Indeed, it has considerable value for a large number of development efforts that share certain characteristics:

- The goal of the development effort is to extend an existing product.
- Requirements for the extensions are well defined because of customer experience with previous versions of the product.
- The extensions are individually less than complex and are understood by those who will implement them.

In overview, the standard development process looks like this.

Initial Business Proposal—Requirements, business assessments, technical planning, staffing. The movers of the product create the business plan that will be used to justify the effort. This involves high-level descriptions of the requirements, estimates of the effort required to implement them, estimates of the sales expected of the updated product, and an assessment of the risk involved. Although this looks like a planning exercise, the actual movers may be planners, developers, or mavericks. The planners who ostensibly prepare the business case and plan will probably gather much of their information from the developers who will actually do the work.

Product Definition—Functional specifications, forecast, development plan. Developers produce functional specifications for the work they will do in later phases. This is intended to be a complete specification that can be turned over to coders, but it can be merely a more detailed description than what was put in the business plan. In this case, the specification is a tool used to get another level of approval to proceed. During this phase, there are other pieces of paperwork and plans that are required to get through the business. This is a key time for determining whether the project really belongs in this software development process or not; if it doesn't belong, the specs will never be completed.

Product Build—Design specifications, code and unit test, test plan. The final functional specifications are formally turned over to coders to be implemented. This phase is the second test for whether the project belongs in this software development process or not; if it doesn't belong, the specs will be obviously deficient and the coders will become the actual designers of the product. At this time, a project that skated through the first phases still has a chance of success, but only if the "coders" are highly capable developers who can violate the process to get the job done anyway. For a project that is well suited to this software development process, this really will be a coding and testing effort, based on high quality specifications produced by highly capable designers. The phase also includes quality certifications and preparations for marketing and support. Somewhere along the line, the organization will announce the product. When this phase is done, the product is ready to ship.

Product Support—Development is no longer in the picture. Development's baby has been adopted by new parents who have no patience for errors or poor performance. The worm turns, however, and a product which bites its marketers is quickly abandoned if there is not another sibling in the development chute.

Closure Questions:

> Is this standard software development process an invention based on ideals of how development ought to work or is it based on practical experience with development?
>
> Do you know how much and why your development process differs from this one?

TOP-DOWN AND BOTTOM-UP DEVELOPMENT PROCESSES

Here are some valid observations in software development. At the most detailed level, these observations are completely true. No one involved in software development has ever acted contrary to the observations.

- At every level, conception of a need precedes design of a solution.
- Conception of a need at each level is always preceded by conception of a need, design, coding, or test at a higher level.
- Conception of a need at any particular level is preceded by the discovery of a problem, during any phase, at any level.

This set of observations leads to the idea of top-down, structured design. That is, you design and implement the top levels, then proceed to the next levels. Top-down, structured design is an iterative process, and does not participate in the sequence of monolithic steps found in the more formal processes.

Then we have another set of observations in software development. Again, the observations are true and a fair characterization of reality. There have been examples where these observations have been violated in software development, but such examples are rare in *successful* software development. Thus, these observations have nearly the same weight in deciding how to develop software as the first set.

- Reuse of code is one of the best ways to improve productivity in developing applications.
- Before developing an application, it's necessary to know that the required low level functions can, in fact, be implemented.
- The maximum application flexibility comes from using low level functions as building blocks to compose higher level, more application oriented, functions.

This second set of observations leads to the idea of bottom-up design. That is, you implement what you know you can implement, as with building blocks, and then you compose your applications from the appropriate building blocks at any level.

Both top-down development and bottom-up development suffer from a single significant flaw. When you work consistently from one end to the other, the result becomes chaotic in the disorderly sense.

When development is done from the top down, the shape and goal of the application is held clearly in mind. However, the top-optimizing decisions made throughout the development process make it difficult to keep low-level functions as clean and robust as they ought to be. The low-level code becomes kludgy.

When development is done from the bottom up, the low-level functions remain clean and robust, but the high-level application view often becomes messy. Ideally, bottom-up development would support classes of applications, but they tend more to lead to awkward applications that never quite satisfy the users.

So what happened to the nice theories about top-down and bottom-up software development? They continue to be used as guidelines, but they are adjusted by the people who build the applications. The theories are linear and software development is nonlinear, so people adjust to make the theories look like they work.

Neither top-down nor bottom-up development is a good choice for the development of most applications (although there are always places where a development methodology can be used). To be workable, top-down development requires extensive knowledge of the implementation base as a sanity check and a balance for all of the implementation decisions to be made as the details are worked out. To be workable, bottom-up development requires extensive knowledge of the target application needs as a sanity check and a balance for all of the implementation decisions to be made as the implementation grows toward the application.

In essence, with all the compelling theories cast aside, top-down and bottom-up development are simply conveniences. That is, we usually have to start someplace and the top and bottom are two obvious places to start. In order to make those starting places work, we have to have considerable knowledge of where we'll end up. We also need some effective techniques to ensure that we'll get to those ending places successfully.

Closure Questions:

> Does prototyping represent a third place to start that is different from both the top or the bottom?
> What other places would be appropriate to start from?

JACK SKINNER'S ENHANCED STANDARD DEVELOPMENT PROCESS

Jack Skinner, having the point of view of a development manager at the time of our discussion of development processes, suggested a variation on the standard software development process that recognizes the fragmentary nature of many product enhancements that are nominally controlled by the standard software development process. Jack's process replaces the fully staged specification, design, and code phases with a less structured and more efficient process. It also uses SWAT teams to handle design crises.

Given that the requirements and business case are available, it is unnecessary to batch all of the specification writing together and all of the coding and testing together. Instead, the individual enhancements are all listed so that developers or small teams of developers can sign up for responsibility for the enhancements they would like to work on.

When design holes are discovered (some usually are), a SWAT team is formed. The team consists of a small number of designers and it works intensively for a few days to adjust the design to close the hole. If the team can't close the hole within a few days, then the hole represents a significant design flaw and a higher level of design must be revisited.

This process cashes in on several factors to gain some significant improvements in productivity.

Development for each enhancement is unitary, allowing for a continuity between specification and code that is not allowed when the two activities are done in batches. This continuity significantly reduces problems caused as developers must (re)learn their designs in order to code them.

If some innovation, prototyping, or learning is required, the responsible developers can change their approach. They've signed up to deliver specifications and code, not necessarily to follow an inappropriate process.

Management can focus attention on critical enhancements to ensure that potential problems are found earlier than they would be if their discovery had to wait until the complete product specifications were written.

Developers feel more involvement in the project because they get to choose what they will work on rather than being assigned problems for which they have neither interest nor training.

Thus, Jack's process eliminates time wasted in waiting for specifications, allows greater flexibility in applying appropriate development techniques to problems, provides better responsiveness to critical problems, and encourages developers to become more involved in the effort and proud of their contributions to the success of the product. What it does not do is to provide one clear, across-the-project point, prior to completion of coding, where the design and function can be reviewed and approved by everyone who cares and a few who don't. Determining whether this is good or bad, and when it is each, is left as an exercise for the reader.

Closure Questions:

How would you adjust this process to take care of the problems that will occur when a later unit of development comes in conflict (breaks when used) with a unit completed earlier?

What kind of mentoring arrangement could you use with this process to help your junior people grow into expert developers faster?

EVOLUTIONARY DEVELOPMENT PROCESS

The evolutionary process is a step forward from the process that was first proposed for structured application development. It keeps the risk low but bypasses the pitfalls of the standard software development process with its monolithic approach to requirements and specifications. The evolutionary process has the following characteristics:

It is a variation on top-down software development, but it is carried to the modular level for synchronization.

It is controlled and measured. Work at the currently explored levels has known requirements; it is supported by the confidence of a panel of experts who believe that the required supporting code is feasible and practical; and when it is finished it is measured against the current design.

It uses a stub and driver approach. Stubs mimic the behaviors of required support modules. Supporting modules that are known to be critical are developed early enough that they can use real code rather than stubs as early as possible. Drivers are cut (freeze points) regularly to show the level of function that is available.

Tools are built to follow (parallel) the design. The toolsmiths are up to date on the design and provide tools to increase the productivity of the rest of the developers.

Phasing of the various modules is out of step. That is, each particular module goes through its own development process, but the schedule of that process is not tied to that of the overall project or to that of subordinate modules. This is a particular exploitation of the fractal nature of the project, following the dictum that "we will produce no module before its time." Looking at the ways in which the modules are handled in this process, you'll immediately notice the similarity to a PERT chart. Things happen at different times, certain needs of the development effort are on a critical path either for time or for resources, and resources can be balanced through the development process with more efficiency than could be achieved with efforts that were in lockstep.

It provides for rework. As progress is made and people understand better what the project is all about, various pieces (modules) will be seen as inadequate, overly complex, unnecessary, or otherwise subject to improvement. The evolutionary project plans for this, sometimes with allowance factors in planning but other times by exploiting the schedule gains to be realized by using designs that are more efficiently implemented than were the original designs.

Layered inspections are used to keep the design consistent and the implementations accurate. The layered nature of the inspections is sometimes according to the standard inspection process (code against design), sometimes according to module structuring (controlling module against support functions, multi-level), and sometimes according to the management structure (check for functional gaps and overlaps in people's assumptions). Both necessary (normally required) and "unnecessary" (revisit early designs to discover inefficient early assumptions) inspections are used.

Closure Questions:

What are the start-up requirements for the evolutionary process in terms of product requirements, base technology, and expertise?

Does the different structure of the evolutionary process offer benefits you need?

Are any different disciplines required for the evolutionary process as compared to the standard process?

LOCATIONALLY FRAGMENTED DEVELOPMENT PROCESS

The locationally fragmented process is one in which the owners intentionally spread the work out among various groups, typically at different locations. The usual motivation for fragmenting the effort is that the resources of a particular location are not adequate for the entire project.

The locationally fragmented process flies in the face of the conventional wisdom that subcontracting is bad. This conventional wisdom is based on historical projects where requirements were poorly communicated and project control was ineffective, otherwise known as "normal" projects.

This process is productive where it is possible to do true top-down development, where interfaces and requirements can be defined without regard for the technology of the underlying solution. The space program is an outstanding example of a project that worked in a fragmented manner. In spite of all the problems and blunders encountered, the space program really did put human beings in space. (For more description, refer to *A Passion for Excellence*, by Tom Peters and Nancy Austin.)

Closure Questions:

> Is there an essential difference between multisite internal software development in a single company and similar efforts accomplished through subcontracted work?
>
> Is software development a sufficiently comprehensive discipline to use such concepts as vertical and horizontal integration?

PHASED BUSINESS PROCESS

A phased business process for software development consists of the timed phases it calls for, plus the documents and agreements that are required in the various phases. The phases are as discussed on page 144 in the section titled "Standard software development process," and they include particular kinds of deliverable results in each phase.

Initial Business Proposal—Requirements, business assessments, technical planning, staffing. The movers of the product create the business plan that will be used to justify the effort. This involves estimates of project effort, estimates of the sales expected of the updated product, and an assessment of the risk involved.

Product Definition—While the rest of the development team is writing functional specifications, the business team is very busy on other things, including cost estimates and forecast assumptions, copyright clearance, financial reviews, and plans for publications, translation, quality, usability, installability, test, development, market support, distribution support, and service support. These all continue through the product build phase, but culminate in associated certifications. That is, plans show the way, and certifications document the successful completion of the plans.

Product Announce—Announcement is a much bigger thing for the business team than for the development team. Thus, it gets its own category in the process. Preparation for announcement involves final cost estimates and forecast assumptions, financial reviews, quality certification, legal clearances, and a business fact sheet, along with a market support plan and an early support plan.

Product Support—In a good business process, a product's time in the field will be carefully monitored and its financial performance carefully scrutinized. In a poor business process, a product's time in the field will be assumed to be revenue-enhancing and any reporting will support that assumption.

Overall, the phased process is characterized by activities and approvals. Activities (for example, document production, plan generation, and drafts of agreements) are always followed by approvals (or disapprovals). Often, the development or planning organization first works like crazy to produce the right stuff, then puts it out to a list of approvers for endorsement and feedback.

Given this mode of operation, a phased business process can be a trying one. While plans often can be accepted and modified easily, an announcement package often requires several rounds of review and correction before being approved.

Worse yet is the normal solution when there is a nonconcurrence; if agreement on a solution is not in the cards, we escalate the issue. Escalation—carrying an issue to high enough management levels so that no one will argue with an arbitrary decision—is a time-consuming process. In some cases, this has been recognized and a limit on how long an escalation is allowed to take is set. Each party must carefully document its own position, and ensure that the other side has been treated with obvious fairness. Each party will also look for alternate sources of credibility, either through expert opinions or through extra channels into the office of the deciding manager. All of this takes precious time, time taken from a too-tight schedule.

Finally, and most damaging of all, the produce/approve structure of the business process is linear. Even though we know we'll cycle a few times, and even though we are frustrated with the inevitability of nonconcurrences, this process locks us in to a linear mode of operation.

You should notice that the planners and managers who have the best success with the phased business process are also those who violate its linearity. They don't wait for approvals—they have the approvers involved in the production of the things to be approved. They do their homework and go looking for the trouble that would otherwise trip them up. The planners you want on your project share a characteristic with the programmers you want on your project: They are tenacious in their search for things that could go wrong, and they establish close ties with those who will approve their work.

As discussed in other parts of this book, this linear process works very well in the right environment. It works when projects build on a well known past and when they incorporate limited and known changes. In these kinds of environments, there's less need for prenegotiation because "everyone knows" what has to happen. There are fewer surprises in store for this product release, because many of the surprises were taken care of in prior releases.

Closure Questions:

Before a project started, how could you tell whether a phased business process would work for it?

If in the midst of the project you discover a conflict between a phased business process and a project itself, how would you begin to correct the problem?

COMMITMENT CHECKPOINT BUSINESS PROCESS

Through a modification in the kinds of agreements between organizations and the involvement of various groups in software development, a newer and more expedited business process can be derived.

This business process for software development is an outgrowth of the phased process, specifically designed to get around the time delays caused by phase reviews, distribution of plans, and nonconcurrences and escalations. Most of the process is the same as the phased process. The key differences are in the home stretch—that time when product release is imminent and delays have critical effects on an already tight schedule.

In the product announcement phase, there is a great deal of activity in forecasting, cost estimating, and requesting approval to release the product. The commitment checkpoint process inverts the order of these activities. Rather than waiting for an approval package, approvers are placed in a partnership role. Their previously more passive role is replaced by an active role in the identification and resolution of problems before the project reaches critical stages. The approval cycle is nearly eliminated by having commitment and agreement when the project is ready for release.

Closure Questions:

Is the increased feedback between approvers and developers an increase or a decrease in the stability of the situation?

How much does the distance between developers and approvers affect the stability and responsiveness of the overall organization?

9

Wonderful Thoughts and Pertinent Points

INNOVATION BY DESIGN

Paul Schumann was a Senior Technical Staff Member in Austin, Texas, before he retired from IBM in 1990. He worked for Technology Futures, Incorporated, and now is with Glocal Vantage Incorporated, also in Austin. Paul laid out a table of innovation categories that can help organizations in characterizing their business and planning their activities.

On one axis, innovations are categorized by what they are related to: product, process, or procedure. This is a kind of innovation that helps to distinguish between areas of business.

On the other axis, innovations are categorized by their scopes: breakthrough, distinctive, and incremental. Breakthrough innovations tend to open whole new areas of business. Distinctive innovations are visible as new entries to an existing area of business. Incremental innovations are usually visible as improvements to an existing entry in an existing area of business.

An organization can use the Applied Innovation Matrix to focus its efforts. If the organization's mission is to enhance existing products, it will have little immediate need for breakthrough innovations. However, if the mission is to devise totally new procedures that can make existing procedures obsolete, any efforts expended for incremental improvements will be no more than training exercises for new people in the group.

But there is a significant lesson to be learned beyond the focusing of an organization's innovative efforts. An organization's investment in innovation must match or exceed its business requirements. That is, if an organization is

Innovation Matrix

	Breakthrough	Distinctive	Incremental
Product			
Process			
Procedure			

© 1990, 1991 Technology Futures Incorporated

Figure 9-1. *The Applied Innovation Matrix*

to produce a new product, process, or procedure, some innovation is essential. Without innovation, there would be no new product, process, or procedure. Using the Applied Innovation Matrix to describe the business need to be satisfied by the organization will clearly expose those areas where innovative efforts will be required. Knowing about such needs, the organization can plan and pursue the levels of expertise, training, and experience required to get the desired innovations.

Finally, notice the tie between innovation and chaos. The mental activities involved in innovation and problem solving are heavily dependent on feedback. Remember the learning curves and sequences of mental models we talked about earlier. Thus, innovation itself is a fractal activity that is an essential part of software development. For this reason, if for no other, expert practitioners of software development must be aware of chaos, and they must learn to exploit it.

Closure Questions:

> What innovation is encouraged in your organization?
> Does that match your product needs?
> How can you use the Applied Innovation Matrix to prepare yourself, those around you, and your organization for the future of your business?

DESIGNERS' SOURCES

Designers synthesize solutions to problems out of three sources: imagination, knowledge, and understanding.

Imagination—This may be one of the most difficult of designers' attributes to measure. It includes—but is not limited to—the ability to concoct new solutions where no solutions existed before, the ability to use different perspectives in order to understand a problem and the solutions that might be applied to it, and the ability to see solutions for the current problem in other areas that might appear to be completely unrelated to it.

Knowledge of implementation technologies and solutions to other problems—This is what the designers bring to the project in the first place, but this knowledge increases in breadth and depth as they pursue their understanding of available implementation technologies or of the specific implementation technologies chosen for the project. If the designer takes the time to study other solutions to similar problems there is a corresponding increase in the ability to solve the current problem, but this is often bypassed in the pursuit of short-term goals.

Understanding of the problem to be solved—Early in the life of the project, this understanding is seldom complete enough for good design decisions, particularly if the requirements are unknown, incomplete, or not commonly understood. Frequently, the designers' understanding of the problem to be solved is a sequence of hypothetical problem formulations, and each formulation in the sequence may be drastically different from both its predecessor and its successor.

Looking at these sources from a fractal point of view, we can see some useful parallels.

Design based on the knowledge of implementation technologies and prior solutions the designer brings to the project usually involves no feedback in the designer's mind between the problem and the solution. Rather, the designer looks at the problem, selects a prior solution that is "close enough," and proceeds to force-fit the problem to the solution. This low-feedback design approach leads to applications that look and act like prior applications. This design approach leads to the good news of applications that look familiar to customers (which may actually be bad news in some cases) and the bad news of leaving the state of the design art exactly where it was before the current problem was attacked.

If, rather than designing with previous solutions, the designer works to understand the problem, a different kind of solution will probably result. In this higher feedback approach, the designer works through stages of understanding the problem before settling on a solution. This design approach leads to the good news of finding a better solution than what was known before and the bad news of not looking as familiar to customers who use earlier solutions to previous problems.

Finally, the use of the designer's imagination is the highest feedback approach. The designer uses the abilities noted above, explores levels of understanding of the problem and possible solutions (lots of feedback here), looks for parallels in other problems and even in other fields of endeavor, and then devises a sequence of solutions to the problem. The finally implemented solution is the unknown news of having an entirely different or entirely familiar appearance to the customer, the good news of having a state of the art solution, and the bad news of having no idea at the beginning of the project what the final result will look like.

A few points are worth noting here.

First, customer involvement in the process becomes more important with a more fractal approach. (Remember the discussion of customer involvement in box 11 on page 36.) With the involvement of a knowledgeable customer or customer surrogate (someone knowledgeable in and understanding of the customer's needs and environment), the devised solutions will remain in the realm of the useful. This result can not be guaranteed without such involvement.

Second, the right approach to solving a problem will involve an intelligent choice of a combination of the three approaches. That is, various factors in the problem environment will dictate whether an advanced or standard approach is required, or whether a new technology is needed to open an entirely new source of solutions for the creation of new business opportunities.

Third, a premature choice of implementation technology can prevent the intelligent composing of the right mix of these approaches. For example, imagination is the one of these three sources that is the most hindered by the "stake in the ground" approach. (See page 88.) Designers who are forced to work through a stake in the ground approach will find that their imaginations are hobbled, and their attempts to expand the understanding of the problem will be similarly constrained. Only strong-willed designers will be able to buck the organization's world view even to conceive of alternative solutions, let alone to propose the alternatives that are imagined. This is one of the key reasons for claims that the stake in the ground approach leads to mediocre design.

Closure Questions:

> For any particular project, how will you decide whether to encourage an imaginative solution or to adapt a prior solution to the problem?
> How can you simultaneously release designers' imaginations from the distractions of prior solutions and focus their energies on innovative approaches that can lead to good, innovate solutions?

PEDANTRY AND DESIGN SKILLS

There are some fascinating thoughts to be derived from the associations of paradigm changes with the nonlinearity of design and the approaches taken in most educational environments. (See page 21.) These thoughts lead to some definite recommendations for organizations in support of design.

First, look at education. From elementary schools, through middle and high schools, into college, and through graduate schools, educators all "build foundations" or "grow from foundations." This is an effective teaching mechanism, because the educators have only to lay the right groundwork and exploit it and the pathways into students' brains will be properly paved and easy to travel. Further, students are carefully taught that there are foundation courses and advanced courses and that they must master the foundation courses before they can handle the advanced material.

The fact of which educators and students lose sight is that this linear presentation of material is a teacher's trick, not a basic fact of human nature. In the rush to educate and be educated, this is so far lost that both students and teachers believe that the linear sequence is natural and right.

Kuhn's work indicates that linear learning is a fiction. The teacher's trick works only through the external application of discipline and the students' inability to resist higher authority. In fact, learning is a one-person-at-a-time path through sequences of the paradigm changes like what Kuhn describes in a scientific community. That is, people form individual mental models giving order to the information they have learned. More information leads to an expanded model or to the replacement of one model with another. By this process, everyone works through a sequence of mental models that each explain the world better or more acceptably than previous ones.

This is something of a dilemma for students, because there is a basic conflict between the teacher's trick and the actual way that people understand things. The unfortunate victims of this cognitive dissonance (distress caused by facts being contrary to the expectations of the authorities who exhibit the facts) are those individuals who firmly believe that learning must be linear yet somehow recognize that they do not learn in a linear manner. When authority looms and the victims' experience is contrary to that of its booming voice, the victims suppress the knowledge of how they really learn (and feel some guilt for getting away with doing it wrong), and further cover up by adopting and promoting the authoritative position.

A fact and an assumption are now waiting in the wings to make their grand entrances.

The fact is that there are very few people who design software. More accurately, there are very few people who devise new conceptual frameworks that can be fleshed out to become successful software. On the other hand, there are many people who copy existing designs, make adjustments to existing designs, or translate a design into code. But copying, adjusting, and translating are not the same as designing. These are creative activities in their own rights, but they are done within a more confining framework than the conceptual framework of a new software design.

The assumption (common to standard software development processes) is that a good design can be defined, early in a software development effort, in enough detail to lay out the entire schedule for the product. This assumption includes the assumption that proper control of a software development project is a simple matter of working hard enough to iron out all the details, after which everything else will follow in sequence. While this assumption is workable in some cases, it is not workable for all software development projects.

Let's explore what happens with people who are linearly educated and involved in the essentially nonlinear task of design. These people expect design to follow the linear fiction rather than to process by the leaps and bounds that characterize the jumps between mental models. If they're real victims of the teacher's trick, as soon as they experience some failures (a very common thing in design) the old feelings of guilt and inadequacy rise to the surface. This, in turn, triggers the old response of imposing authority and forcing the situation into the "right" mold. For them, the "right" mold involves better estimates, more refined plans, tighter schedules, closer monitoring, and more predictable measurements of results. Their past, and a fiction, have prepared them to be micromanagers. If these are the people who are in control of the project, beware because they will impose a linear control on it; however, the project will only succeed if it is opened to nonlinear selection of alternatives.

Victims of the fiction of linear learning have suppressed their experience of changes in mental models. Never having practiced (or allowed themselves to acknowledge having practiced) such changes, they are not able to see, experience, or imagine the changes in mental models that are the essence of good design.

Good designers are adept at trying out new mental models to see how they fit the problems at hand. Whether they experience great leaps of imagination or borrow insights from those around them, they find ways to extend what they have seen and what they can imagine. Whether this is the result of a natural ability or something they've learned to do under duress, they compose mental models until they find some that work. The mental models that work become the frames around which software designs are built.

Closure Questions:

> How will you form partnerships so that those who prefer a single mental model can balance those who prefer never to use the same mental model twice (and vice versa)?
>
> What will your products look like if everyone in the organization uses mental models exactly the same way?

THE PURPOSE OF BUREAUCRACY

A favorite human pastime is the bashing of bureaucracies. Bureaucracies are viewed as inhuman, inhumane, malignant, malicious, and perverse. Yet bureaucracies are one of the most productive vehicles ever defined for carrying on the everyday business of caring for the needs of an enterprise and the multitudes of people that must deal with it.

What is the cause of the discrepancy between these two views?

In programming terms, a bureaucracy is a multiprocessing computer, people are the processors, and policies and procedures are the programs. The processors are imperfect, their performance varying from day to day, depending on their moods and health. The policies and procedures are imperfect, being the statements of what is expected to happen most often rather than what actually happens.

Early work on defining bureaucracies was intended to eliminate favoritism and prejudice in the work place. Max Weber documents seminal work on bureaucracies in his *Theory of Social and Economic Organizations*. The bureaucracy was to be an organization with well-defined jobs, a place where people could earn advancement and recognition by the achievement of their job goals, rather than by the whims of biased supervisors. Yet we all have the uncomfortable feeling that this is not a description of today's bureaucracies.

Bureaucracies can actually come into existence in a couple of different ways. (Watch them—they are a lot like software development.)

In one case, a business person is overworked and decides that some of the work can be handled by a lower-paid employee. The new worker is hired, the expected rules are explained, and work proceeds. That's a bureaucracy. There's a policy maker and a policy enforcer. As the amount of work increases, some of the rules are changed and additional policy enforcers are added to the staff. As appeals for exceptions to the rules are sent to the policy maker, the rules are changed, often to handle highly specific circumstances. In this way, the policy statement grows. Growing, it often becomes cumbersome. The supporting staff learns to rely on the book rather than to bother the policy maker.

This works in a small business but tends to fall apart in a large business. Notice the parallel with software development. For a small program, you build a first solution and then fix it as problems crop up.

In larger companies and situations, bureaucracies are defined differently. Policy makers think more carefully about their decrees. Rule books are defined, organized, and stored in designated places so that everyone who needs them can get to them. Policy enforcers are trained in the use of communications devices and the rule books. Because it is still a matter of policy enforcers and policy makers, all of whom are people, there are still appeals and exceptions made, but the weight of the organization dictates that these are not for the faint of heart. Rule changes become more difficult, and they occur less frequently.

Again, this looks like the development of a larger program. In linear terms, you accumulate requirements, design the bureaucracy, and write the rule book. You debug the policy through the day-to-day working of the bureaucracy until it runs well enough. Then a small staff of maintenance policy makers supports the bureaucracy until the next major change.

But look again at the net effect of the bureaucracy. High-priced people have their productivity and decision-making responsibilities enhanced by the use of lower-priced people who enforce policies (follow rules). For normal cases, the policies say what to do and it happens quickly. In exceptional cases (a good bureaucracy will identify such cases very quickly), a policy maker can step in and determine what should be done. This is even self-checking, because a high number of exceptional cases will motivate a policy maker to adjust the rules so that the normal policy enforcers can handle the job.

So if bureaucracies are all such good things, why don't we like them?

Interestingly enough, we do like some bureaucracies. The ones we like, we never see. Good bureaucracies are the ones that support your needs so smoothly that you don't notice them. They include the auto maintenance shop where you don't have to fight to get work covered by a warranty and the cooperation between the medical clinic and the insurance company that arranges for you to never see any billing activity between them.

One of the reasons given for American business being so far behind Japanese business is the respective techniques for automating processes. American businesses automate processes as soon as the processes can be made to work. Japanese businesses resist automation until they've fussed with the process, tuned it, tried to replace it, and gone through many cycles of continuous improvement. Robert J. Kriegel and Louis Patler have many related comments in their book, If it ain't broke . . . BREAK IT!

Automating too early ensures that you're stuck with a cumbersome process forever. Had the equivalent happened with automobile standards, we'd all still be driving Model T Fords.

The same thing can happen with a bureaucracy. If policies are made too early and enforced with no flexibility, the bureaucracy will remain cumbersome for its entire existence. Actually, such a bureaucracy will probably get even more cumbersome as it patches itself in reaction to needs of its environment.

Closure question:

How will you lead your software development organization to avoid premature "automation" of your early processes?

Box 33. *Automating too early*

The bureaucracies we don't like are like programs that are poorly designed for the needs of customers. They fail in particular ways.

Their goals are not the goals of the organization—When a bureaucracy is in place to support a sub-goal of an organization (for example, controlling expenditures), it loses sight of the larger organization's goals. This is the case when your job is to develop software, and you can save $100,000 in development costs by buying a $10,000 work station, but the financial controllers by policy are not allowed to authorize that expenditure.

The policies are poorly defined—When the policies that control a bureaucracy don't fit the situations encountered by the bureaucracy, hassles are guaranteed. A possibly artificial, and extreme, example is the state that requires proof of insurance to be registered on the state computers. Out-of-state drivers are automatically in violation, and subject to whatever other policies might be lurking behind the scenes.

The policy enforcers are underqualified or poorly trained—Having the best policies and intentions in the world may not help if the policy enforcers don't know how to deal with their customers or how the policies are to be applied.

Some policy enforcers enjoy making other people uncomfortable—When the people who enforce policy are irritated or contrary, they can easily interpret policies to the detriment of the people with whom they're working. They can also overlook policies that might help the people with whom they're working. Yet we should be careful here. The standard admonition is, "Never attribute to malice that which can be adequately explained by stupidity or ignorance." This is sometimes difficult, because we can never quite see what is going on inside the bureaucracy, but it's a safe bet that "they" are "out to get us" far less often than we might imagine.

Most of the people within bureaucracies have taken unfair criticism. They are the victims, as much as those on the outside, of poor policies, poor training, and the poor attitudes of the people we all deal with. We should notice several things.

What bureaucracies do to us, we do to other people with our software.

Bureaucracies are improved by proper training and motivation of policy makers and supervisors. Our software is improved by proper training and customer awareness of everyone in the software development group.

Many bureaucratic problems would be avoided if properly trained and motivated policy enforcers could be allowed to deal with customers in pursuit of customers' goals. Many functional and usability problems with software could be avoided if the products themselves supported varying user needs.

But look at what all of these suggested improvements do. They prepare people to handle feedback. They open the organization to chaos and allow people to handle it productively. They expand an unrealistic concept of order into a practical and responsive concept of order. This requires the policy maker to take a new view of the world, but that's what awareness of chaos does to all of us.

Closure Questions:

> With the similarity between bureaucracies and software, is there a business opportunity in converting the policies of a bureaucracy into application software?
> Is there precedent in the software industry for application support packages that accommodate the changing of policies?

PARETO'S LAW—THE 80-20 RULE

From *Murphy's Law and other reasons why things go gnorw!* by Arthur Bloch, Pareto's law states,

> "20% of the customers account for 80% of the turnover."
> "20% of the components account for 80% of the cost."

These examples indicate the general situation that can be observed in nearly any environment, including several examples in software development:

> The software function that is used 80 percent of the time is implemented with only 20 percent of the development resource for the whole project.
>
> 20 percent of the people in a development project account for 80 percent of the design, code, documentation, and testing of the product.
>
> 20 percent of the people in a development project account for 80 percent of the hassles experienced by everyone in the entire project.

Of course we recognize that the numbers 80 and 20 are only approximations, but the point remains that there is exceptional leverage exerted on projects because of the efforts of small numbers of people. We can gain extraordinary benefits observing and utilizing the patterns that show where a 20 percent effort can realize 80 percent productivity.

In terms of chaos, 80 percent of the application fits within an area of order, and thus is accomplished with little effort. The rest of the application, the 20 percent that crosses boundaries and is in areas of disorder, takes 80 percent of the effort.

In his book *Rethinking Systems Analysis and Design*, Gerry Weinberg suggested that, "developers should exploit the 80–20 rule by terminating their projects when they have completed 80 percent of the planned function (with 20 percent of the effort), and immediately begin efforts for the next project instead of completing the first one."

In their book, *If it ain't broke ... BREAK IT!*, Robert J. Kriegel and Louis Patler quote Sandy Mobley, "If you try to become proficient at what you are weak at, it will take an inordinate amount of time. That means you don't have time to keep improving at what you are already good at, so that skill gets rusty and you end up mediocre at everything. The so-called well-rounded personality is really, in my experience, very very rare." Sandy Mobley is a manager of training at McKinsey & Co., the giant management consulting firm. In her description, she displays awareness of the 80–20 rule and the fact that there are areas in which you can learn and develop skills much more readily than you can in other areas. In terms of chaos, your productive areas for learning and developing skills are chaotically compatible with your internalized world view. Your counterproductive areas are chaotically incompatible with your internalized world view.

And now, as usual, it's time for a disclaimer. Remember that you and the world are always changing. Every once in a while, it will be necessary for you to go through a paradigm shift. When you do, your areas of order and your areas of disorder, your 80 percent areas and your 20 percent areas, will change. Using the wisdom of Sandy Mobley, that means that your productive areas for developing skills will also change. Recognize that fact and exploit it. Review what you're learning and what you're doing on a regular basis. If you've changed paradigms between reviews, you'll discover that some of those things seem more right than they used to and some other things will seem less right. When that happens, you have yet another question to answer—What will you do next?

But the 80–20 rule can be misused as well. Avoid abusing the 80–20 rule by following these examples and looking for others in your own organization.

> Don't assign a "total control" person responsibility for the early design stages of software development. This level of control early in a project is dangerously stifling to the overall effort.
>
> Do assign a "total control" person responsibility for the final validation of product functionality. You don't want anything to fall through the cracks at the expense of the customer.
>
> Don't rely on a testing organization to remove 80 percent of the errors in a product. The cost of removing defects during test is orders of magnitude higher than doing so during design and implementation.
>
> Do train your entire development team in practical methods of verification, causal analysis, and inspections. A little of their awareness will prevent errors that would be difficult to remove later in the effort.

The general admonition here is to focus efforts effectively. Look at everything you do, pick the parts where you can be most effective, and give the rest to someone else. Don't waste your time on parts where you're not productive. In an organization, swap responsibilities around until everybody can be highly effective in what they do. Don't let anyone have a responsibility in which he or she is unproductive and uninterested. There are sure to be better things he or she can do.

Closure Questions:

> How might you determine whether people are working in one of their 80 percent areas or in one of their 20 percent areas?
>
> How might someone get ready to be highly productive in a particular area?
>
> What relationship would you expect between job boundaries and individual productivity?

TASK-ORIENTED GROUP MANAGEMENT

Managers often believe that they can direct and control a project by keeping the reins in their own hands and assigning individual tasks to those who work for them. This is viewed as a simplification, since each worker has only that task to pursue. Ideally, each worker can simply perform the task and everything will come together smoothly. Note that this approach is usually, but not always, associated with micromanagement.

If a task could be completely and unambiguously specified, it could indeed be turned over to a competent, independent individual or group. The result would be a collection of components or work products that would fit together effortlessly and correctly.

Notice the similarity between task management in software development and time and motion studies in manufacturing. Given the idea that manufacturing tasks could be defined in great detail and the most efficient sequence of motions determined for each task, manufacturers studied the actual times and the actual motions of people performing those tasks. But the choreography approach to manufacturing didn't work. Manufacturers found that people got bored with the repetitious activities, lost concentration, and started to make mistakes. The attempt to completely define jobs and focus attention on just the jobs failed, even in the simplest environment that could be devised for human endeavor.

Task management doesn't work for individuals or for groups. Software development tasks can seldom be defined well enough for task management to work.

Three problems make this an unworkable general approach:

First, specifications are seldom complete. Where they are incomplete, the group working on the task will fill in the missing details to the best of their understanding (not part of their task, remember). Only if the assumptions of the task workers conform to the assumptions of other task groups will the results fit together successfully.

Second, specifications are often ambiguous. This is another opportunity for mismatched assumptions.

Third, even if a task is completely and unambiguously specified, some leeway will be allowed the task group. The group will use this leeway to optimize the "how" of their task. Because of the boundaries on the task, the optimization will necessarily be local optimizations, good for the task but of unknown impact outside the immediate area of responsibility. Local optimizations such as these are almost as severe in their damage to software systems as the more obvious problems of mismatched interfaces. (See page 19.)

It is a forlorn hope to expect that people in a highly controlled environment will pay attention to anything but what the controllers pay attention to. The killing contribution to the situation comes from the feedback in communication between the task controllers and the task workers, plus the lack of information in areas where the controllers assume that the workers know what's expected.

Consider a large job as an area that is divided. Each smaller part represents a task to be assigned to someone. In theory, it should be simple to draw lines to delimit each task. (The dashed lines in Figure 9–2 represent these limits.) However, the problems noted above guarantee that the boundaries are seldom where they need to be. Further, the people who are to accomplish the tasks will intentionally or unintentionally move the boundaries. Thus we will always see gaps and overlaps. The gaps are the traditional cracks through which things can fall. The overlaps are causes for turf battles.

In practical, everyday terms, the gaps and overlaps combine with the control-oriented environment to cause some frequently encountered problems. These are some problems caused by the gaps:

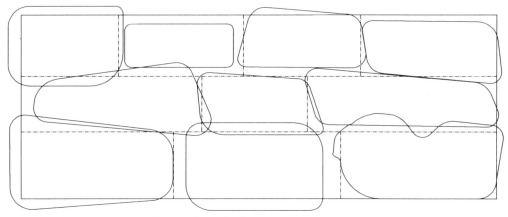

Figure 9–2. *Tasks as parts of an area*

People are careful not to exceed their boundaries, so things fall through the cracks.

People hide behind their boundaries when things fail, so that the focus is on escaping blame rather than on accomplishing the job.

People who care about the whole job are labelled as troublemakers. They stick their noses into the gaps, which are beyond their job responsibilities, and so where their noses don't belong. They "make work" for people who don't want their boundaries expanded.

Now look at the problems caused by the overlaps:

People appear to be petty when they argue over which of them should handle the overlapped area.

The different orientations for the two tasks cause the involved people to look at the overlapped areas differently. This means that solutions in the area will be different depending on who finally gets the responsibility.

With equally valid claims to overlapped areas, people have to escalate to higher authorities to get decisions on who should have the extra responsibility.

Note the legalistic nature that becomes part of everyone's job under task management. Everyone becomes involved in boundary watching. The organization takes on a defensive, fearful, argumentative, and petty flavor that tends to stifle teamwork and cooperation. Higher-level managers get involved in escalations about boundary disputes although they don't have the required technical or situational knowledge; their decisions are made based on factors that have nothing to do with the dispute.

The alternative to task management is something I'll call responsibility management. That isn't a really good name for it, but it will do for now.

With responsibility management, you define jobs by their central responsibility, not by the boundaries of their activities. You also assign complete coverage of the overall job as part of the responsibility. The results of this kind of management are interesting.

Boundaries are no longer meaningful. There are no boundaries to constrain people's efforts or for people to hide behind.

Teamwork becomes a necessity. If the job is done poorly, everyone has a share in the failure. When the job gets done well, everyone shares in the glory.

Escalation is no longer a way of life. Part of the team responsibility to get the job done is to communicate to ensure complete coverage and to negotiate resolutions to problems.

Those who uncover problems are heroes rather than troublemakers. Problems are things to be resolved to get the job done, not threats to the people who own particular tasks.

Overall, we can use this formulation to recognize that task management is much like slavery, while responsibility management requires working partnerships and people who support other people to get the job done.

Having expressed part of the case for responsibility management, it's still necessary to recognize that it's the fractal nature of working relationships that make task management what it is. And, given the nature of fractal things, we should expect that there are cases where task management is exactly the right technique to use to get a job done.

Keeping in mind the lessons we learned about the Pillars of Software Engineering on page 74, we can see a direct correlation between the three requirements for the use of software engineering and the use of task management.

Well-defined, independent requirements—Where the requirements are independent and well defined, it is clear where task boundaries can be drawn.

Well-defined implementation base—A well-defined implementation base consists of the common knowledge required to serve as a framework for communication. Having this practically eliminates the perceptual and personal factors that move boundaries and reinforce conflicts between task views of work.

Expert practitioners—When people fully understand their technological and organizational environment, task views fit within the overall environment and task-related conflicts are minimized.

With all three of these requirements, it becomes clear that there are areas in which task management can work and work well. We should expect those areas in many of the environments where full use of software engineering techniques will be effective. However, it should also be clear that most jobs in software development will be handled much more effectively by responsibility management than by task management. This is particularly true when the efforts involve large or complex projects, innovation beyond minor or isolated improvements, or significant interaction with customers. It is also particularly true about practically any new project you can think of.

Closure Questions:

How can you tell whether people are trained to take task assignments or responsibility assignments?

How might a group change from being task oriented to become responsibility oriented?

KINDS OF MEASUREMENT

Classical measurement theory notes three domains for measurement—processes, results, and inputs. I mention this because I want to take a different point of view and I'd prefer the reader to know that I'm not inventing things out of whole cloth just for the sake of having things to say. There really is experience and reason behind everything you're reading in *Exploiting Chaos: Cashing in on the Realities of Software Development*.

The useful distinction that is pertinent to our discussion is the distinction between adjustment measurements and success measurements. Adjustment measurements are mostly about what can be done to improve a process. If we listen to W. Edwards Deming, we use adjustment measurements to indicate if a process is stable and to validate whether process changes lead to such improvements in a process as increased stability or reduced variation. Success measurements are mostly about whether a process is cost-effective and whether the results of a process are suitable for use.

Notice the difference in perspective between the classical and the adjustment/success views of measurement.

In the classical view, the emphasis is on where you can do the measuring. The assumption is that any measurement can be used to improve the process. You prefer to measure the process because that's where things are really happening. If you can't measure the process, you try to measure the results. Measuring results is a little indirect, but it gives you a chance to adjust the process if the results aren't usable. Finally, if you can't measure either the process or the results, you'll measure the inputs. This is even more indirect, but if it's all you can measure, that's what you do.

> *What would happen if the batter in a baseball game were to focus on measurements for success rather than on process measurements? We could envision the batter looking so hard at the scoreboard that he doesn't even see the pitch crossing the plate: strikeout!*
>
> *Likewise, we could imagine a software development company that focused so much on profit that it failed to invest appropriately in its people, processes, and customer involvement. Its result would be the same as the batter's—failure.*
>
> *Closure question:*
> > *How might you use both success measurements and adjustment measurements in your work?*

Box 34. *Measurement myopia*

If this last seems too far-fetched for you, consider social services programs that tend to be measured on good intentions and resources (inputs) thrown at problems rather than on processes or results. The software development version of this is the project that is planned and directed in accordance with the

"Free" measurements are measurements that occur naturally in a process. Measuring the size and dimensions of a manufactured part is relatively "free."

"Introduced" measurements are measurements that are imposed on or inserted into a process. In manufacturing pipe, it might be possible to introduce flow rate measurements by adding some stages to the manufacturing process.

The temptation of each is to measure when it's neither appropriate nor productive. "Free" measurements are taken because they're there. "Introduced" measurements are invented and taken because people believe that it's important to measure things.

But taking and tracking these measurements, giving in to the temptations, requires project resources. The more you measure, the more project resources you use for measurement rather than production. If you're not careful about the measurements you use, you can tie up inordinate amounts of project resource and hurt, rather than enhance, project results.

Adding the resource drain to the feedback nature of measurements, we can clearly see the danger in measuring things. Imprudent measurement can cause project unpredictability and use so much project resource that it totally paralyzes the project group. Measurement paralysis can be deadly.

Closure questions:

How do you know whether your project measurements are meaningful, useful, or productive?

How might you eliminate counterproductive measurements?

Box 35. *Measurement paralysis*

leader's favorite theory with no feedback from reality. Such a project seems unlikely to succeed, yet the approach has in fact succeeded. Knowing what we know about chaos and personal discipline, we would conclude that the leaders' theories were close enough to reality and that the developers' personal discipline bridged the gaps to make the projects work.

In the adjustment/success view, the emphasis is not on where the measuring can be done but on the purpose of the measurement. The goal is to keep the bounds of chaos as close as possible, thus improving our chances of making the process work successfully for us.

A good example of this comes from archery. As beginners, we might shoot arrows and barely manage to keep them within a one-meter circle. We can then try to master all the skills necessary to hit the bull's-eye, or we can try to master the smaller set of skills that we need to shoot consistently and get the arrows to hit within a tenth of a meter circle. If we can learn the latter (process improvement), we can then easily learn to stand differently to move our results to the bull's-eye (adjustment for success measurements).

For software development, this view of measurement is particularly useful. Such success measurements as profitability and customer acceptances are of little use in tuning the software development process. Corresponding adjustment measurements include the expertise of developers, the suitability of the development process and tools, and the smooth integration of customer contacts that will help to develop the right product. Notice that the two sets of measurements are in apparent opposition, but they are both necessary for the overall success of the organization. This example also shows that success measurements at one level might be adjustment measurements at a higher level. The chaotic view thus shows just how carefully decisions have to be made in the software development business (and nearly all others). We have contradictory world views covering the same area of business; the best decisions can be made by understanding both views or by recognizing and nurturing both views.

Closure Questions:

> Does your organization distinguish between success and adjustment measurements?
>
> How do you determine whether your investment of resources is appropriate for your organization?

10

And in Conclusion, . . .

After reading *Exploiting Chaos: Cashing in on the Realities of Software Development* the reader should be aware of some significant things.

First, nearly any software development scheme can be made to work, given the right people, the right training, the right environment, the right project, and the right customers.

Second, it is of no practical use to pretend that all the conditions of the first point are true if they are not in fact true. Indeed, such pretense is the most significant proximate cause of most failures in software development.

Because people are learning creatures and because learning involves feedback, we can safely say that every human endeavor has a fractal nature. We can also safely say that those misguided people who ignore that fractal nature will continually be surprised at the results of their endeavors. As a kindness, we'll call those misguided people "victims." The surprises will come even though the "victim" will have done "all the right things" and things "should have worked."

If the surprises are unpleasant, the "victims" will typically believe that they didn't do "all the right things" quite correctly and merely need to try a little harder the next time. If the surprises are pleasant, the "victims" will believe that they really did "all the right things" and that the good results were simply their due.

In essence, these people view their efforts as incantations to magical worlds. The results of their endeavors must then be the acts of capricious beings who sometimes fail to respond properly to the incantations.

The fractal view is a more productive and manageable view of reality.

The fractal view recognizes that the results of feedback sometimes lead to stability and sometimes lead to instability.

The fractal view recognizes that results can often be unpredictable and that it's therefore necessary to watch what happens rather than to assume that past patterns will hold forever.

The fractal view recognizes that paradigm shifts will be necessary from time to time, in order to bring a more orderly and productive understanding of a changing environment.

The fractal view recognizes that there is an immense benefit to be gained when it is possible to exploit an area of order to use the patterns found there.

The fractal view recognizes that there are no universal tools or magic approaches that can be "just right" for all needs and all situations.

Some readers will feel like this chaos stuff means they should give up. After all, if everything is so chaotic, why should they try to do any better? The answer, of course, deals with areas of order. We have areas of order today that we never had before. We understand more than we ever have before about software engineering, software development, personal discipline, and the world as a whole. As a specific example, the proofs of correctness that we know how to do today were vague academic hopes in the 1960s.

Rather than giving up in the face of this chaos, discover and invent new areas of order that you can exploit. Exploit areas of order wherever they can be found or defined. Be prepared to eliminate an area of order if there are larger benefits to be derived from another view. Remember the unpredictability that accompanies all of our efforts and check both your results and your assumptions. And, last but not least, use positive personal discipline to bridge the final gap between a process that is almost good enough and the reality it is intended to support.

It's not necessary to try to increase disorder to take advantage of chaos. Rather, our understanding of chaos allows us first to know when we need to look for more productive views, and second to know where and how to apply our efforts most productively.

Closure Question:

How will you use what you've just read?

Appendix:

Answers to closure questions

CHAPTER 1: CHAOTIC FOUNDATIONS

Introduction to Chaos (page 4)

How do you decide when you will use a computer system to do your work?

Some people let their work loads determine when they will use the computer. Others, using shared systems that may slow down when they are fully loaded with users, will organize their work to use the computer when response is fast and do other work when the response is slow. The former approach, which does not use feedback, sometimes wastes time. The latter solution affects the performance of the computer, probably changing its response time.

Can you exploit fast times when they occur, or do you even think about the performance of a computer system when you devise your plans?

Refer to the previous answer. Sometimes adding a little complexity to your planning can make your work move faster.

Do you expect your computer support to run like clockwork?

On shared computer systems, only novices believe that things will run the same, day after day. You don't have to let the chaos dominate your attention, but you can exploit it.

Chaos in Clocks—Chaos is Always There (page 7)

How many places can you observe feedback that is supposed to keep things neat and orderly?

We're surrounded by feedback. Nearly everything that we do involves feedback intended to keep things working. Discussing things with peers, getting and giving job direction, learning new ideas and skills, and driving to work all involve feedback. The better question might be, "Where do we not see feedback?" We don't see feedback in those few, unique cases in which something is supposed to happen but nobody cares about the precision or the effectiveness of the result.

If you observe feedback systems closely, can you see chaotic behavior within the bounds set by the feedback?

In most feedback systems, we simply ignore deviations as long as they're within acceptable limits. If we were to look, we would see chaos.

Can you identify some natural examples of feedback and chaos?

Pick any you want, they're all around. A river meanders, raindrops rise and fall in a thundercloud, insect and animal populations show wonderfully chaotic distributions over time. Anything having to do with the "balance of nature" will involve feedback and show chaotic behavior.

Chaos in Water and Wax—Control Often Exaggerates Chaos (page 10)

Are there disorderly parts of your job that you routinely ignore or adjust for because they don't fit in with the official things you are supposed to do?

This is such a common phenomenon that we seldom notice it, yet we have a term for it: the "unwritten law." You can see these parts of your job if you consider your reaction to a co-worker who does things "by the book" (or possibly your co-workers' reactions when you do things by the book). Notice that the evaluation of by the book as being good or bad depends on social and cultural criteria, not the content of the book.

Is your performance rated better when you ignore these things or when you adjust for them and make the process look better?

The answer depends on the social and cultural criteria where you work. It's often wise to know whether your organization values apparent process success or adherence to processes. This is one example where it's better to know the ground rules before trying to make changes, whether the changes are to the process or to the ground rules.

Chaos in a Rainstorm—Adjust to Chaos or You'll Be All Wet (page 11)

What does your organization do to see if its areas of order are about to close up or to find new areas of order that might be productive?

Ignoring these problems is a common oversight among organizations. People want to believe that things will continue as they are, so they fail to look for the obsolescence of their technology, products, or services. If your organization does anything to avoid these dead ends, congratulations, keep up the good work, and look for even better ways to avoid the dead ends. If your organization does nothing to avoid the dead ends, I wish you the best of the miraculous luck you're counting on for having a good future.

What tools and concepts do you have to help you exploit existing areas of order?

This is an exercise in creativity. Your organization has at least one existing area of order, and it is trying to exploit that area. But competitive products, professional societies, literature in your field, and creative people in your organization can help to identify additional areas of order that might be productive for you.

How will you find or create new areas of order when you need them?

Actually, it's better to find and create areas of order constantly in your organization. When you need them it's too late to create them without disrupting the organization. Still, it may be beneficial for everything to get shaken up once in a while to keep people from becoming complacent. The same creative people mentioned in the previous question can provide help, but you'll want to have even more of your own creative people involved in inventing new areas of order.

Box 1—*James Gleick:* **Chaos, Making a New Science** *(page 2)*

How often do you read literature outside of computer science to find ideas that can provide a new perspective on your work?

This is a gold mine. Some of the most surprising, productive, and profitable ideas in software development were simply transplanted from other fields. I'd recommend that more than twenty percent of your reading should be outside of your field of expertise.

Can you exploit such transference of ideas from physics, psychology, history, language studies, journalism, and political science?

Of course you can! It may take a little practice, but try to draw parallels between the other fields and your own. Once you begin, you'll find it easier and easier, then more and more productive. This question merely suggests fields with known successes in transferring ideas to software development.

Which will you explore next?

However you prefer to learn, there's material available for you. Bookstores now carry books and audio tapes of interest in many fields. Libraries have videotapes on a wide variety of educational and informative topics, and public broadcasting stations regularly cover a wide spectrum of material. Pick your subject, pick your medium, then go get it.

Box 2—Learning how to program (page 5)

How would you recognize a part of your job that wasn't chaotic?

The parts of your job that aren't chaotic are the parts that you know completely, that never change, that you do "like clockwork," and that you probably do for unknown reasons. If you identify such a part, I suspect that your next step should be either to stop doing it (it isn't really needed) or to automate it (why are you spending brain power on a no-brain task?).

Box 3—Dripping water and mathematical chaos (page 7)

Can you adjust the water flow so that it produces all and only drops of water, yet any increase in the flow becomes a stream with no drops?

You should try this one, even though it can't be done. In the intermediate flow state between drops and a stream, you'll see long drops that look like strange streams, but it's clearly not a continuous flow. You'll also see the water "wiggle" from side to side in the middle of these long drops.

Is the boundary between the two flow rates orderly or disorderly?

The approved answer is "disorderly" because we can't quite call the water behavior dripping or flowing and because of the path the water takes. Still, looking at just the rate of flow, averaged over minutes, it is quite orderly.

Box 4—Requirements feedback (page 8)

If you can think of ways to avoid the feedback of gathering requirements, why do you have any confidence that the resulting requirements will be useful?

This is a cautionary question. Defining requirements in a vacuum is a common practice and historical failing of the software development community. The only way to ensure a predictable schedule for defining requirements is to eliminate the feedback, yet the only way to have a chance of getting good requirements is through feedback from customers and clients. There should be no confidence in requirements defined without feedback from customers or good customer surrogates.

Box 5—Chaos and software development control (page 9)

How would you know if your project control kept you from seizing opportunities?

Project control will always prevent you from seizing opportunities. The challenge is to make sure that you know about as many of the opportunities you're passing up as possible. When you know about the passed opportunities, you'll have a chance to think about them later and decide whether to pursue them or not. Of course, if you fail to think about them and evaluate them at all, you won't stay in your business for long.

CHAPTER 2: FLOW AND CHANGE

Catastrophe Theory (page 17)

What was the cause of the last failure in software development you experienced?

People seldom begin a software development effort without knowing something about how to develop software. But if they neglect to use a matched set of process, tools, situation, developers, and application, they will encounter pressure away from their selected area of order. Thus, a failure in a software development effort is often associated with a catastrophic transition, and so the next question becomes necessary.

In retrospect, can you see the key characteristics of a catastrophic transition in that situation?

Look for an area of order where things should have worked well, and pressure from a variety of sources that made your life difficult in that area of order. Then look for a sudden change in how things were done, possibly a war-room approach, people giving up a normal part of their business lives, or other effort-focusing stratagems.

How can you help to prepare your group to survive and thrive if a catastrophic transition is forced on it?

Two approaches can help with potentially catastrophic transitions. The first is to intentionally use several areas of order at once. If your organization is large enough, you can have software development teams that each use different world views but share experiences so that they can recognize problems within any particular team. The second is to actively pursue knowledge of the wide variety of software development processes and techniques available in the business and academic communities. Active pursuit includes the full intention to incorporate the best of the ideas into your own organization, helping to ensure that you are ahead of any forces that push you toward a catastrophic transition. In other words, whenever you can, soften the possible blows by being ready for them and by taking your catastrophes a little transition at a time.

Bubbles and Function Charts (page 21)

Do you know of any useful application that consists of a single function with no peripheral supporting functions?

Yes, there are some, but they're very limited. Probably the most famous is the "Hello, World" program written by every beginning C language programmer. That program has the sole function of printing the greeting, "Hello, World." The next most famous example comes from IBM's mainframe operating system, MVS. The IEFBR14 program has the single function of returning control to the calling point using standard interfaces. Other than examples like these (learning exercises, interface preservers, or single function support routines), all useful applications have multiple functions.

What is required of a utility support function that is useful with multiple major applications?

The key to reusable support functions is the use of common interfaces. If the major applications are significantly different or implemented with different languages, the support function may have to be tolerant of different data representations.

Would you expect the same data structures to work in different applications that are based on different paradigms?

This might happen by design, but is unlikely to happen by accident. This is one of the big flaws in the idea of preserving existing code. Often, people will try to save development time in a software development project by retaining an existing set of programs. However, the data structures tend to be so embedded in the program that it's more work to retrofit the programs than to rebuild them for the desired data structures.

Paradigms and World Views (page 23)

How many paradigms (world views) can you identify in the current field of computer science?

This list could go on for a long time, but consider such categories as language (for example, COBOL, FORTRAN, C, PL/1, FORTH, PASCAL, and PROLOG) which carry their own ways of building applications, formality (for example, ad hoc, structured programming, proofs of correctness, data flow, control flow, and object-oriented), which carry their own theories and world views, and optimization (for example, Reduced Instruction Set Computers, Complex Instruction Set Computers, optimizing compilers, and personal expertise), which often seem to influence people to nearly religious debates about rightness.

How often do such theoretical dichotomies as Reduced Instruction Set Computers and Complex Instruction Set Computers prevent practical implementations?

If nearly any theoretical aspect of computing is taken to its extreme, the result is impractical. It might be different if we had computers that were infinitely fast, but our technology forces us to compromise on many theories. That doesn't prevent the theories from being useful, it just means that we have to keep our balance.

Do you have a blind spot because of your own current specialty?

Yes. That's our nature. We always see the world from our current perspectives, and our current specialty is a significant part of our world view.

How would you step above a possible blind spot to see if it existed?

This ties back to the discussion in Chapter 1 about reading outside of your field. There are many benefits to be derived from getting a broad perspective on things. The more perspectives you can understand, the less likely it is that a blind spot will sneak up on you.

Layers of Reality (page 25)

How might you know if your world view interfered with solutions to your design problems?

There are two excellent clues you can look for. The first is if you tend to run into endless problems in refining your designs. That is, every time you make a design decision, it seems to lead to additional problems that are the same size as the one you just resolved. An extreme programming parallel is in writing straight line code to look something up in a table. Until you think of loops, the lookup is a difficult problem. After you think of loops, the lookup is nearly trivial. The second clue comes when your design must be changed (as they all must). If a change in the kind or number of situations to be handled requires a change in your design, you have a world view problem with the design.

When was the last time some novice asked a question out of ignorance and you responded, "Why didn't I think of that?"

If you can't remember the last time, you've just uncovered a problem. It's difficult to keep a fresh point of view and your inexperience with "Why didn't I think of that?" should be a warning sign. If you are a respected leader in your group and use the phrase regularly, you're probably in good shape and should continue your explorations.

What techniques could help you to remember other points of view?

There are lots of mind-broadening techniques available. Some of the key ones include maintaining lots of contact with your customers (and not just the same ones all the time), getting novice points of view (bring novices into your organization or hire temporary testers for your products, and then listen to all of what they say), pursuing new information both inside and outside your field, participating in professional societies and academic partnerships, and so on. The real problem here isn't in remembering the points of view but in reaching out so that they can touch you.

Gause Windows (page 27)

What product has given you the pleasure of using an application tool that fits Don Gause's ideas, where learning more about the tool was simple because it extended what you first learned?

I hope you're fortunate enough to have experienced at least one of these products. They do exist. The fascinating thing about them is that you find them more often in the realms of computer games than in business applications. There's a lesson in there somewhere.

What products have required you to learn whole new sets of rules and thoughts?

If you've used computers at all, you've had experience with products like these. Keep in mind, though, that it's not necessarily bad to have to learn whole new sets of rules and thoughts. That may be the introduction to a new and highly productive world view. But following Dr. Gause's ideas, it might be better to have a small set of new rules and thoughts to learn rather than the entire set that is required for the most complex use of the application.

Which set of products did you like better?

No, the approved answer is not, "The second kind." The best answer is, "It depends." If you've experienced products in both categories, and found some in each that you liked, then you have a basis for your own decisions that's far better than if you only experienced one or the other. There's more to learn from a variety of experiences than from many repetitions of the same experience.

What is it about people that makes the second kind of product so much more common than the first?

One answer to this question is that designers tend to look for consistency rather than usage in their designs. That is, designers make all functions equally accessible. The usage view would lead designers to ease of access to the most commonly used functions and extension of the access techniques to the rest of the functions. There are plenty of other answers as well, so you don't have to like this one. Another answer is that some applications that evolve over multiple releases do not have a consistent design for the incremental functions. This leads to different world views by function and makes it more difficult for the user to learn how to use the application.

Myopia—Some Limits on What We See (page 29)

If you have problems to be solved, do you want them to be solved by people whose myopic bounds are smaller than or the same as yours?

This is not a multiple choice question. The approved answer is no! If the myopic bounds of the people who are helping you to solve problems are smaller than or equal to yours, they can't do anything with the problem that you couldn't do. If you're the leader of a group, your group will do much better if each person has a contribution to make. Thus, you don't need lots of duplication of what you can already do, you need group bounds that are wider than yours. With wider bounds for the whole group, you can solve problems better and all of you can grow at the same time.

How might you find people with different myopic bounds who could contribute to your projects?

Recruiting is always a difficult problem, and the concept of myopic bounds strongly suggests that you be tolerant in your recruiting activities. You need to look for the intelligence the candidate has that makes it possible to contribute to your projects, the communication skills the candidate has that make it possible for people on the project to function as a team, and the technical knowledge or learning capabilities the candidate has that minimize the time required to integrate him or her into a project team. Then resist the temptation to hire the person who is comfortably "just like me, just like Sam, just like Sue." To avoid myopic traps, you need different points of view and should intentionally hire to achieve variety and balance in personality types, points of view, and technical capabilities. There are personality type tests that can help you to achieve some of the needed balance. However, you'll probably have to make your own judgement calls on points of view and technical areas of expertise. As you do this, you should probably tell the candidates that you're hiring for variety. For some, this will be intolerable and they should work in environments where they are comfortable. For others, this will be an additional inducement to join your group.

Having seen changes in the past, do we have any reason to believe that the future will involve no further change?

The most classic case of myopia is the belief that what we have now is all that we will ever have (and that nothing will be taken away). This is actually the least likely future of all. The future will differ from the present, and those who fail to change will fail both personally and professionally. Consider the risks. The greatest risk is to make no changes—failure is guaranteed. A slightly lower risk comes if you change for the sake of change—failure is no longer guaranteed, but random action may not be the most productive course. The lowest risk comes from intelligently selected change—success isn't guaranteed, but neither is failure, and you'll still have an edge on those who choose the other two options. And, in a final commercial for this section, you'll have a much better chance of making intelligent choices if you broaden the bounds of your myopia.

Simulated Annealing (page 31)

How might you use the concept of simulated annealing to overcome a cultural aversion to risk taking?

"Cultural aversion to risk taking" means that people in your organization have habitual responses to proposals that include, "We've never done that here," "It'll never work," "They'll never approve that," and many others. That set of responses is goal directed, the direction being to do what we've always done. The simulated annealing approach indicates allowing responses in the opposite direction. So in such a group you might designate a risk taking group and observe their results to justify changing the habitual responses. Or you might seek out risks to take to break the habitual view of risk. But keep your balance here. Remember the answer to the last closure question in the previous section. What this organization perceives as high risk is really low risk. Consider clarifying the perception, in addition to using the simulated annealing concepts.

What kinds of results would you expect from any project that is not allowed to back away from bad or less than optimal decisions?

When an organization makes decisions "once and for all," you would expect the results to be fragile. Using the parallel concept of cooling metal, the results would be crystallized in arbitrary rather than uniform and consistent ways. Allowing decisions to be changed is an essential part of good software development.

Box 6—A structured programming catastrophe (page 15)

How could you marshall forces like Mills' and make change happen in your organization?

Harlan Mills had several things going for him in his work on structured design. He had a project to which his people could contribute. He, the technology, and the project all required that the people grow in their technical expertise. He had people who were capable and flexible, he had credibility as a leader of software development, and he had an infectious passion for the project and the technology. In short, he had a situation and the personal attributes that add up to strong leadership. But these were not things that he inherited. He made most of them happen. You can do the same thing if you will insist that your people grow, if you trust them, learn how to be a leader and then actually lead, and take on challenging projects with vision and passion. All of this is within your grasp, if you decide to make it happen.

What would you do if the transition happened to you rather than to the organization?

Some people will view this question as a threat. It shouldn't be. If you rather than your group make the catastrophic transition, that's all right. Just because you're the leader (or a significant influence) doesn't mean that you always have to be in conformance with the final result. If you learn something during the project, you'll be more able to handle various situations in the future. What you should do if the transition happens to you is to say so (admit it or brag about it, whichever you'd like) and learn to master the new world view.

Box 7—Catastrophic sidetrack (page 16)

What might you do if you were a programming leader and your team members demonstrated that they just wanted to code for explicit requests?

First, you should recognize that there is a problem. Programming for explicit requests is one of the least productive ways of programming that exist. Next, as a leader, you should de-emphasize lines of code as a measurement and encourage your team members to learn how to use generalized code and to improve productivity. Finally, you should work to define, adopt, and support conceptual frameworks that can define more productive areas of order for your group. Consider getting more education, using new methodologies, and improving communication with your customers as techniques to cause the next transition.

What similarity do you see between this view and an organization that is firmly in crisis management mode?

Both represent trivial responses to business needs. When organizations and people work this way, they become victims of their own poor practices—easy prey for more far-sighted competitors in their environments.

Box 8—Local optimization (page 19)

Which of the decisions that you make routinely are optimization decisions?

The probable answer to this question is, "All of them." If you are lucky, most of the things that have to be done fall into obvious areas of order. There, you probably won't even feel as if you're making a decision. Decisions are called for when things fall on boundaries between areas of order or when you're defining areas of order. Of the two kinds of choices, the latter are the most productive. Those are the decisions that guide behavior and world views (global optimizations) rather than defining special cases (local optimizations). But, of course, a balance is needed.

How might you know whether your decisions bring order or disorder to your organization?

There are three things to look for: consistency, compatibility, and guidance. Consistency means that you are pursuing a predictable and probably understandable area of order. Compatibility means that your decisions are in accord with the other decisions being made in the group and you reinforce the group's areas of order. Guidance has two parts: one is leading, the other is following. If your decisions establish guidance for the organization or follow the guiding standards set for the organization, you reinforce or establish order for the organization. How you blend these attributes will depend strongly on your leadership role in the organization. If your decisions aren't consistent, if they are contrary to decisions made by the rest of the group (subject, of course, to the concepts of simulated annealing), or if they degrade the group's guiding principles, you bring disorder to your organization. However, the goodness or badness of this order or disorder can't be judged outside of the context of the organization.

Box 9—The baby duck syndrome (page 22)

How would you identify developers with desirable imprints for your projects?

An assumption in this question is that there is such a thing as a desirable imprint. That's probably all right, since we can guess that imprinting is inevitable and we'll have to select real people for our projects. Identifying developers with tolerable imprints requires you to have a knowledge of technologies and processes other than the ones you're using on your project. It also requires that you be able to step back from your imprints to look at the developer's. Interviewing is one productive way to identify imprints. During the interview, you can ask for comparisons of processes and technologies, or set up some role-playing situations to see how the developer responds. The most conclusive way to identify imprints is to observe the developer at work. There, you will see visible evidence if the developer's imprints are in conflict with the tools he or she is using. But be careful. Don't confuse a learning curve with a contrary imprint.

What might you do with developers who are imprinted in ways that will conflict with your project needs?

You have roughly four choices. You can help them to change, not a problem if you and they are flexible enough. You can help them to find jobs that are more aligned with their imprinting. You can tolerate their reduced productivity (which may still be quite high). The fourth choice is to change the project to conform to the imprinting of the developers. Each of these has its advantages and should be considered as a fully viable option.

CHAPTER 3: ORDER AND BOUNDARIES

The Psychology of Order (page 34)

What will you see in your organization if it is actively pursuing a common area of order?

The signs of coherence in an organization include the things that people talk about, the heroes people revere, and the actions that are taken in the organization as a matter of course. When a group pursues a common area of order, you will see the people using a common set of reasons for doing things. The same reasons will be the significant attributes of the group's heroes. And people will talk about those reasons. When the group isn't pursuing a common area of order, people will talk about why things in the group don't make sense. The people who are respected will not be the people who get official recognition, and the decisions that are made will be made for short-term reasons rather than long-term reasons.

What key factors can you use to resolve apparent disruptions in the organization?

Disruptions are most often the result of disparate world views. A leader can guide an organization into an area of order for its endeavors by using a vision of what the organization should become, a mission stating who the organization's customers are and what product or service the organization is to deliver, a set of goals that are concrete achievements for the group to make, and a set of values that are important to everyone in the organization. These things provide guidance for all decisions and an identity and a purpose that will unify the group's efforts. Rather than trying to negotiate agreement on the details of what is to be done, attention to the guiding standards eliminates most such disagreements.

Bounds of Chaos (page 37)

How might you know where the bounds for your processes are?

For some processes, it's easy to determine the bounds of the process since the bounds are formed by the assumptions used in defining the process. For other processes, feedback is sufficiently complex that the original assumptions are no longer pertinent—it doesn't take much. Sometimes, you can find the bounds of your process by simply watching. The situations where the process becomes disorderly (hits the bounds) and the situations that the process simply doesn't handle adequately will show them to you. At times, you may need to probe and search to find the bounds, but you'd hate to have them sneak up on you and be a big surprise.

As you take your risks, do you care whether your feedback information is direct or indirect?

This question, since it leads into the following section, has an approved answer. Wherever possible, you want your feedback to be direct. Levels of indirection in feedback lead to incredibly chaotic behavior, like the behavior we see in the stock market.

The Stock Market (page 40)

What measurements in your software development environment reflect outcomes?

Typical counts and statistics about software are outcome measurements. These include lines of code, customer satisfaction, test cases executed, and numbers of defects. Few software development measurements relate to the actual processes involved in designing and developing software. For example, there are no measurements of how people write code, of how causal analysis is actually performed, or of how effectively code is written to accommodate proofs of correctness.

Does your organization attempt to manage to the numbers or to the process?

For most readers, the answer will be "to the numbers." At higher organizational levels, the processes of developing software are arcane and not well understood. However, the numbers can be manipulated and reported as though they meant something (which, indeed, they occasionally do). Managing to the process appears to be an artistic endeavor because of the lack of related numbers.

How might you get the benefits of using both outcome numbers and process measurements?

Nearly all of the outcome numbers associated with software development are ambiguous. They don't correlate with any of the desirable attributes of software. An increase in lines of code can be associated with a decrease in product function and reduced quality. A decrease in bugs found might be associated with a decrease in product quality because the cause for the decrease is reduced resources for causal analysis and testing. But if you ensure that the people know the appropriate development technologies and methodologies and pursue the organization's guiding standards with discipline, then the numbers can be used to indicate the situations where something needs to be explored. That is, an increase or decrease in the numbers doesn't say that the project has gotten better or worse, it just says that something has changed and ought to be examined to see if the news is good or bad.

Chaos Within Acceptable Boundaries (page 41)

How do your measurements show how your processes help to produce your product?

Typical measurements indicate how a process works or whether the results of the process are acceptable. Thus, measurements don't help much at all in relating a process to a product. This is a process-design consideration rather than a measurement consideration.

Do lines of code or person-months have anything to do with software product function or quality?

Lines of code and person-months are measurements of complexity and investment, not of function or quality. For a given design approach, lines of code and person-months are the best estimating tools available for the size and cost of a project. But change the design approach or the implementation language and these estimates will change drastically, without any change in product function.

Multiple Areas of Order (page 42)

How can you recognize an organization that smoothly supports multiple areas of order?

Probably the best indicator that you as an outsider can see is that the people in the organization appear uniformly friendly and cooperative. When an organization smoothly supports multiple areas of order, the people understand and deal with the different perspectives involved.

What kinds of boundaries would you expect to see in such an organization?

Such an organization probably won't have boundaries as such. The people in the organization will direct you easily to the group with particular responsibilities. But, when it comes down to a question of who handles a particular piece of a particular situation, you'll probably find that the people enter negotiations where people in a boundary-oriented organization would enter legalistic proceedings.

Imposition of Artificial Boundaries (page 45)

Where have you seen "just a little wrong" theories that caused problems in software development?

The examples must, of course, come from your own experience. But you'll probably come up with examples where someone fine-tuned the theory (or a product design) so much that it ruled out some practical necessities or made it awkward to use in some required situations. Or you might recall examples where the choice of a standard implementation language was just slightly out of synch with the application needs, so a special class of support routines had to be written in at least one other language to make the implementation work well. Be careful with this last set of examples, though. This description could also apply to a software development effort that intentionally exploited two areas of order.

How might you intentionally set up productive boundaries for your projects?

The possibilities here are endless, but they need to be handled with care. If you know of a highly creative exploration of a particular area, you might impose standards (boundaries) that would prevent the use of more traditional solutions to the associated problem. This technique has been used for projects ranging from the development of IBM's first transistorized computers to the creation of application generators. Another way to set productive boundaries is to insist on adherence to certain standards. Of course, there's a responsibility that accompanies your setting of intentional boundaries. You must observe carefully and patiently to ensure that the results are actually as desired. When you use boundaries to make particular things happen, you should be prepared to accept and learn from some project failures without assigning fault to the people involved. After all, they're your boundaries.

Patterns and Perspectives (page 49)

What common practices do you know of that prevent the use of patterned techniques?

Probably the most common practice preventing the use of patterned techniques is that of coding the examples. This practice leads to programs that specifically check for department identifiers rather than having an externally defined, tabular definition of department identifiers. Even when not coding the examples, people tend to code the current process. To really use patterned techniques productively, it's necessary to implement an abstraction. Specifics belong in external definitions where possible or in support routines where necessary.

Other than decision tables, operating systems, and spreadsheets, how many examples of pattern-based tools can you name?

This one I can't even begin to answer for you, but you probably use more pattern-based tools than you realize. Look at the application packages you use the most—they're the most likely candidates. The most flexible of these are probably pattern-based.

Do you have views of your application needs (or anyone else's, for that matter) that could be used as the basis for pattern-based tools?

The approved answer is yes. The odds are that nearly everything you do with a computer is an example of what lots of other people are doing. If you abstract from your particular use to a general pattern of the needs of most (all) of the other people doing similar things, you have the basis for a patterned tool.

Implementing a Philosophy (page 52)

What conceptually fragmented products have you enjoyed using?

Again, I can't describe your exact experience. However, I can guess that your answer will include only products that satisfied two conditions. First, they satisfied an absolute need. They did something that you had to have done. Second, they were the only products you ever used to satisfy that particular associated need. I'd even guess that you don't explore the tool or use many of its capabilities beyond what you initially acquired it to do. The reason for that guess is that learning each new capability is like learning a whole new product (conceptual fragmentation, remember?) and that tends to be a frustrating experience.

How would you expect your customers to respond to your product if you could not describe its purpose, use, and structure in a straightforward, concise way?

Software developers want their customers to crow with delight over how wonderful a software product is. But the customers may not see the beauty of the product in the same way as the software developer. The developer loves the internal interplay of structures and components, the customer simply wants a tool to accomplish a job. Your hoped-for customers want conceptually coherent tools, and you should expect them to be upset with you if you do not satisfy their wants and needs.

Box 10—*Keeping the pool clean (page 35)*

If your group is gyrating wildly, how will you know whether to introduce an exciting, unifying idea to your people or to take them away from the problem for a day?

Patience may be the key word here. Wild gyrations over a short period of time may simply be the birthing pains of a new idea that can help your group significantly. You don't want to disrupt this disruption. But if the gyrations continue for an unreasonable length of time, they will take on a life of their own. This is what you want to disrupt, and a getaway day, a reminder of the guiding standards for the group, or the introduction of a new idea become necessary.

Box 11—*Customer involvement (page 36)*

Why do software development organizations believe that they can satisfy unknown customers?

This is a funny question, or at least one of the answers is. Software development organizations believe that they can satisfy unknown customers because most successful software development organizations have done just that. But the successes of those organizations can't be attributed to the lack of customer knowledge. Instead, the successes came in spite of the lack. Consider a shotgun pellet. When a shotgun pellet shatters a skeet (that clay thing you shoot at for practice), you could call that pellet successful. But that doesn't promise that all shotgun pellets will be successful, it just says that enough of them were in the vicinity to get the job done. The software development organizations that succeed with unknown customers are like the pellets that shattered the skeet. We don't know how many other software development organizations failed while using exactly the same customer knowledge—none—but we can guess that there must have been a bunch of them.

A second answer to the question is a bit more subtle. Some of the most wildly successful products in all marketplaces, not just software, have been products that were used for purposes that their designers never intended. You should strive to satisfy your customers as much as you can, but should do so in such a way that your product is extendable and exceeds what your immediate customer needs. This opens your opportunities to achieve surprise successes.

Box 12—*W. Edwards Deming: Out of the Crisis (page 41)*

If you see messages that feel like indictments coming from a figure with the success and stature of W. Edwards Deming, what would be a good business action for you to take?

The answer is simple to state but sometimes difficult to implement. A good business action would be to explore the indictments to see if they provide you with knowledge that you can use to improve your organization. The difficulty is that people are quite good at pretending that apparent bad news doesn't exist. If you see such denial in your organization, the organization may be due for some therapy.

Box 13—Generations of languages (page 47)

How can you turn the generation idea to your use in your work?

As you broaden your experience within an application area or across application areas, keep your eyes open for patterns of processing, patterns of specifications, and sources of errors. Exploiting the patterns and eliminating the sources of errors for your customers will lead you along the generation path. Incorporating advanced technologies along the way also will help to show you new patterns and ways to define new generations of your products. As a user, document your wish list and the generalizations you'd like to see in the products you use, and send them to software development organizations. Wouldn't you like it if product improvements were ideally suited to your needs? Software developers aren't very good at reading minds, but you can help them understand what you need.

Box 14—Tom Peters: Thriving on Chaos (page 48)

Is your organization stagnant or constantly changing?

I hope your answer is somewhere between the extremes in the question. "Constantly changing" carries overtones of so much change that the work of the organization can't be accomplished. Another description of this is that there is so much feedback and so much adjustment that the organization is in total disorder and therefore unable to function. "Stagnant" carries overtones of so little change that the organization will die from a bad case of obsolescence. The vibrant, dynamic organization is constantly changing, but the changes are chosen to be improvements (and allowed time to work), to disrupt disorder (look back to the answer for box 10 on page 191), or to force re-evaluation of an area that has not changed for an excessive length of time.

How can you create and exploit stable forces for change in your organization?

This question points to cultural influences in your organization. If you make heroes of the people who are innovative, recognize and reward innovations that contribute to the organization's success, and measure leaders on their attempts to find productive changes to make, you will encourage as an organizational culture a very stable force that still views change as a desirable way of life.

Box 15—Menuing philosophy (page 51)

What other common aspects of software development depend on having well-thought-out designs?

The answer to this question is really too simple. Good software development is critically dependent on having well-thought-out designs. The point of the question is this: If there's any aspect of your software development efforts that is not well thought out, it is either wrong or it is an experiment that is attempting to find out what might be right. Further, even aspects that have been well thought out should be revisited from time to time, because the world is constantly changing and analyses from the past may be invalid in today's environment.

How would you describe a working, coherent interface between software and users?

I hope you used such words as, "conceptually coherent," "relevant to the user's world view," "repeatable and extendable," and "delivering high function with low user effort." There are many criteria, but the key point is in the eyes of the user. Users don't want to master tools, they want to get work done. They need tools, and they need interfaces that make the tools so obvious and natural that they require no conscious attention. Given that such an interface is currently improbable, users want the closest approximation possible.

CHAPTER 4: WHAT CHAOS WE SEE IN SOFTWARE DEVELOPMENT

Methods and Technologies (page 55)

What parts of software development can you think of that depend on feedback but seem inherently orderly?

The parts you describe in your answer to this question are probably parts where experts perform their magic with high personal discipline. Causal analysis and high quality debugging might fit in this category.

What parts of software development can you think of that appear disorderly but don't have obvious feedback?

Here, you probably described parts where people are isolated from the others who receive their results or utilize their services. Remember that feedback leads to both areas of order and areas of disorder. Where you see disorder without obvious feedback, it might be time to introduce some feedback.

Problem Solving is Chaotic (page 57)

How would you know if a particular problem fits with a particular problem-solving technique?

Even as you answered "try it" you probably wondered why I asked this question. Unfortunately, there are many people in software development who believe that their favorite tool is the answer to all problems. Because of the inherent unpredictability involved in software development, we need to keep our eyes and minds open.

Should we expect any particular problem-solving technique to be applicable and productive for all problems?

The trivial and obvious answer to this question is no, but you need to achieve a balance. While no single technique can be universally applicable, you don't want to have one technique for each problem. You should explore problem-solving techniques to find which ones work for you and other people in your organization, and occasionally you should try new ones to keep your perspectives fresh. But it's also good to keep a primary set of problem-solving techniques in your bag of tricks.

Requirements Gathering is Chaotic (page 59)

What can you say about the relationship between the effectiveness of requirements and how happy the customer will be with the resultant product?

Since the word "effectiveness" is in the question, you would expect customers to be highly satisfied with the resultant product. But remember that requirements change over time. Given the best and most effective requirements, an extended development cycle without upgraded requirements can lead to a failed product. A requirements-gathering process should be active over the entire development cycle.

Who should be involved in defining the requirements for a product?

The obvious, flippant answer is everyone. The obvious wrong answer is "no one." Given the learning involved on all sides in gathering and defining requirements, the practical and desirable answer is, "real end-user customers, designers from the development team, and planners from both communities." And, as noted in the previous answer, requirements should be continuously validated throughout the development cycle to avoid the following interchange:
Development: "Here's what you ordered."
Customer: "That's no longer what I need."

Design is Chaotic (page 60)

Experienced developers can point both to projects that produced high-quality and imaginative products when the design was tightly controlled, and to projects that produced good results when the design group retained considerable flexibility. Can you identify a common factor that makes both work?

Yes, I'll beat on this topic, probably becoming a real nag. Theories of how software development ought to work are often based on successes from the past. But successful software development always happens when the involved people use the processes and controls as tools to make the right things happen.

Is it possible to predict the success or failure of a project by looking only at the process or processes that are supposed to be used?

Somehow I don't think you could have read this far in the book if your answer to this question is yes. The feedback involved in software development makes it chaotic. The creativity and learning involved make the prediction of final results even less predictable. Processes simply repeat things that have been done before. Still, carefully defined processes can provide support structures that help people to apply their creativity and personal discipline to make things work well. Looking strictly at the processes ignores the most critical factors in software development, the people.

Forecasting is Chaotic (page 62)

What other business aspects of software development cross from chaotic to fictitious behavior?

Whenever a part of the business is based on wishful thinking (to be carefully distinguished from hope followed by planning and exploration), it will cross that boundary. As such, this is a trap for the parts of the business that are often left as afterthoughts: marketing and support training come to mind.

Are your forecasters accountable for the accuracy of their forecasts?

This is a sanity check question. Forecasters often work their magic, then go on to the next project that needs a forecast. Some educational feedback is essential to the successful use of forecasting as a business tool.

When you start up a software development effort or propose one, how will you specify the role that forecasting will take in the effort?

Just as software development tools need to be matched with applications and people, so forecasting should be matched with the project. The involvement of potential customers is also important. You should work with your forecasters to use the services they can provide (maybe more than you might think) while watching out for fictitious results (which may be unintentionally fictitious).

Overload Makes It All Worse (page 64)

How do you react in an overload situation—by working harder, by overlooking quality or details, or by finding ways to simplify, eliminate, or reduce the overload?

The expeditious answers tend to be the most dangerous, as they lead to more overload. Postponing a problem, pretending that the problem doesn't exist, taking shortcuts, and hurrying through a job are all examples of expeditious answers. You will never correct an overload situation by dealing with its symptoms. You correct overload by making most of its symptoms unnecessary.

Which of the overload-handling techniques have you mastered?

As with problem-solving techniques, you'll need a bag of tricks to help you to resolve the situation. Probably the two most important things to remember are your most productive attitude and the most significant source of overload symptoms. The most productive attitude about overload is intolerance: As long as you tolerate overload and simply try to plow through, you'll stay in the overload situation. The most significant source of overload symptoms is "the way we do things around here." When your organization suffers from overload, it's past time to change your way of doing business.

Chaotic User Interface (page 65)

What would you expect of an application with no consistency or self-similarity in its user interface?

I'd guess you wouldn't buy an application like this unless it were the only one with the desired function in existence. But the inconsistent user interface will be a source of frustration that will be hard to dispel. If you're developing products, you'll want to provide user interfaces that have at least enough consistency to allow users to get started without training courses.

Where an application (for example, a spreadsheet) requires function with another shape (for example, printing), would you expect the user interfaces of the parts to be completely consistent with each other? (Does the printing user interface take formulas, or does the spreadsheet interface require single responses to queries for parameters?)

We can easily justify some inconsistencies in user interfaces, based on the needs of the various functions. But the impact on the user can be minimized, and the differing functional needs featured, if the application uses a cohesive interface style.

Chaotic Code and Data Structures (page 68)

Given the similarities we've noticed between user interface guidelines, design principles, coding structures, and data structures, should we expect that consideration for any of these should always take precedence over any of the others?

Every once in a while, you have to ask a question that has the answer imbedded in it. This is such a question. Software development is, and probably will always be, a balancing act. Whenever you approach a software development effort, you should identify the aspects of the effort that are the most critical, give those aspects a half a point higher priority, and then proceed with the effort giving balanced attention to all the aspects that pertain. To pursue any aspect at the expense of all others is to court disaster.

Are we wearing blinders if we try to believe that any particular part of an application can be fully completed (functionally, structurally, or by interface) before the rest of the application can be begun?

This is also an "obvious" question. We need to remove our blinders to all kinds of things if we want to be successful in developing software. The pertinent blinders involve not only these noted parts of an application, but also the business parts of development and the environment in which the whole organization exists.

Strange Software Development (page 69)

Assuming that your development processes have multiple stable states, how might you identify variables in the environment that might influence the processes toward more desirable states?

Dichotomies in an organization provide considerable information. When people talk about doing a balancing act between schedule and quality, between performance and storage, and between long-term and short-term results, for example, the associated dichotomies tell you about variables you can use. Looking at the entire set of dichotomies you can find, pick the priorities that characterize the organizational state you find the most desirable. Then capture those priorities in the guiding standards for the organization and support them with your most diligent efforts. This will give a strong cultural influence toward the state you desire the most.

What tendencies within an organization might make the organization cycle around if the tendencies were unchecked?

Probably the strongest such tendency in an organization is the tendency to change optimization criteria. For example, an organization might focus on producing code for a while, then focus on exercising test cases, then focus on performance, then focus on quality, then focus on schedule, then go back to test cases, then focus on quality, and so on. Each point of focus would be a current hot button, possibly something an executive asked about in the last status meeting. But the changing emphases within the group would cause different stable states and fragmented efforts that would be counterproductive for the overall project.

Box 16—SWAT Teams (page 56)

Have you seen a project of any size that did not require SWAT teams at some time?

This is unlikely. All the dynamics of software development indicate that problems will crop up from time to time and that the most difficult problems will involve multiple groups. That makes SWAT teams (or a war room approach, task forces, or whatever you'd like to call it) nearly inevitable.

Have you seen SWAT teams abused? How have they been abused?

This is very likely. Used sparingly, SWAT teams help to resolve problems quickly and effectively. But given their successes, people get tempted by the "more is better" idea and start to use SWAT teams everywhere. This is counterproductive and can actually stop a project in its tracks (and has done so).

Box 17—Working harder (page 63)

How do you know when an overload situation can be resolved by working harder and when it requires working smarter?

This is a distance question. If you can honestly and intelligently see how to reach the end of the project or the boundaries of the overload with a small increment of effort, working harder can be the best answer. However, if you're far from the end of the project (again, be honest and intelligent when you evaluate this) or if it requires a large increment of effort to reach the boundaries of the overload, working harder is suicide. In the latter case, the overload is a symptom of a broken project and you need to solve that problem to make the overload disappear. In looking at overload situations, be very careful not to fool yourself. You're fooling yourself if you think you can cannibalize your emergency response resource (SWAT teams and so on) to make up the difference. You're fooling yourself if you de-emphasize your attention to quality in order to increase production.

What balance between working harder and working smarter would be most productive in your organization?

The typical answer to this question leans incorrectly toward working harder. To achieve and maintain a competitive edge, working smarter is best. Of course, in a really exciting organization people work hard at working smarter.

CHAPTER 5: HOW SOFTWARE DEVELOPMENT TRIED TO AVOID DISORDER

Although some of your favorite techniques aren't in this chapter, will you evaluate them from the chaotic point of view?

Obviously, I hope your answer is yes. Otherwise, you may be missing some important insights into how your favorite techniques work. Wouldn't you like to know improved ways to use them? Wouldn't you like to know about any hidden traps that you might be able to avoid?

Software Engineering (page 74)

How do you keep in touch with theoretical and practical work in the area of software engineering?

Look at what you do today to stay in touch with current and coming technologies. Are you sure that those efforts are adequate?

What kind of partnership can you form with the software engineering community so that they can look for methods and techniques that would be applicable to your environment?

Think about working with consultants from local universities, establishing study projects with other people in your organization, even benchmarking (as associated with the Malcolm Baldrige National Quality Award), and paying for memberships in professional societies as ways to stay up to date on software engineering.

How closely does your environment match the environment required for successful use of software engineering techniques?

This depends on your organization, obviously. The odds are that your organization has some of the attributes required, is close on others, and is quite different in some ways. You can compare your environment with that required for software engineering disciplines, and decide what you should do with your organization. This is a far better approach than the wishful thinking used in some organizations.

Pillars and Foundations of Software Engineering (page 76)

What kinds of preproject activities could you use to ensure that your project could use existing software engineering techniques?

Once you see the pillars, the answer to this question should come easily (even if making it happen isn't so easy). Hiring, training, experience, technology, and requirements are the keys. Make them happen.

Are there other ways to expand the bounds of the applicability of software engineering?

This is part of the reason why you should try to stay in touch with the software engineering community. Many people are working towards advances in software engineering technology. When these advances become practical and available, you could be among the first to benefit from them. Also, appropriate leadership of your organization can encourage the increased self-discipline that will also expand the bounds of your use of software engineering technologies.

Can software engineering help to build software right the first time?

By itself, software engineering can't help to build software right the first time. The creative front-end efforts (requirements and design) have to be well defined and established before current software engineering disciplines can add their benefits.

Do It Right the First Time (page 77)

Does your organization have a balanced mix of people that will enable it to handle the disorder of learning and invention while gaining the benefits of order?

This question is to focus your attention on your group. You can do something right the first time if you recognize the dynamics of doing so and have people who will make those dynamics work for you. But if the mix of people in your organization isn't sufficiently diverse or flexible, you won't get the dynamics that can make it happen. In that case, you should use some other approach.

Is it possible to develop a new product in a totally orderly fashion, perhaps by using a well-defined set of requirements?

This is a lead-in question. Typically, developing a new product is a more disorderly endeavor than developing a release of an existing product. However, outstanding requirements can help you to develop a new product with a mostly orderly process.

Requirements (page 83)

Consider requirements listed in a document, stated as a simple point by point list of requirements, gathered by people with widely diverse backgrounds. What is the value of this document?

Such a document has minimal value, if any at all. There's so much room for interpretation in individual items in a list that getting any understanding of a complete set of requirements based on a complete list is nearly impossible. Add the diverse backgrounds of the people who contributed to the list, and you guarantee that an implementation based on those requirements will miss the need.

If your product requirements show signs of being put together without having one or more of the six categories covered, how will you proceed with the project?

The choices are simple here. You have three. One is to muddle through in spite of the deficit and hope that it won't hurt the product too much. The second is to fix the deficit, bringing the requirements up to usability. The third is to find another way to handle the requirements, possibly by having customers work directly with developers.

What tools might you acquire that might help you to do your whole project better?

Ah yes, another lead-in question. Increasingly, there are tools available to help with software development, including requirements gathering. These tools fit under the heading of Computer Aided Software Engineering (CASE).

Computer Aided Software Engineering (page 85)

Have you heard CASE advocates claim that their favorite tools can solve all software development problems?

Don't take the easy way out and say that CASE advocates are like snake oil salesmen. It's natural for people to believe that their particular world view applies to everyone and everything. CASE tools have considerable value and you can derive significant benefits from finding tools that are suitable for use in your organization.

Did they explain the associated world view so you could understand the area where you could believe the claims?

This is one of the key points in selecting CASE tools. If the world view associated with the tool is conformable to world views in your organization, and if the tool provides for import and export of information so that you can integrate the tool with others, you probably have a winner for your organization.

Do your criteria for selecting or rejecting CASE tools include procedural, declarative, or object-oriented considerations?

The broader your perspective, your way of looking at your projects, and the tools available to you, the better your decisions will be when you select or reject CASE tools. This will depend on the technologies and methodologies in use in your projects, as well as whether you're early or late in your project cycle. Early in a project it's easy to adopt a new technology, but it's more difficult later on.

Object-Oriented Processing, et al (page 88)

Do you have enough experience with object-oriented techniques to evaluate their use in your project's disciplines?

Many available software development methodologies require significantly different world views for their productive use. Often, a methodology or technology can't even be evaluated adequately without mastering the associated world view. Examples include not only the object-oriented view, but declarative languages, artificial intelligence engines, and smooth end-user interfaces.

How might you demonstrate that the area of order for your favorite implementation and design disciplines is adequate to the needs of the application you're building?

You should at least try to think about this before building your product. You'll eventually get an answer based on sales of the product, but it would be much better for your peace of mind to have explored the fit.

Stake-in-the-ground Design (page 91)

How could you use several stakes to offer some comfort and security to your peers who prefer the stake-in-the-ground approach?

Using stakes gets dangerous when people confuse trials with requirements. Using several stakes actually provides some protection against the danger by retaining the notion that there are still choices to be made. Be careful, though, so that you don't get trapped into thinking that the initial set of stakes is a complete set of the possible choices. Your best answer may still come from another solution.

If your development group is large, how could you clearly identify stakes so that you could reap their benefits while avoiding their traps?

Identification is the key part of this question. As long as you can identify stakes and have people treat them appropriately, you can reap the benefits of the approach. You might identify pilot projects as explorations of particular stakes.

What management style would be the most dangerous in a group using stakes?

Still another lead-in question. The most dangerous management style when using the stake in the ground approach is the style that insists on full change control, locking the project into the first stake that was chosen.

Micromanagement (page 93)

Do you see the micromanagement symptoms in your organization?

Most people have some tendency to use micromanagement techniques, so it would be a surprise not to see some of the symptoms.

What education and experience might you pursue if you discovered that you were a micromanager and wanted to learn better habits?

Antidotes for micromanagement attitudes include education and experience in team building, leadership, and empowerment. In addition, taking an active role in increasing your people's expertise and capabilities will help you to understand that they need room to contribute rather than restrictions to prevent failure. Failure is a key point. Your people need opportunities to fail so that they can grow and learn to avoid future failures.

Fire Fighting in the Midst of Chaos (page 95)

What can you say about organizations that receive reports of trouble and respond either in knee-jerk fashion or by ignoring the reports?

> First, the two organizations have immense commonality. They both exhibit undifferentiated responses. The difference is in the attitude they have toward the world. The knee-jerk organization has an error-prone attitude: every trouble report means something is wrong, fix it. The ignoring organization has an attitude of denial: no trouble report has any merit. Neither is appropriate in real software development, but both are common.

What can you learn from all the things in this chapter that might help you with your work?

> The good news and bad news in this chapter should help you to recognize the balance that is needed in your organization. You should see some things here that reflect things that you're doing well. You may also see some things here that indicate ways in which your organization could improve.

Box 18–Frederick P. Brooks, Jr.: "No Silver Bullets" (page 72)

Do you have a favorite "silver bullet" that would solve all software development problems if people would just wake up and use it?

> People commonly identify single causes and single solutions to complex problems. If you have identified one of either, consider the following observations: First, get a firm grip on your pride and whatever it is that you identified. The odds are that you have identified something significant and worth pursuing. Second, try your solution or create a solution that handles the cause you identified. You'll probably find that there are other causes and other solutions. That's all right. Third, with your new knowledge of causes and solutions, pursue the set you feel is most significant. Collections of partial solutions are still highly significant in software development. We need all the help we can get.

If so, how drastically will the software development industry have to change to exploit the benefits of your particular "silver bullet"?

> The really fascinating thing about silver bullet solutions is that they work within particular areas of order. If the software development industry fit completely within one area of order, we could expect a small number of silver bullets to make things much better. Therefore, the software development industry could simply get in the same area of order and things would be wonderful. Unfortunately, that's not

too likely. Remember that this is a chaotic business and inherently has multiple areas of order. It would not work to force the entire industry to occupy a single area of order. But use your silver bullet in the area of order where it's appropriate. Fixing one area is much better than leaving all of the areas untreated because you can't fix them all.

Box 19–A need for order and a chaotic organization—a broken team (page 73)

What would you expect to happen if you formed a team of people who are not suited to the jobs involved?

You should expect strange results if you formed a team that was not suited to the job at hand. In many cases the people involved will have the flexibility to adjust to the new environment, but in many cases they won't. With the most flexible people, you'll get some success. But the more likely result is high levels of frustration for you and the rest of the people involved.

Do you want heavy-duty innovators on a straight coding job? Do you want coders (no matter how experienced) performing an innovative design job?

These are examples of mismatches that could lead to disaster. People have things that they do well and that they enjoy doing. You'll get the best results if you form groups with people do those particular things well, who enjoy doing those things, or who want to grow into doing them. Innovators are not ideally suited to the job of coding from a specification. Coders are not ideally suited to the job of creating an innovative design.

Box 20–Frederick P. Brooks, Jr.: The Mythical Man-Month (page 77)

If you haven't read *The Mythical Man-Month* recently, why do you think you are immune to the mistakes and oversights that are preventable based on the knowledge contained in this classic?

That's a nudge. There's lots of good information in the literature of computer science, and the information presented by Frederick P. Brooks is excellent. You can learn lessons from Brooks or you can learn them from painful experience. If you're involved in software development for very long, you'll learn those lessons one way or another. I recommend the less painful way.

Box 21–Philip W. Metzger: Managing Programming People (page 78)

How often do we succumb to the arrogant tendency to define our development processes solely based on our own experience? Why might you think that you could successfully define a process or build a product without looking at the wisdom and experience of people like Frederick P. Brooks and Philip W. Metzger?

Again, there's wisdom in the literature that you can get without going through a lot of pain. Even if you disagree with such authors as Frederick P. Brooks and Philip W. Metzger, being aware of their ideas and experiences can help you to avoid some major problems.

Box 22—Customer surrogates (page 79)

What customer surrogates drive your projects?

Every application program is written for some customer. The development group that has a clear idea of the attributes of that customer has a much better chance of implementing a cohesive application. If each developer has a unique and individual customer surrogate in mind, the application will probably be fragmented.

How might you ensure that you have the best set of customer surrogates for your work?

One way to get good customer surrogates into developers' heads is to have the developers meet and work with real customers. Another way is to have the developers work at the customers' jobs until they understand some of the frustrations and other considerations. A third way is to incorporate customers into the development team. A fourth is to have designated team members who have good customer surrogates in their heads and who will serve as arbitrators of all decisions related to customer needs and desires. There are lots of workable techniques. The one technique that is not workable is to simply assume that everyone knows what customers want and will provide it.

Box 23–Mixed organization with flexible needs—a broken team (page 82)

Are the world views represented in your organization conformable?

You need variety in your organization, but that variety requires that the involved people understand and respect each other. World views will be conformable if people allow them to be. World views will never be conformable if the people in the organization wear "turf battle" glasses.

Do you have a vision, mission, goals, and a set of guiding values to help to keep your organization on track?

When a variety of world views is represented in an organization, something is needed to keep the entire organization productive and on track. Having an established vision, mission, goals, and guiding values is an excellent way to encourage the unity of purpose that will do so.

How many chaotic failures in organizations can be traced back to incompatible assumptions that lead to conflicting responses to feedback?

The flippant answer to this question is "all of them." While that's a good approximation, the answer is incomplete. Remember that feedback leads to chaos and chaos is inherently unpredictable. Incompatible assumptions are the obvious way to get conflicting responses, but the inherent chaos is another way. Turning the question around, we find a cautionary note. Conflicting responses don't necessarily come from incompatible assumptions. It's reasonable to check on people's assumptions, but it may be counterproductive to try to fix people's attitudes when they aren't really in disagreement.

Box 24—Dataflow processing view (page 87)

If you don't know the flow of data in your organization, what confidence do you have in the mutual support of your processes?

There's lots to be learned about the information-processing needs of an organization from the flow of data throughout the organization. Without knowing the flow of data you may have high confidence, but the confidence may well be misplaced. Consider learning about data flow, and use the flow of data within your organization as a real learning tool. I think you'll be pleased with what you learn and surprised at the misconnections you'll find between your processes.

Box 25—Orderly organization with unknown requirements—a broken team (page 90)

What kinds of mindsets would lead people to form teams such as those broken teams?

Other boxes describe several different kinds of teams, some functional and some dysfunctional. The message of each of these team boxes is that functional teams are compatible with their development needs and that dysfunctional teams are incompatible. The typical mindset that leads to dysfunctional teams has two key attributes. The first attribute is the conviction that a particular world view is the right world view. The second attribute is the conviction that there is no need to validate the first one. I used the word "conviction" in this, but it's not that intentional. The odds are that the people with those convictions aren't even aware of them. Left to their own devices, they wouldn't become aware of the convictions until the trauma of a project failure forced them to be.

Is there something you can do to ensure that you don't do that to any of your people, and nobody does that to you?

When you're in the leadership role, you can guard against the phenomenon of dysfunctional teams by applying what you've learned here. Establish the guiding standards for your organization, pursue those standards in your decisions, and watch carefully for the signs of resultant disorder. If you discover disorder, you may have to adjust the standards or adjust the people. Possibly, you can retain the standards and organize the group so that people have responsibilities suitable for their significant contribution.

If you're not in the leadership role, your actions must be a little different. Try to have an influence on the guiding standards, to ensure that you can work within them in good conscience. Watch carefully for signs of disorder arising from your efforts. If you discover disorder, you have three obvious options (and maybe a few less-obvious ones as well). First, work with your peers and the organization's leaders to resolve the disorder. If it's not possible to resolve the disorder, vote with your feet (and find a more suitable place to give your unique contribution). In between the two, if you choose not to leave the organization you can often carve out a niche where you can give your contribution without being a proximate cause of disorder.

Box 26—Pilot induced oscillation (page 92)

How would you know if your attempts to control were causing problems?

One of the best—if somewhat shocking—ways to find out if you're overcontrolling is to stop controlling at all. Pilots learn to let go of the control stick completely. Take a vacation, if you can delegate responsibility to someone who won't make any decisions. Assign yourself to a task force otherwise, so that you just don't have time to make the controlling decisions. If work (or a particular kind of work) stops or if work goes more smoothly while you're "away," you've been overcontrolling the project. This might be traumatic to the people who might have learned to wait for your decisions.

What micromanagement techniques are deadly to software development organizations?

The dual answers are "all of them" and "none of them." For the second answer, there are places in software development where micromanagement works. I suspect that the number of such places is considerably smaller than the existing number of micromanagers. For the first answer, micromanagement is basically incompatible with most software development efforts. As many micromanagers as possible should work to overcome their handicap.

Box 27—Real fire fighting (page 94)

What might you conclude about any software development organization that focussed on one single point of view, one single approach to business, or one single method for solving problems?

I would conclude that such a software development organization would survive as long as its current product sold well. Then, it would become a business failure. No business survives forever without adapting to the changing world around it, and I certainly would not expect a software development organization to have any more stability than any other business.

CHAPTER 6: WHAT SOFTWARE DEVELOPMENT SHOULD DO

Chaos, Good and Bad (page 98)

Have you experienced situations in which the lack of a "devil's advocate" allowed a disaster to happen?

Even if you haven't experienced such a situation, you've probably seen them in the news. Feedback leads to chaos, which includes both areas of order and areas of disorder, but the feedback usually allows us to identify and occupy areas of order. Lack of feedback can lead to situations that are worse. Without a contrary voice, lacking a system of checks and balances, disaster is all too likely.

Have you been on a project that was scuttled because no two people could pull in the same direction?

This is another version of inadequate feedback, but one that never seems to become newsworthy. Often, when an organization has no guiding standards and has ineffective communications it never really becomes effective.

How would you steer a course between these two extremes to produce the best possible results?

The first case often comes from overwhelming but narrow guidance, the second from lack of guidance or guidance that people in the organization do not endorse. To steer between the extremes, you need leadership skills and guidance standards that are balanced, comprehensive, and commonly adopted by people in your organization. Leadership skills and the balance of values (for example, "make the best decisions" provides much better guidance than "support the leader") help to prevent the first case, because effective devil's advocates are balancing influences. Leadership skills and a significant agreement with the guiding standards help to prevent the second case.

Can your current process deal with multisite development?

The level of communication required for multisite development differs significantly from that required for single-site development. Also, even if the balance of work is carefully considered, the communications between sites will tend to increase the bounds of feedback, which are the bounds of chaos on the project. If those concerns haven't been addressed in using your current process for multisite development, your process can easily be a barrier to progress rather than a tool for achieving progress.

Is it flexible enough to allow different people, groups, and goals to contribute positively to your product?

A process should have enabling as well as controlling and bounding features. This is a lead-in question for the next section.

Controls Versus Enablers in Software Development (page 103)

How would you know if you had a good balance of controls and enablers in your projects?

Two key indicators in your answer should be project success and what people say when they talk about the control mechanisms. But project success or failure happens far too late to be useful in improving the balance within a project. So, listening when the project's people talk is key to achieving a good balance. But there's one additional thing that has to be done, even before you believe what you hear. People can only report based on what they know and what they feel. People on the project need to be aware of the possibilities of control and enabling so that they can reach good conclusions and tell about them. Part of the leadership responsibility is to provide training and experience in control and enabling.

What relationships do you need between your people to make the enablers work most effectively?

Any discussion of enabling and empowerment is incomplete unless it includes leadership and trust.

Teamwork (page 104)

How do you know your effectiveness when you are trying to take care of these teamwork issues *and* make technical decisions on a project at the same time?

When the teamwork issue touches a relationship between you and one of your peers, an associated technical decision is actually helpful in forming a good working relationship. Both can be handled at once. In general, you should handle consistent levels of teamwork issues and technical decisions. Thus, a high-level leader should deal with major teamwork issues and make technical decisions that provide major guidance for the team. If there is simply too much for the leader to do, requiring a choice between teamwork issues and technical decisions, the leader should always choose the teamwork issues. The alternative degrades the team.

What ideas can you extract from the parallel between a team and a collection of technologies for organizations that might exploit multiple technologies in a single project?

There's no new news in this question, just a strong reminder about making the most effective use of people and resources. To exploit multiple technologies, you will apply each where they apply, in their own areas of order, and make the interfaces between them as smooth and as clean as possible. To allow team members to contribute their best, you will allow each to adopt responsibilities according to his or her capabilities and desires, and make all their interactions as cooperative and smooth as possible. The self-similarities in the various aspects of software development provide some real opportunities for those who care to notice and exploit them.

Prescriptions for Exploiting Development's Fractal Nature (page 105)

When can you most productively select the tools you will use in support of your project?

The approved answer is "It depends." Major tools for the project may have to be selected some time before the project begins, so people can be trained and gain some experience in their use. At the other end of the spectrum, we find tools that turn out to be needed on the project although that need was not predicted. Those tools, of course, have to be invented after the need becomes apparent. You need to look at the selected implementation technology for the project and acquire a reasonable set of tools to make that technology work most effectively. Then you need to monitor project activity to ensure that things are working smoothly and that immediate-need tools are implemented or acquired appropriately.

What balance can you achieve in your selection of tools and processes between absolute knowledge, which comes too late to be useful, and theoretical guesswork, which comes too early?

The simple answer is fifty percent. If you wait until the need for a tool is fully apparent, the wait for the tool will have an impact on the project's schedule. But the cost for some tools is quite high, so you'll want to be a little careful that you don't blow the entire project budget on accumulating tools that "might be needed." The key word to keep in mind is, in fact, balance. If you strive for a productive balance rather than following an absolute priority, your decisions will probably work out well.

Separate the Processes According to Their Goals (page 106)

Can we expect different groups to have identical goals for their respective processes? If so, why do they have separate processes? If not, how would you keep them working toward the common project goal?

This is the (by now) familiar idea of having people work in appropriate areas of order. Normally, you should expect different groups to have different immediate goals for their processes. The second part of the question points out that two groups working in the same area of order should probably have the same process or processes with significant commonality (unless they're experimenting to discover possible improvements, of course). For the third part of the question, an organization really needs common guiding standards to keep the various groups aligned. The guiding standards include the organization's vision, mission, values, and goals. Part of the leadership responsibilities for the organization includes enrolling people in support of the guiding standards and keeping the guiding standards in tune with the needs of customers and the people in the organization.

Business Process (page 107)

What parts of a good business process require knowledge of the technology being used?

Planning, estimating, and tracking require knowledge of the technology, and will be fictitious exercises without it.

How could you demonstrate that a business process enhanced or degraded a development project?

With a good working partnership between people using the development process and people using the business process, you can get consensus about the impact of the business process on the project. This requires the business people to have some knowledge of what's going on in the development effort and the developers to have some understanding of the business. Without such cross understanding and without the good working partnership, any conclusions about the relationship between the processes will be based on presumption, not on reality.

What kind of people could design good business processes and what would he or she need to know?

Because of the close similarity between processes and programs, you'd really like to have a good designer involved in the creation of a business process. But just being a good designer isn't nearly enough. A thorough and practical knowledge of the business would also be needed, as well as a good working knowledge of the development processes to be used. It might be a good idea to consider the set of processes as a system, and to design the entire system as an entity, rather than to create the collection of processes one at a time.

Implementation Process (page 108)

If this section deals with a topic that is so critical, why is it so short?

I'll keep the answer short, too. The section is so short because its content is spread throughout the book.

Management Process (page 108)

What signs can you look for that might indicate conflict between a management process and either a business or a technical process?

The standard signs of disorder in an organization are sufficient. People tend to take their processes personally; when the processes conflict, you'll hear lots of we-they griping in both camps. You'll see decisions that are made but never implemented quite completely. Also, you'll see indications that the people involved want to tighten the controls on the other group as a means of damage control.

Select Workable Processes According to the Situation (page 109)

What parts of typical projects and situations are considered in selecting processes?

Too often, current situations aren't considered when selecting or defining processes. People tend to define their processes based solely on their beliefs about what contributed to their past successes.

Business Process (page 109)

What indications should you expect to see if your chosen business process is incompatible with the selection factors discussed above?

Incompatibilities will show as areas where lots of special decisions have to be made. By tracking the sources of the problems, you will be able to identify the conflicts and begin to change the processes to adjust.

Does your process address all of the factors that apply to your customers and products?

You probably don't need to address all the factors, but you should at least consider them when you define or adopt your processes. Then you should watch for the signs of incompatibility in case you need to adjust.

Implementation Process (page 111)

What indications would you expect to see if your chosen implementation process were incompatible with the selection factors listed above?

The answer here is the same as to the similar question in the previous section. The areas where you spend most of your special case efforts are strong indicators of incompatibility between processes and needs.

Does your process address all of the factors that apply to your technology and people?

The most probable answer to this question is no, but the process shouldn't have to handle all the factors in complete detail. A process, particularly in software development, is a framework that allows people to focus on their work. Consider all the factors when you define your processes, then watch for signs of trouble.

Management Process (page 112)

If the management process is out of synch with the needs of the project, which is most likely to suffer?

Ultimately, the project itself will suffer. The management process is not something separate that continues no matter what. It is simply one of the processes involved in getting a job done and it is subject to potential for gain and susceptibility to flaws just like other processes.

What indications should you expect to see if your chosen management process were incompatible with the selection factors discussed above?

You should have this answer down pat by now. Refer to the similar questions in previous sections.

Ensure that the Processes Are Compatible (page 113)

How would you know whether your candidate processes would work well together?

Enough system modelling to see if your processes will work together would be highly appropriate. You can expect that processes defined independently, without consideration for other processes, will not work well together. This is true both in their initial form and in adjusted forms as people try to make the system work. Processes defined to work together stand a much better chance of actually doing so.

How can you gain the benefits of specialization while avoiding communication blockages?

Allowing people to work in their area of interest and ability while including responsibility, negotiation, and the pursuit of common purposes, you will satisfy both parts of the question. You may also need to provide training in related skills and education about how you expect the group to function.

Measure Your Results (page 114)

What can you predict for a project when its people twist their measurements to agree with the estimates or the plans?

This is another of those questions where the right answer is obvious but software development teams choose the wrong answer anyway. The right answer is that distorted measurements significantly increase the probability that the project will fail, making it almost a certainty. This really hinges on the definition of success. When there is a strong emphasis on the measurements rather than on what is being developed, people tend to lose track of the importance of the project. Once the project direction is lost, we can probably start to write its obituary.

Verify/Challenge the Selected Processes Constantly (page 114)

If you suspect that your project or process isn't working properly and your process measurements look normal, how would you decide what action might be necessary?

This looks like a situation where a getaway day might be appropriate. When the measurements are all within expected ranges but the project seems to be headed for trouble, you need to know three things. First, are the measurements worth anything? Despite your original hopes, the selected measurements for the project may not indicate anything significant. Second, are the measurements being faked? This is intolerable in a project and may require a change in emphasis by all its leaders. Third, is the process, or any process in the project, getting in the way of productive work? Through various discussions, interviews, and other feedback mechanisms that are part of a getaway day, you can find very good indicators about the workings of the processes. There may be process problems, there may be measurement problems, or your suspicions may themselves be derived from marginal sources. Whatever you find out, you can adjust as appropriate, use the getaway day to enhance communication in the group, and reinforce the guiding standards for the group.

Box 28—Flexible maintenance team (page 99)

Would this situation (and the product) be less or more stable, over the long run, if developers and maintainers were isolated from each other?

Any temptation to isolate the groups from each other should be resisted. These teams are clearly working in an area of order that is strengthened by short feedback paths. Increased isolation would lengthen the feedback paths, increase the bounds on the area of order, and decrease the stability of the relationship. This is an invitation to disorder.

How might more formal control and rigor help or hinder the efforts of this team?

This issue should be handled very carefully. More formal control and rigor would be appropriate only if it would help the groups to increase their knowledge of related activities and to ensure that problems would be fully accounted for. If the increased control and rigor became distracting or interfered with communications between the groups (really, not theoretically), it would cause separation of the groups, leading to the isolation problems noted in the previous question.

Box 29—Dynamic development team (page 101)

What companies can you think of that already use some of the techniques mentioned for this team?

Hopefully, the companies you mentioned are dynamic, up-and-coming companies. This kind of development doesn't fit well with more stable, traditional companies. If you find more traditional companies with this kind of team, you should also expect to see considerable internal turmoil in the company, and you might see moves to transform the company to make it more dynamic.

Box 30—Time-critical maintenance (page 105)

If your situation calls for time-critical maintenance, do you want to have team members who thrive on putting out fires? Or would you prefer to have team members who prefer to prevent problems? Could you productively compose your team of members from each camp?

These questions deal directly with the chaotic aspects of the situation. Team members who thrive on quick fixes are people who give chaotic kicks to the system based on short-term needs. In a software maintenance group, this is a strong influence toward disorder. On the other hand, having people who thrive on prevention will be unlikely to give the kind of problem response that is necessary. Initially you might compose your team of members from each camp, but to do so productively you'd want to use a buddy system. You'd want each quick fixer to be paired with a preventer, and vice versa. Possibly a better team makeup would be to have experienced team members (those with a long range view but the willingness to solve immediate problems) at the core of the team. These core team members would also serve as mentors to junior members of the team (those who initially thrive on quick fixes) to help the junior members to achieve the maturity and long-range view required as they too grow to become core members of the team.

Box 31—Breakthrough development (page 110)

What business areas can you think of where a broad, highly varied exploration would be productive?

The business area is probably less important than your competitive situation. If you are well established with a product, you need to take care of your existing customers, both by maintaining support for their current work and by expanding what you can help them do in the future. If you are breaking into an existing product area or defining a new one, breakthrough development would be highly appropriate.

CHAPTER 7: A PROCESS THAT EXPLOITS CHAOS

Overview (page 121)

Does your most used development process consider the kinds of work to be done in a variety of situations?

Consider a range of opportunities hinted at in this question that are related to this section. The section actually describes a network of processes, which is one way to handle a variety of situations. Yet the question is asked as though you had only one process. If one uniquely specified process is to handle a variety of situations, the process must have considerable built-in flexibility. In the extreme, this amounts to having no process at all.

Can your process or processes support a variety and mixture of needs for innovation, discipline, rigor, and productivity?

This question is more aligned to what your process or processes actually do rather than to the variety of situations that are to be covered. Every productive software development process must support innovation, discipline, rigor, and productivity. If your processes don't do that, you and the people around you are blocked from your best contribution.

What do your processes look like?

This is a lead-in question for the next section. Nearly all software development processes lend themselves to some kind of visualization, whether it's the waterfall process, the spiral process, or this next process, which looks like a laser.

Laser Analogy (page 122)

What other analogies might you use to devise productive processes?

After exploring the laser analogy for this process, you might want to explore other analogies.

One example might be the embryonic development of animals. As animals go through their embryonic development, they pass through forms that mimic stages of evolution. You could devise software development processes that were staged to roughly parallel the generations of languages. The first, prototype stage would be a collection of programs that handled the individual needs of the application. The second, base application stage would use the requirements gathered from the first stage to build a traditional application. The third, generator stage would use customer feedback and the capabilities of the application to build a generalized product for a class of applications. The fourth stage would again use customer feedback and the experience with the generalized product to build an artificial intelligence or object-oriented application that would have immense flexibility and extensibility.

Another example might be the cooperative efforts required for the stage production of a new play. The software development industry might not be ready for this level of division of labor yet, but stage productions entail amazing numbers of responsibilities and high levels of cooperation between all of the people involved. With the increasing emphasis on processes, the possibility exists that some particular scheme of labor division may be so highly productive that the software development industry would naturally adopt it. In terms of chaos, this simply means identifying a unifying area of order that covers more of software development than we've covered in the past.

Project Staffing (page 123)

Is your current management scheme up to the challenge of the movement of people and ideas required for this fractal process?

A management scheme based on specific responsibilities and on obtaining and holding human resources—people—will not be up to the challenge presented by this fractal process. A management scheme based on resource pools to be allocated according to personal and project needs will do much better. People and ideas must flow if this fractal process is to work. Management must enhance rather than restrict the flow.

Does the culture of your organization show enough respect for everyone in the group to allow this process to work?

High levels of mutual respect are required if this fractal process is to work. Turf battles can be deadly to the project and the process. The only reliable way to keep the project and process going is for the organization to have guiding standards (superordinate goals, or a compelling set of vision, mission, goals, and values) and full respect for people with differing areas of expertise. The project must be led in a positive way.

Work Flow (page 124)

How might work flow and idea flow happen without people flow within a group?

Olson's first law of computing is "There's always another way." If you must have a fixed organizational structure, you can still get the idea and work flow required to make this fractal process work. If the people can't go to the work, let the work come to them. Departments can serve as resource pools and various parts of the development work can be adopted within a department based on the skills of the people rather than the name of the department. Idea flow can always be handled by various kinds of get-togethers, formal and informal; it can be encouraged by the physical layout of the work facility; and it can be encouraged by shoving people out of their offices from time to time. Once again, the key factors are supporting people in the best contribution they can give, having strong guidance for the entire group, and maintaining high levels of mutual respect.

When the size of a group requires high formality in communications, how might you devise ways to continue the flows without jeopardizing that formality?

Translated into different terms, how do you get high levels of order in an area of high feedback? The key points in this question are timing and documentation. If the formality of communication is to be so high that every exchange of information must be documented in detail, then the project had better be one that clearly satisfies the conditions of the Pillars of Software Engineering. Fully documented communication means slow communication (and "slow" might be the reason why it has to be fully and formally documented), so any required learning is feedback and the bounds of chaos will be large. More particularly, since this question indicates size as the reason for the formality, you can approach the communication in two stages. The first stage is very intensive, informal, and potentially disorderly—information interchange and negotiation. In this stage, people actually communicate what they're doing and what they're concerned about, and they work through the alternatives that are always available. The second stage transforms the results of the first stage into the documentation needed for the formality of communication, which probably is required so that the rest of the group can know what's going on. The formality helps to extend the area of order for overall communication in the group, but that's still just an extension. As groups get larger, communication needs can impose ever-higher burdens on the people in the project, tending to overwhelm their ability to produce with the need to communicate.

Another way to handle required formality is actually complementary with the method noted above. If the reason for the formality is to have full knowledge of what is going on, you can use computer conferencing as a preferred means of communication. For this to work, the communication must actually be less formal, so that people can express opinions and explore alternatives without being locked into early guesses. But the computer conferencing method of communication is inherently documentable. People can then explore and share ideas, document their agreements, and have all the background of decisions available for others who may want to understand how and why particular decisions were made. This assumes, of course, that the reasons for the formality are positive in terms of the people and the project rather than negative in terms of assessing blame.

How does communications in the fractal process compare with communications in the surgical team as described by Frederick P. Brooks?

One of Brooks' reasons for forming "surgical teams" was to significantly reduce the amount of communication required in a software development project. If you have a project of 200 people, there are 19,900 possible communication links between them. If you can organize those people into groups of 10, you will have 20 teams, and the number of possible communication links between teams will be reduced to 190. To make this work, you have to formalize communications somewhat, having team leaders (or team spokespersons, however you want to do it) communicate with other team leaders. The team leaders must remain aware of what's going on in their teams and return information to their teams based on their communications. This kind of communication is compatible with the fractal process but a bit more variable. The reason is that team size may vary drastically between parts of the process.

In a cycle department, you might find a full surgical team, but in a splinter department, a team is most likely to be just one person.

Times for Various Projects (page 126)

What are the times involved in various kinds of efforts in your existing process?

Software development processes are typically defined according to how they should operate in steady state. That is, they ignore startup phenomena, the training and learning curves required for building up the levels of expertise in the group, and they have no provision for capturing work products (retaining the value of the past investment) if the project should need to be shelved or terminated. But all of these things are very real. They can often make the difference between a project that succeeds and one that fails.

How well does your process work in crisis situations?

Crises are specifically called out in this question because they will happen in every software development project, but they are seldom mentioned in software development processes. Crises will come from a variety of sources, including the process itself (feedback leading to unpredictable disorder), external factors (the business is changed so the project must change drastically to respond), and personal factors (a key person on the project took another job and so the project must take a different tack). The unpredictability of these things makes it difficult and generally unproductive to have the process account for them. However, the process should have some kind of red flag built in to signal, "Don't respond to the extraordinary with ordinary thoughts and efforts."

Terminating a Project (page 127)

Do you ever consider dropping a project or stopping the use of a process?

On a project of any size and of any duration, it's almost inevitable to consider dropping the project or changing processes within the project. Our response is often to reject the idea out of hand because the current process and project may be rotten, but "It's OUR process and OUR project." In other words, we're hesitant to change from what we're doing to something else. But we might find that change isn't so intimidating if we look at what's involved in terminating a process or project and what's involved in converting to a new project or process. Balancing the impact of change against the consequences of no change, we can make a better judgement about the best course of action.

If a process is terminated too abruptly, what happens to the people who are involved?

This tends to be one of the most painful and personally dislocating aspects of process termination. Note that this question is about process termination, not project termination. People must always go through a paradigm shift (change in world view) when switching from one process to another, and changes in world view are traumatic. Having everyone make the change at once increases the negative (that is personally rather than mathematically negative) feedback in the situation and you can expect high levels of dissatisfaction to surface immediately. If you can possibly telegraph the punch and have the people actually become involved in making the change happen and shaping it, you can soften the impact of the paradigm shifts and spread them out over time. You'll need to balance the immediacy of the need for the change, the dislocation caused by the abruptness of the change, and the bonding you can get in the group by having them involved in making the change happen.

CHAPTER 8: MORE POSSIBLE PROCESSES

With all of these possible processes, how will you know it when "the right processes" for you come along?

There are some criteria for a right process noted in this section, but there's a more important answer. There is no such thing as a process that is just right for a project! With the changes in the world, in the project, and in the people, you should always be looking for a process that is close enough. Remember the discussion in Chapter 1, when we talked about drip chambers and grandfather clocks as processes that are close enough. What you really need to identify is a combination of three things. First, is the process close enough to what is required for your situation? Second, is your personal discipline and the personal discipline of the others on the project adequate to bridge the gap between close enough and just right? Third, do you and the others on the project believe in the process enough to apply your personal discipline to bridging the gap? If your answer to all three questions is yes, you've found a process that will work.

What will you get if your group doesn't decide explicitly on a process or set of processes?

Don't be too hasty about answering "chaos" to this question. You're very likely to get disorder if there's no explicit decision about processes, and larger projects will be more likely to fail than smaller ones in that case. However, there are a couple of ways to muddle through to success even with an explicit decision. Personally, I'd rather know whether one of my projects fits into one of these cases or not; guessing about project success tends to be less productive than working to achieve project success. One path to success is to have a group of people who have common experience and so much mutual respect that their process is an inherent part of their group identity. Where this is true and the process is close enough, you have one of the most productive situations possible. A second path to success occurs when the project group is small enough and the dominant personality in the group enforces a process on the rest of the group. Again, the process has to be close enough, but you can expect the path to be a little more rocky than the previous one, since there is a natural resistance to following an imposed process rather than a process adopted through participative consensus. There are probably other ways that a project might stumble into a successful process without an explicit decision, but the lack of a decision significantly increases the probability of a chaotic mismatch between the process and the project. I hope that you will take a more businesslike approach.

Notice that the next section talks about a "process" that doesn't necessarily include explicitly selected processes.

Skunk Works Process (page 136)

Considering the culture and politics of your current organization, how would you recruit people for a skunk works project?

The most important criteria for a skunk works project are always buy-in and expertise. However, the culture and politics of the organization can have a significant impact on your recruiting techniques. If the organization is strongly oriented toward getting approvals and making carefully evaluated decisions, you will recruit mavericks (people who are frustrated about the system getting in the way of progress) for your skunk works. You will need to find or be a shelter point in the organization, protecting the project people from outside interference while supporting their needed interactions with other parts of the overall organization. If the organization is at the other end of the spectrum, working through empowerment and positive leadership you will recruit simply by announcing the startup of the project and dealing with the excited people who volunteer. If you intend to establish a skunk works project, look carefully at the existing culture and politics of your current organization and make sure that you have the appropriate shelter and support. Then identify the places in the existing organization where the right kinds of people for the skunk works project will exist, and do your recruiting there.

How could people in your current organization prepare themselves for skunk works opportunities?

People prepare themselves for skunk works projects by increasing their expertise in critical areas, by learning the capabilities and deficiencies of existing and alternative processes, by demonstrating their determination to make the right things happen for projects within the organization, by being highly productive in team endeavors, and by making all of this visible in their everyday work. The skills are those needed in a skunk works project, and the visibility is what allows others to identify them when a skunk works project is to be formed.

Rapid Prototyping (page 138)

When you learn something, is it more often by incremental trial and error or by blinding insight?

People all learn differently. Most people will learn through a blend of incremental understanding and blinding insight, but the balance will vary from person to person. Thus, your immediate answer to the question will be a highly individual answer. Because things tend to look more incremental in hindsight than they really were, your answer will also be slightly skewed toward the incremental side. The implication of your answer also tells something about how you would tend to use rapid prototyping. You will tend to use rapid prototyping in roughly the same way that you learn, but the balance between the two is an essential part of being productive with rapid prototyping. If your particular answer tends toward incremental learning, you should periodically and intentionally go against your natural tendency and create a prototype that differs significantly in philosophy from your existing prototype.

What other approaches can be used in conjunction with rapid prototyping to further enhance the effectiveness of each?

This is a lead-in question for the next section. Customer involvement with rapid prototyping gives one of the most synergistic combinations you can devise for determining the product you should build.

Mike Barnhouse's Customer-Involved Development Process (page 141)

In your existing processes, how do you negotiate the balance between the need for compressed schedules and customer demands for products with high function and high quality?

One of Mike's reasons for defining the customer-involved development process was that development groups tend to squeeze the customer out of the process in order to satisfy tight schedules. Using this approach, products tend not to achieve usable function, quality, and interface until about the third release. Thus, the Barnhouse process should not be viewed as a process with a longer cycle time than the equivalent standard process, but as a process with half the cycle time of the standard process that leads to acceptable levels of function, quality, and interface. When you look at your negotiations for schedule, you should also look at the actual time it takes to deliver customer satisfaction.

Japanese Process (page 143)

How does your software development process enhance your organization's future?

In an organizational sense, this is an optimization question. Work that is specifically directed toward a single purpose often satisfies that purpose and that purpose only. (There's no surprise there.) In software development, that usually means that the same function has to be rebuilt for each product and that changes in use or interfaces force significant changes in product components. If, instead, work is done to achieve the desired purpose but it is done in such a way that it leaves a positive legacy for the organization, the result is usually of higher quality, easier to reuse, and saves the organization considerable effort in the long run. What's most interesting is that if design is approached in this way, the resultant design is more elegant and the function can be implemented with less effort than is required for the more single-minded approach. There is a demonstrated improvement in product characteristics if developers work toward more than just the immediate goal.

What areas of investment, other than reuse, can give you the kinds of leverage the Japanese hope to derive from their current software development efforts?

The accumulation of working code and platforms (reuse) is a big benefit of long term thinking in software development efforts. You can get additional, corresponding benefits from an accumulation of productive tools (CASE) and from the expertise accumulated by highly productive developers. Reuse gives product parts that don't have to be custom built for each use. Tools are the equivalent of capital investments that make workers more productive. Expertise is the power and leverage that gives the basics of competitive advantage.

Standard Software Development Process (page 145)

Is this standard software development process an invention based on ideals of how development ought to work or is it based on practical experience with development?

The standard development process is actually a combination of both. The basic structure was based on an idealization of the aspects of software development, and then the process was reshaped through experience. However, the standard development process was invented a long time ago. Considering what the software development industry has experienced and learned, you might expect that a newly devised software development process, starting from a different and hopefully more practical set of ideals, might look very different. Think like the person who looks back at younger years and wonders, "If I knew then what I know now, what would I have done differently?"

Do you know how much and why your development process differs from this one?

This is a question whose answer I clearly can't predict, nor can I provide an approved solution. However, I suspect that your knowledge of the differences between your process and the standard process depends critically on your knowledge of your process. So this question might have been asked, "How well do you know your development process?"

Top-down and Bottom-up Development Processes (page 147)

Does prototyping represent a third place to start from that is different from both the top or the bottom? What other places would be appropriate to start from?

Given a set of choices, it's easy to assume that there are no others. So we might be tempted to say that the only choices are top-down design and bottom-up design. But that kind of thinking can block you from looking at some productive alternatives. Top-down and bottom-up are terms relating to code. Prototyping looks at functionality and user interface rather than code, so it does represent a third place from which to start. Object-oriented programming represents a bottom-up approach within an entirely different world view. It might be productive to figure out what a top-down approach in the object-oriented world view would be.

Jack Skinner's Enhanced Standard Development Process (page 148)

How would you adjust this process to take care of the problems that will occur when a later unit of development comes in conflict (breaks when used) with a unit completed earlier?

There are several choices, and determining which is best will depend critically on the people in the group. One choice is to have a bug zapper team that will step in and resolve such conflicts. This might have the disadvantage of degrading people's pride of accomplishment, depending on how the teams interact and the levels of mutual respect within the organization. Another choice is to recall the development team for the first unit and have both teams work together toward a solution. This has advantages as far as pride of ownership but could appear punitive if handled improperly. A third choice is to regress the new unit and add the combination of the new and old units to the work list for bids. This opens the door for a partnership between bug zappers, developers from the team for the first unit, and developers from the team for the second unit. Each of the choices (as is the case with practically all choices) has positive and negative aspects, and you should make your own choices carefully.

What kind of mentoring arrangement could you use with this process to help your junior people grow into expert developers faster?

You could associate an advanced developer with every item on the work list and set that person up as a designated mentor for anyone who asked for that particular item. This would allow junior people to gather knowledge from a variety of mentors or to join the camp following for a particular mentor. Similarly, you could also associate a junior developer with every item on the work list. The answer I'd prefer to hear is that a work item is given to someone only if both a junior developer and an advanced developer sign up for it. The team members could then determine both the kinds of work they want to be involved in and the mentors and proteges they would like to have in their partnerships.

Evolutionary Development Process (page 149)

What are the start-up requirements for the evolutionary process in terms of product requirements, base technology, and expertise?

The start-up requirements for the evolutionary process are nearly identical to the start-up requirements for the standard software development process. Its main innovation is in the scheduling of effort and resources. The second innovation is in the use of inspections intentionally to inject accumulated expertise into components that were implemented early. The evolutionary process does require the early specifications to be complete enough to support the scheduling innovation.

Does the different structure of the evolutionary process offer benefits you need?

If you have a project without enough staff to handle fully parallel development, the process has something to offer you. You can document your specifications, then schedule the work with a smaller team, and still have some confidence in being able to track and measure progress. Also, if you know that you have some learning to do as the project progresses, the use of retro-inspections in the evolutionary process allows you to proceed with the confidence that the entire product will reflect expert implementation throughout, which might not be the case without those inspections.

Are any different disciplines required for the evolutionary process as compared to the standard process?

Not really. The evolutionary process is a simple restructuring of the standard process, exploiting some of the ideas from the Skinner process in a more controlled and more fully planned way.

Locationally Fragmented Development Process (page 150)

Is there an essential difference between multisite internal software development in a single company and similar efforts accomplished through subcontracted work?

The obvious answer is yes and no. In either case, the inevitable communications problems dictate that each organization approaches the linkage in conformance with the Pillars of Software Engineering. That is, the requirements and technology base should be well defined and the people involved should have the necessary expertise from the start. The difference is the temptation in the multisite case to relax the conformance to the pillars and to have information flow that is peripheral to the effort but useful to the developers. The former is dangerous while the latter tends to be good.

Is software development a sufficiently comprehensive discipline to use such concepts as vertical and horizontal integration?

Being a more conceptual discipline than those usually described as vertical and horizontal, software development can, indeed, be approached with either a vertical or a horizontal approach. The vertical approach corresponds to the company that develops a computer along with its associated operating system, compilers, tools, application generators, and applications. The horizontal approach corresponds to the company that develops particular compilers or particular applications for a broad range of computer hardware and operating systems.

Phased Business Process (page 151)

Before a project started, how could you tell whether a phased business process would work for the project?

Two of the simplest ways to have confidence in using a phased business process are previous success in doing so and conformance to a business equivalent of the Pillars of Software Engineering. In each case, this implies having the knowledge of what has to be done and the experience needed to carry it through successfully. Without those two, it would be good to have scheduled time to learn and practice the skills necessary to make the process work.

If in the midst of the project you discover a conflict between a phased business process and the project itself, how would you begin to correct the problem?

This question can best be answered by identifying the areas that can possibly be changed, then identifying the balance of changes that is appropriate to the situation. You can change the business process, change the project, change the people, or get out of the business. (Maybe you have a few other choices as well.) Look for such things as the business process being broken (replace it), the project being in bad shape (get out of the business, fix the project, or start over), and people who resist the processes (educate the people or adopt process closer to the ways the people like to work).

Commitment Checkpoint Business Process (page 152)

Is the increased feedback between approvers and developers an increase or a decrease in the stability of the situation?

Most often, you'd expect this increased feedback to improve the stability of the situation. In some cases, for example, if there are personality conflicts between the people involved, you might see instability.

How much does the distance between developers and approvers affect the stability and responsiveness of the overall organization?

This is a clear case of reducing the bounds of chaos by shortening the feedback cycle. The commitment checkpoint process bypasses an entire set of problems that can be quite painful in the standard business process.

Box 32—Process origins (page 131)

What are the origins of your processes?

This one I can't answer or predict for you. The purpose of the question is to encourage you to look at your processes and identify those that are the most likely to require new definitions. The ones that are experientially based and have never gone through a conceptual refit are the ones to look at first. But for all of your processes, it's productive to look at the origins to see if they still bear any resemblance to your projects and your organization.

CHAPTER 9: WONDERFUL THOUGHTS AND PERTINENT POINTS

Innovation By Design (page 154)

What innovation is encouraged in your organization? Does that match your product needs?

An honest evaluation of innovation in your organization, possibly in comparison with the visible innovation of your competition, will give you a good idea about whether your organization encourages appropriate levels of innovation. Innovation is unpredictable in detail but can be explicitly encouraged by recognizing your innovators as heroes and by ensuring that innovations are incorporated into your products. Innovation can be suppressed through overly detailed planning, extensive reliance on cost justifications for exploratory efforts, and overloading innovative people with highly constrained work. In some organizations, innovation is encouraged in speeches, and it is part of what the organization's leaders brag about, but it is discouraged in practice. Watch for this as you look at innovation in your organization.

How can you use the Applied Innovation Matrix to prepare yourself, those around you, and your organization for the future of your business?

The Applied Innovation Matrix helps you to correlate the business you're in and the innovation that is required for that business. You can also use the Applied Innovation Matrix to document which areas of innovation are successfully pursued in the organization. The difference between the two matrices indicates potential new areas of business (stuff you're good at that you don't yet deliver to your customers) and areas where improvement is necessary (stuff that you don't do but that is needed for your business). By adjusting the suppressors and enhancing the encouragers, you can change the climate of your organization to be more encouraging of innovation in those areas. With education and practice, you can get good at producing innovations in those areas. Technology Futures, Incorporated and Glocal Vantage have additional and more comprehensive uses of the Applied Innovation Matrix available for their clients.

Designers' Sources (page 156)

For any particular project, how will you decide whether to encourage an imaginative solution or to adapt a prior solution to the problem?

The obvious answer to this question is to use what works. With this answer, the capabilities of the designer are less important than the existence of working code.

However, you also want your designers to gain experience and maturity in producing good designs, so there may be times when it's appropriate to risk being accused of having an NIH (Not Invented Here) attitude and ask the designers to produce a totally new solution. In balance, you'd like to have designers who know how to design well, and then have them learn about the best available designs. With experience and knowledge they will have the best chance of making their own choice between build and buy, and produce significantly advanced designs when the choice is to build.

How can you simultaneously release designers' imaginations from the distractions of prior solutions and focus their energies on innovative approaches that can lead to good, innovate solutions?

You might need a careful balancing act between reduced and increased freedom to make this happen. For example, IBM reduced the freedom of computer designers when the decision came down to produce no more vacuum tube computers. However, the freedom to create in the area of transistorized computers was unbounded. Your approach will actually depend on the designers on your project. Some designers seldom look at previous designs while other designers seldom look elsewhere. It will probably be productive to have your designers get away from their offices, possibly to attend classes on topics that are not obviously related to their immediate jobs. Ideas stolen from other disciplines have been highly productive as seeds for innovative designs.

Pedantry and Design Skills (page 158)

How will you form partnerships so that those who prefer a single mental model can balance those who prefer never to use the same mental model twice (and vice versa)?

This requires more than simply identifying the two attitudes and throwing the people together. The key ingredient in forming the required partnership is mutual respect. It may be necessary to put the people together and give them a problem that they must solve jointly, with clearly identified aspects expected from each. If they don't start with mutual respect, seeing success in a collaborative effort will help a lot.

What will your products look like if everyone in the organization uses mental models exactly the same way?

The flippant answer is that your products will look as if you have far more people than designers. This question is intended to caution you against the temptation to hire people who are just alike, trying to achieve success through cloning. With mutual respect, you can get much more successful and robust products if your staff has a wide variety of viewpoints and capabilities.

The Purpose of Bureaucracy (page 161)

With the similarity between bureaucracies and software, is there a business opportunity in converting the policies of a bureaucracy into application software?

This is exactly what happens in expert systems when you capture the expertise of someone knowledgeable in the field and encode that knowledge in rules for the expert system. You create an application that can make decisions using the same knowledge as the expert practitioner. The same can be done for the policies in a bureaucracy. But be careful. As we've discussed, the policies of a bureaucracy may not be quite what makes the bureaucracy work. If you encode the policies but leave out the human disciplines that bridge the gaps between policies and realities, you'll implement a broken application. Also, there's the question of whether the bureaucracy represents the most effective and efficient set of policies. It may be that several cycles of improvement would be necessary before the encoded bureaucracy would make a good application.

Is there precedent in the software industry for application support packages that accommodate the changing of policies?

Expert systems, application generators, and object-oriented applications all tend to accommodate policy changes. By easing and isolating the specifications of policies, each of these software development approaches provide flexibility analogous to policy changes.

Pareto's Law—The 80–20 Rule (page 163)

How might you determine whether people are working in one of their 80 percent areas or in one of their 20 percent areas?

If you know about peoples' productivity rates or how they work, you can look at their results and get a very good idea. Their productivity will be much lower than their potential if they're working in a 20 percent area. You can also talk to them and see if they're frustrated. Frustrations tend to be much higher when people are in a 20 percent area than in an 80 percent area.

How might someone get ready to be highly productive in a particular area?

This is the same as developing expertise. You need education, experience, knowledge of the work of others, and some understanding of the conceptual bases that apply to the area. With all of this, assuming that the area is of interest, he or she will develop the area into an 80 percent area.

What relationship would you expect between job boundaries and individual productivity?

This is a lead-in question for the next section. Taking the question at face value, I would expect to see very high productivity if the boundaries of a person's 80 percent areas correspond to the boundaries of his or her job. However, it's impossible for someone else to define a job so that it matches the boundaries of the 80 percent areas. Read on.

Task Oriented Group Management (page 166)

How can you tell whether people are trained to take task assignments or responsibility assignments?

The most obvious clue about whether people are task oriented or responsibility oriented is to look at their approach to those with whom they work. If they are inclined to ask for approval for all new actions and if they tend to get nervous as other people get jobs similar to theirs, they're probably task oriented. Their focus is on the boundaries and they work very hard to ensure that the boundaries are clearly defined. If they are inclined to take action without approval and seek to negotiate with people who have neighboring responsibilities, they are probably responsibility oriented.

How might a group change from being task oriented to become responsibility oriented?

This is a tall order, and one that requires leadership support. The change requires a different world view; the leader must exemplify the desired world view and reinforce it with every decision. The reinforcement will include an intolerance both for things falling through the cracks and for blaming problems on other groups. The reinforcement will also include strong support for people who negotiate to prevent boundary problems and for people who adopt problems from other areas because they take their responsibilities seriously. The leader will have to demonstrate considerable patience even while showing that only the responsibility world view is acceptable.

Kinds of Measurement (page 169)

Does your organization distinguish between success and adjustment measurements?

This is a cautionary question. Many organizations don't distinguish between the kinds of measurements they use, and so their improvements to their processes are not as effective as they could be. Look carefully at the measurements in your organization to see if they help you to make appropriate decisions. Decisions with unfortunate results might be the result of the chaos of software development, a mismatch between the process and the reality it's to support, or the use of an unfortunate set of measurements.

How do you determine whether your investment of resources is appropriate for your organization?

The criteria will vary from organization to organization. It's possible to be trapped as a result of time delays in investments. For example, today's profits are the balance of revenues (the results of past investments) against today's costs. If you improve today's profits by cutting today's costs (shedding people), you're destroying your future because of your past mistakes. It is necessary to keep costs within reason, nothing is unbounded after all, but costs should be controlled based on more than a simplistic view of today's numbers. You should also look at what is needed to produce your product. Since you need high levels of expertise and productivity in particular areas to accomplish your mission successfully, you must invest to achieve those levels. If wishful thinking or inappropriate measurements lead you to neglect those levels, you'll bear the pain because of the results you fail to achieve.

Box 33—Automating too early (page 160)

How will you lead your software development organization to avoid premature "automation" of your early processes?

This is a balance question. You want to automate things as quickly as possible so that your critical resource, your people, is applied to significant rather than mundane efforts. However, you don't want to cast your processes in concrete when they're at such a preliminary level that they actually degrade your productivity. Keep two answers in mind. First, you only understand your processes after you've used them for a while and after you've made significant improvements to them. Don't automate the processes until you've gone through enough improvement to understand the effect of change on the processes. It's entirely probable that only the second or third process for a particular purpose should be automated. Second, when you do automate your processes, do so in generalized and flexible ways that allow the automated processes to be improved easily.

Box 34—Measurement myopia (page 167)

How might you use both success measurements and adjustment measurements in your work?

Since we're close to the end of the book, you're allowed the flippant answer "appropriately." This box is simply a common example to illustrate the danger of using success measurements where adjustment measurements are needed. But the real confusion in the kinds of measurements comes because people use definitions very differently. For some people, the pursuit of profit includes an incredibly rich fabric of interrelated factors (revenue, cost, investment for return, product competence, customer satisfaction, quality, and many more) so that they do quite well in making their decisions based on that pursuit of profit. For other people, the same words (pursuit of profit) mean nothing more than a simple subtraction of numbers and direct action on accessible parts of those numbers. In the former case, the use of various measurements will be appropriate. In the latter case, the use of the measurements will be suicidal. But both people use the same words, can walk into a meeting and discuss the topic, and will walk out in full apparent agreement. Yet neither understands the other. Such is the problem with words.

Box 35—Measurement paralysis (page 168)

How do you know whether your project measurements are meaningful, useful, or productive?

First, put away the idea that free measurements have to be used; they don't. Even gathering and reporting free measurements uses project resources. If the measurements don't help you improve your business or product, they're not worth it. Second, look at the measurements and evaluate whether a change in the measurements gives you any more information than the knowledge that something changed. Measurements that indicate the causes of problems are generally more useful than measurements that indicate the existence of problems. Third, look at the costs of taking the measurements and see if they're a significant portion of the costs of producing your product. You want to use measurements to understand what's happening in your project, not to increase your project's costs. Using unnecessarily expensive measurements is simply not good business.

How might you eliminate counterproductive measurements?

This isn't as easy a question as it might seem. In software development some measurements achieve sacred cow status, and they can't be easily dislodged from the organization's culture. For these cases, it may be necessary both to devise ways to use these measurements in ways that don't interfere with the main work, and to devise productive measurements that you can use privately in their place. You can sometimes eliminate counterproductive measurements that haven't achieved sacred cow status simply by showing that they cost more than they are worth. However, sometimes you'll have to replace them with something more useful.

CHAPTER 10: AND IN CONCLUSION, . . .

How will you use what you've just read?

This answer is yours and yours alone. Thank you for reading *Exploiting Chaos: Cashing in on the Realities of Software Development.* I sincerely wish you success and satisfaction in applying what you've read here.

Bibliography

Adams, James L. *Conceptual Blockbusting*. Reading, MA: Addison-Wesley, 1986.

Arfman, Robert W. "The Japanese Software Industry: A Comparative Analysis of Software Development Strategy and Technology of Selected Corporations." Cambridge, MA: Massachusetts Institute of Technology, 1988.

Beckhard, Richard and Harris, Reuben T. *Organizational Transitions*. Reading, MA: Addison-Wesley, 1987.

Bloch, Arthur. *Murphy's Law and other reasons why things go gnorw!* New York: Price-Stern-Sloan, 1977.

Brooks, Frederick P. *The Mythical Man-Month: Essays on Software Engineering*. Reading, MA: Addison-Wesley, 1975.

Brooks, Frederick P. "No Silver Bullets." *Unix Review* 5:11 (November 1985), pp 39–48.

Buffington, Perry W., Ph.D. *Your Behavior is Showing*. Nashville, TN: Hillbrook House, 1988.

Crosby, Philip B. *Quality is Free: The Art of Making Quality Certain*. New York: Mc-Graw-Hill, 1979

Danforth, William H. *I Dare You*. St. Louis, Mo: American Youth Foundation, 1965.

Deming, W. Edwards. *Out of the Crisis*. Cambridge, MA: MIT Center for Advanced Engineering Study, 1985.

Drucker, Peter. *Innovation and Entrepreneuring*. New York: Harper & Row, 1985.

Gause, Donald C. and Weinberg, Gerald M. *Are Your Lights On?* Cambridge, MA: Winthrop, 1982.

Gleick, James. *Chaos, Making a New Science*. New York: Viking Penguin, 1987.

Hawking, Stephen, W. *A Brief History of Time: From the Big Bang to Black Holes*. New York: Bantam Books, 1988.

Jackson, Michael, *Principles of Program Design*. New York: Academic Press, 1975.

Kriegel, Robert J. and Patler, Louis. *If it ain't broke . . . BREAK IT!* New York: Warner Books, 1991.

Kuhn, Thomas S. *The Structure of Scientific Revolutions*. Chicago: The University of Chicago Press, 1970.

Mandelbrot, Benoit. *The Fractal Geometry of Nature*. San Francisco: W. H. Freeman, 1982.

Mayo, Elton. *Social Problems of an Industrial Civilization*. Cambridge, MA: Harvard University Press, 1945.

Metzger, Philip W. *Managing Programming People*. Englewood Cliffs, NJ: Prentice-Hall, 1987.

Miller, George A. "The Magical Number Seven, Plus or Minus Two: Some Limits on our Capacity for Processing Information," *The Psychological Review*, 63:2, (March 1956) pp 81–97.

Peters, Thomas J. *Thriving on Chaos: Handbook for a Management Revolution*. New York: Alfred A. Knopf, 1987.

Peters, Thomas J. and Austin, Nancy K. *A Passion for Excellence*. New York: Random House, 1985.

Rubinstein, Moshe F. *Patterns of Problem Solving*. Englewood Cliffs, NJ: Prentice Hall, 1975.

Saunders, P. T. *An Introduction to Catastrophe Theory*. New York: Cambridge University Press, 1980.

Smith, Preston G. and Reinertsen, Donald G. *Developing Products in Half the Time*. New York: Van Nostrand Reinhold, 1991.

van Laarhoven, P.J.M. and Aarts, E.H.L. *Simulated Annealing: Theory and Applications*. Boston: D. Reidel, 1987.

Weber, Max. *Theory of Social and Economic Organizations*. New York: Free Press, 1947.

Weinberg, Gerald M., *The Psychology of Computer Programming*. New York: Van Nostrand Reinhold, 1971.

Weinberg, Gerald M. *Rethinking Systems Analysis and Design*. Boston: Little, Brown, and Company, 1982.

Index

Page numbers in boldface type are primary discussions of the related topic.